Trevor Snow

A graduate of Brasenose College Oxford, Trevor Snow made teaching his career and was Head of Modern Languages at Taunton School for over twenty years before starting up his own company taking people on holiday to France.   His love of France and long experience of visiting the country, including two periods of living there, have given him a deep knowledge of the different regions and their culture.
He lectures on a wide range of topics to do with France, but this is his first book.

The Best of France

Trevor Snow

Trevor Snow

peakpublish

Peakpublish
An imprint of Peak Platform
Hassop Station
Bakewell
Derbyshire
DE45 1NW

First published by Peakpublish 2010

Copyright Trevor Snow 2010
All rights reserved
The moral right of the author has been asserted
Cover Design Trevor Snow and Chris F Coley

Printed in England

No part of this publication may be reproduced, stored in a retrieval system, or transmitted, in any form or by any means, electronic, mechanical, photocopying, recording or otherwise, without the prior permission of the publishers.

A CIP catalogue record for this book is available from the British Library

ISBN: 978-1-907219- 06-1
www.peakplatform.com

To my grandchildren, who live in France, in the hope that they will grow to love the country as I do.

Contents

Page 1   1 Cathar Country

Page 26   2 In the Footsteps of Cézanne and Pagnol

Page 59   3 Treasures of the Riviera

Page 91   4 Bastides of the South West

Page 127   5 The Heart of France

Page 148   6 The Valley of Kings

Page 191   7 The Magic of Brittany

Page 231   8 Houses, Gardens and Artists

Routes, distances and road numbers in the **How to get there:** sections are taken from the appropriate Michelin *Local* or *Regional* Road Maps.

1 Cathar Country

This tour is built mainly around the historical event that brought this part of France to prominence: the Albigensian crusade in the early 13th century. Narbonne, however, owes much of its interest to its place in Roman history, while Rennes-le-Château's fame, or should it be notoriety, stems from events that took place there towards the end of the 19th century, but both places have a connection with the crusade.

Where to stay:
Make your base for this tour either near Narbonne or Carcassonne. Both are worth discovering and both give easy access to the foothills of the Pyrenees, which are the setting for most of your visits

The *Château l'Hospitalet* is in its own vineyard between Narbonne and the sea. The restaurant is good and they have an interesting range of their own wines. Around the main courtyard are a number of boutiques selling locally produced goods and, of course, you can buy the château wines.

If you prefer to stay near Carcassonne, choose the *Château de Floure*, a Château-Hôtel in the Relais du Silence group. The rooms are beautifully decorated, each in its individual period style. For setting, ambience and cuisine this is a little bit of luxury.

How to get there:
For the Château l'Hospitalet, follow the route de Narbonne Plage for 10 kms from Narbonne through the hilly garrigue (scrubland) called the Montagne de la Clape.
For the Château de Floure, leave the N113 at the sign to the village of Floure, 11kms east of Carcassonne.

Excursions: 1 Cathar castles in the Corbières
2 Narbonne
3 Béziers and Minerve
4 Rennes- le-Château
5.Carcassonne and Montségur

To put you in the picture about the Albigensian Crusade 1209-1229:
The stated motive for the crusade was the suppression of the Cathar religion, considered a heresy by the Catholic Church. For Cathars, God reigned over a spiritual world of light and beauty while the Devil governed material things. They could not, for example, accept the divinity of Christ made man, and yet strove to follow his precepts. *Cathar* comes from the Greek word for 'pure', their priests were called *parfaits* (perfect) and tended to set a better example of a Christian way of life than many Catholic priests. They did not consider themselves as heretics, but it is easy to see why the Catholic Church did.
Catharism was widespread and tolerated in the liberal society of the south, which was ruled in part by the kings of Aragon, in part by the counts of Toulouse, technically vassals of the king of France, but in fact pretty much independent.
Attempts by St Bernard of Clairvaux (1145) and by St Dominic (1205) to bring the Cathars back into the Catholic fold did not work. Raimond VI of Toulouse refused to abandon his support for the so called heretics and was excommunicated in 1207. The following year he was accused of being behind the murder of a papal legate. This provoked Pope Innocent III to call for a crusade against the heretics, which, significantly, would also allow appropriation of the lands of their main

protectors, the count of Toulouse and his nephew Raimond-Roger Trencavel, viscount of Béziers and Carcassonne.

The crusading army assembled in Lyon in the spring of 1209 and marched down the Rhone valley. Raimond VI of Toulouse, a cunning politician, pre-empted the invasion – and his certain defeat - by meeting the crusading army at St Gilles (on the Rhône delta) and swearing to 'take the cross' himself, thus putting himself and his lands under the protection of the Pope. His nephew was not granted the same privilege, as the papal legate leading the crusade, Abbot Arnaud-Amaury of Cîteaux, decided that a show of force was required. The count and viscount were allowed to return home, but the crusading army soon captured Béziers (see Excursion 3), then Carcassonne (see Excursion 5). It was during the siege of Carcassonne that Raimond-Roger Trencavel was treacherously taken prisoner and later died in his prison of dysentery (though some say he was poisoned by his captors).

If this is starting to read like a story from the 'Boys Own Annual', the events of the next 40 years continue in the same vein, with massacres, betrayal, military ineptitude, political machinations. In 1229 under the terms of the Treaty of Meaux (pronounced *mow*), the then count of Toulouse, Raimond VII, was forced to agree to the marriage of his daughter to the brother of the King of France, Alphonse de Poitiers. This meant that on Raimond's death all his lands would be integrated into the kingdom of France, unless he managed to produce a male heir. In spite of taking a new wife, he was unable to do this and so when he died in 1249, the independence of the *Midi* effectively died with him.

Another thing:
If you want a cheese that is creamier and more tangy than some of the stuff you find in supermarkets at home, look for the label *Brie de Meaux*. The French reckon it is the best. The town of Meaux lies to the north east of Paris in the region called Brie.

Excursion 1: Cathar Castles in the Corbières

A leisurely day's drive will allow you to enjoy the beauty of this rugged countryside and appreciate the difficulties facing the 13th century crusaders in their heavy fighting gear in the heat of summer, finding their way in hostile territory. Even today, with the benefit of roads, the landscape seems wild and impenetrable.

How to get there:
From Narbonne take the N9 towards Perpignan. After about 15kms take the D611A>D611 to Durban-Corbières. Its castle featured little in Cathar history, since its lord quickly swore his allegiance to the king of France. The next 20 kms of lovely scenery will bring you in sight of the Château d'Aguilar, perched on its hilltop. This fortress was not much involved in the Cathar struggle either. Captured in 1210 by Simon de Montfort, it was reinforced in 1257 by King Louis IX (St Louis) because of its strategic importance as an outpost guarding the frontier with Spain (which was north of the Pyrenees until the 17th century). Along with other border fortresses it was known as one of the *fils de Carcassonne* (sons of Carcassonne).
Only 1km further on you reach Tuchan, centre for the Fitou wine *appellation*. Go to the Cave Coopérative to taste, and even purchase this decent red, in the unlikely setting of a disused chapel.
After Tuchan take the D14 to Padern and Cucugnan, and a little further, on the D19 (direction Maury), you come to the turning for the Château de Quéribus. The steep road up to the car park is signposted.

Another thing:
If you think the name 'Cucugnan' sounds funny (to French people it sounds childishly vulgar), so did the 19th century writer Alphonse Daudet, who included his version of the old Provençal story under the name *Le Curé de Cucugnan* in his *'Lettres de mon Moulin'* (English translation in Penguin). The

village makes the most of its fame, with a presentation of the story in the tiny Achille-Mir theatre in the village square.
The journey time to Quéribus is about an hour, but add on another hour if you stop at Tuchan and Cucugnan, which will bring you to Quéribus in nice time for lunch – before or after a visit to the château.

To put you in the picture about Quéribus: Since the massacre at Montségur in 1244 (see Excursion 5), Quéribus had become the centre of the resistance of the heretics. It is easy to see from its position why it was able to hold out for another 11 years. However, please note that there is hardly anything left of the crusade period castle. It was modernised *later* in the 13th century and modified again in the 16th to keep up with current standards of artillery.

There are conflicting versions of its eventual surrender in 1255 without bloodshed to the king's army: was the commander, renowned for his courage, tricked into surrender, or was he made to realize that he no longer owed allegiance to the count of Toulouse? At all events he was allowed his freedom, his lands were not confiscated and it seems that the Cathars in the fortress were allowed to go free too.
Quéribus became another of the French king's frontier fortresses, another 'son of Carcassonne'.

Visit:
A 20 minute walk from the car park *(uphill, and take water with you if it's hot)* brings you to the castle, where the unusual shape and lighting of the *salle gothique* of the keep have given rise to theories about its solar symbolism.

You get spectacular views over the Roussillon plain as far as the Mediterranean. The peak that stands out when you look south towards the Pyrenees is the Canigou, sacred to the Catalans – its flowers are gathered and made up into crosses to bring happiness and protection to the houses they adorn.

Opening times: October to March, 10am-5pm (-6pm in March, October); April to September, 9.30am- 7pm (-8pm in July, August)

Entry: 5€. This includes the show 'the sermon of the curé de Cucugnan' in the Achille-Mir theatre in Cucugnan

Where to eat:
Enjoy a picnic lunch - and views that are nearly as good as from the castle itself - beside the castle car park. Be warned that it is often windy up here, even in fine weather. There are also good value restaurants in the vicinity. Try *L'Auberge du Vigneron* in Cucugnan or *L'Auberge du Vieux Moulin* in Duilhac.

Begin your afternoon excursion by continuing on the D19 to Maury, where you turn right onto the D117 to St-Paul-de-Fenouillet. There, the D7 (later D10), direction Cubières, will take you through the spectacular Gorges de Galamus. It is worth stopping in one of the lay-bys to get out and look more closely at the deep gorge. You may just see in the shadows the Ermitage St-Antoine-de-Galamus, built into the rock. At Cubières turn right onto the D14 to Duilhac. Just before the village you will see the sign to the château de Peyrepertuse, one of the most spectacular of the Cathar fortresses and the most difficult to spot as you drive towards it from Cubières, so well does it blend with the natural rock on which it is perched.

Another thing:
The road numbers may change (D7 to D10) because you cross from one *département* to another. The D stands for *Départementale*. The N roads (*Nationale*) keep the same number for their whole length.

This part of the journey will take about 30 minutes – more if you stop at the Gorges de Galamus. Look out for good views of the Canigou along your route.

To put you in the picture about Peyrepertuse (*meaning: 'split rock' in Occitan*)**:**
There is mention of a fortress here as far back as the 8th century, but the remains you see today date from the 12th and 13th centuries. At the time of the crusade it was part of the kingdom of Aragon and so was not attacked by Simon de Montfort. However, Montfort did confiscate other lands belonging to Guillaume de Peyrepertuse, who then occupied nearby Puylaurens and was duly excommunicated for his Cathar sympathies. Records show that Guillaume was back in Peyrepertuse in 1240 when it was besieged by the royal army. There was no way that the fortress could be taken by force, but Guillaume surrendered it to the king of France against forgiveness for his previous 'sins'. As at Quéribus, there is no mention of any burning of Cathars. King Louis added an upper section to the fortress, the Château St Georges, which is reached by the vertiginous stairway, called the Escalier St Louis. Peyrepertuse, an impressive example of 13th century military architecture, became the most important of the 'sons of Carcassonne' guarding the border with Spain.

Another thing:
Occitan was the language widely spoken in the south of France until about 1900, even though French had been the official language since the 16th century. In the latter part of the 20th century it had something of a revival, and is now taught at school and university level and you can find TV programmes in Occitan on FR3.

Visit:
It will take about 20 minutes to reach the castle on foot from the car park. *Take water with you and wear walking shoes.* It is not so much the remains of this *citadelle du vertige* that make the visit worthwhile, but the fantastic views over the Corbières, as far as the Mediterranean.

Opening times: November to March, 10am-5pm (closed in January); April, May, October, 10am-6.30pm; June to September, 9am-7pm (-8.30pm in July, August)
Entry: 5€

Make your way back to Narbonne by the D14 to Padern. Then take the winding D123 through the magnificently rugged country of the Mont Tauch (pronounced 'tosh'), branch onto the D410 at Maisons and follow this road until it joins the D613. This will bring you back, through more wild looking country, to Narbonne. If you are returning to Carcassonne, turn onto the D611 after St Laurent, and follow signs to Fabrezan and Fontcouverte to the N113.
From Peyrepertuse allow a good hour to get back to Narbonne or Carcassonne.

Excursion 2: Narbonne

I certainly recommend you spend a whole day here if this is your first visit.

To put you in the picture:
The title '1st daughter of Rome' etched in stone on one of the roundabouts as you come into Narbonne from the A9 motorway refers to Narbo Martius being the first Roman colony to be founded outside Italy, in 118BC. For the Romans Narbonne was a site of strategic and commercial importance. It was the junction of the *Via Domitia* (south-north) and the *Via Aquitania* (going west towards Bordeaux) and also a sea port on the delta of the river Aude. Gradual silting up of the estuary and the dramatic alteration of the course of the Aude after major floods in the 14th century meant that Narbonne was no longer effective as a seaport. This, along with the ravages of the plague and the Hundred Years' War, contributed to its decline. By the Revolution it had only a few thousand inhabitants and had lost the right to have its own archbishop.
Lying at the heart of the Languedoc region, Narbonne's economy has long depended on wine production, but the problem has been that for much of the 20th century the wine produced was rather ordinary - quantity not quality seemingly

the watchword. But since I first came to Narbonne in the 1970s, the wine has become better and better, the town has grown in size and prosperity, so that it is now a major tourist centre in the region.

Begin your visit by savouring the Mediterranean sights and smells of the market in Les Halles, a splendid *Art Nouveau* construction of steel and glass. Then cross the bridge and stroll along Les Barques, the tree-lined promenade alongside the Canal de la Robine (which has linked the Canal du Midi to the coast south of Narbonne since the late 18th century). You will come out onto the Place de l'Hôtel de Ville, where you will see a stretch of the Via Domitia, unearthed by chance during maintenance to underground pipework in February 1997. To his credit the Mayor decided that the square should be pedestrianised and the Roman road become a feature, all in time for the tourist season the same year. Looking north, the Via Domitia follows the line of rue Droite, and on the south side of the square it crosses the mediaeval Pont des Marchands, lined with shops. Make the time if you can to explore these picturesque streets.

Another thing:
The huge plastic amphora with its flow of plastic red wine that decorates the first roundabout after the A9 motorway exit was voted one of the best (or is it worst?) examples of bad taste in a national survey by a French magazine.

Visit: Cathédrale St Just *(*pronounced *Joo)* **et St Pasteur**
The present day cathedral is the third or maybe even the fourth church built on this site, which in fact comprises the old and new Archbishops' Palace (both mediaeval), cloister and cathedral. Of the earlier churches only the 9th century bell tower remains. The first stone of the present Gothic cathedral was laid in 1272 and the chancel completed by 1332. Constructing a transept and nave on the same scale would have meant building out beyond the town's defensive wall at a time in the Hundred Years' War when the English were threatening, so work was stopped and over the centuries there has never been enough money to complete the job. From the

outside, the double flying buttresses and the sheer volume of the building make it elegant and imposing, even unfinished.

Inside, you will be struck too by its beautifully proportioned architecture. If you look at nothing else, head for the chapel behind the altar where you will discover a magnificent 14th century stone reredos. Plastered over in the 18th century, perhaps because certain scenes were considered too old-fashioned for the more sophisticated views of the time, it was only rediscovered in 1981 when the statue of the Virgin, placed there in its stead, was lent to the Louvre for an exhibition.

The beauty of the sculptures and the graphic representation of the scenes of Purgatory and Hell make up for the fact that, in spite of meticulous restoration lasting 20 years, some panels are irreparably damaged. It is a real gem that ranks with the wall painting of the Last Judgement in Albi cathedral. I particularly like the little local touch of the souls on their way to purgatory being transported in a basket used for carrying grapes at the wine harvest.

Visit: Archaeological Museum (*in the New Palace*):
On your way between the cathedral and the archaeological museum, step into the Cour de la Madeleine. On the wall facing you, you can just make out what is thought to be the lintel of the Mihrab (sanctuary of a mosque), testament to the fact that in the 9th century the Moors occupied territory this far north.

On the other side of the Passage de l'Ancre is the entrance to the archaeological museum. Amphorae and artefacts from the Roman period abound, including a huge anchor found in the Etang de Bages, indicating that ships of considerable draught came up through the lagoons to the port of Narbonne, difficult to imagine today.

However, the *pièce de résistance* of the museum is its collection of Roman wall paintings, considered the best in France. These come from a late 1st century AD villa, uncovered by chance during the digging of the foundations for a new block of flats in 1973. The colours of these remarkable decorations are still vivid and make use of *trompe-l'oeil* technique and perspective, while the row of apples on a shelf would not be out of place in a Cézanne still life. Before leaving the Archbishops' Palace, it is worth climbing the 162 steps for the view over Narbonne and the surrounding country from the top of the keep, built on the ramparts of the Gallo-Roman town by Gilles Aycelin, Archbishop of Narbonne and Chancellor to King Philip the Fair. It is a fine example of a late 13th century keep, of which Victor Hugo said:

> *At the centre is a keep so fine that in truth*
> *One would not paint it all in a summer's day*
> (La Légende des Siècles 1859)

Where to eat:
There are a number of pleasant brasseries or cafés that serve snacks and light lunches in the main square and the adjacent rue Droite and cours de la République.

How to get there:
Parking is often at a premium in Narbonne. The best bet is to drive to the town centre following signs for centre ville (town centre) and les Barques (the gardens alongside the Canal de la Robine). Use the underground car park whose entrance is on Les Barques, just by the easily recognised covered market (Les Halles).
If you are staying near Carcassonne, it takes about 45 minutes to Narbonne by the N113. Spot the Cathar warriors on the hillside just to the left of the N113 as you approach Narbonne.
The cathedral is open daily: May to September, 10am-7pm; October to March, 9am-12 noon, 2-6pm
The Archaeological Museum: April to September, 9.30am-12.15pm, 2-6pm; October to March, 10am-12 noon, 2-5pm (closed Monday) Entry: 5,20€

Excursion 3: Béziers and Minerve

If you are staying near Narbonne, I suggest you drive towards Béziers first and walk round Minerve in the afternoon. If you are staying near Carcassonne, visit Minerve in the morning and the Béziers area in the afternoon. Either way, have lunch at Minerve.

To put you in the picture:
Raimond VI had cleverly avoided the loss of his own lands by putting himself under papal authority at the meeting at St Gilles on 18th June 1209 (see introduction). The Papal legate, Abbot Arnaud-Aimery therefore marched his army of crusaders to Béziers, whose young lord, Raimond-Roger Trencavel had been refused protection by the church, making his lands the number one target for the crusaders.
Before the crusaders reached Béziers, Trencavel retreated to Carcassonne with the Jews of the town and some of the more notable heretics, because Carcassonne, as you can understand when you see it, was easier to defend. The Catholics of Béziers refused to give up the remaining heretics, as demanded by the crusaders, and some foolhardy inhabitants even ventured outside the walls to taunt the besieging army. This was their downfall. The pursuing crusaders were able to get into the town and capture it. As an example, the town was razed to the ground and the inhabitants, Catholics and heretics alike were massacred, Abbot Arnaud-Aimery supposedly giving the infamous order: 'Kill them all, God will recognize His own'.

How to get there:
From Narbonne take the N9 towards Béziers rather than the motorway. You will have a pleasant drive through a 'sea of vines'. On the way, you will have the time to make a little detour to see the mysterious Oppidum d'Ensérune, a settlement that goes back to the 6th century BC. The museum is historically interesting and the views, as far as the Pyrenees and the Cévennes, superb. From the 'oppidum' you see immediately below you the Montady lake that dried up in

1247. The field system looking like the spokes of a wheel is due to the channels that drain off excess water into an aqueduct leading under the hill to Capestang (see below).

Just outside Béziers have a look at the impressive flight of 7 locks, the Ecluses de Fonseranes on the Canal du Midi. Note the 'olive' shape of the locks, worked out by Pierre Paul Riquet, the canal's designer, to give better resistance to the pressure on the walls from the surrounding earth. There is no need to go into the town, but from here you do get a good view of the cathedral that dominates the Béziers skyline.

Once you have seen the cathedral -greatly rebuilt after the 1209 massacre- and imagined the carnage of that event, take the D11 towards Capestang. The name means 'head of (the) lake', which shows the extent in ancient times of the lakes that formed the delta of the river Aude. Follow road signs to Carcassonne (the D11 becomes the D5 when it enters the Aude Department). From time to time you will cross or drive alongside the Canal du Midi, a triumph of 17th century engineering and recently designated a World Heritage site. Some 12 kms after Capestang turn right onto the D607 (D907 as it changes Department). The Cité de Minerve is signposted from now on. After about 8 kms you take a minor road (D10E) that twists its way through rugged, inhospitable country the remaining 6 kms to Minerve, site of the second massacre of Cathar heretics by the Crusaders, in July 1210.

The journey time to Béziers from Narbonne is about 30 minutes. Add on 30 minutes if you stop at Ensérune and another 30 minutes if you linger to watch the activity at the flight of locks. Béziers - Minerve is about 45 minutes.

Coming from the Carcassonne direction, take the N113 (direction Narbonne) to Lézignan-Corbières, then the D611 to Homps, the D910 via Olonzac to Aigne, then the D177 for 1km till it joins the D907. Turn left and after 1km fork left onto the D10E to Minerve. Journey time: about 45 minutes.

To put you in the picture about Minerve:

After the capture of Carcassonne the new viscount, Simon de Montfort (see Excursion 5*)*, spent a difficult winter, failing to take the castles at Lastours (north of Carcassonne) and suffering the loss of several castles that he had previously taken, as well as the capture and murder of a number of his men. By spring 1210 he had received reinforcements and set out on a campaign to put an end to these rebellious uprisings by local lords sympathetic to the Cathars.

Minerve was on his list of heretic strongholds because of denunciation, according to contemporary sources, by the wine producers of Narbonne who were at odds with the inhabitants of Minerve more for commercial reasons than religious zeal. So Montfort laid siege to the town on about June 15th 1210. It is easy to understand that the fortress, without the 19th century bridge, was extremely well protected by its location. But Montfort was well aware of the 'Achilles heel' of Minerve, as of many fortresses of the region in the hot summer weather: water.

He set up 3 catapults to bombard the city gates and in particular the well. You can see a replica of one of these devices on the far bank of the ravine opposite the well. The defenders sent out a raiding party by night to burn it down, but the fire was discovered in time and the catapult, appropriately known as the *malvoisine* (literally 'bad neighbour'), continued to do its worst. Eventually, on about July 20th, the lord Guilhem de Minerve, realizing that they could not hold out much longer, and realizing too that Minerve would suffer the same fate as Béziers if taken, came out to parley with Montfort.

Abbot Arnaud Aimery agreed to spare the lives of the inhabitants, including all heretics – even the men and women priests, who agreed to convert. Some crusading knights were outraged, because they had come to wipe out the heretics, not allow them to live even as Catholics. However, the Abbot reassured them: 'very few will convert'. And so it was: a funeral pyre was set up outside the town and some 140 were burnt to death, many leaping of their own accord into the flames, according to a contemporary (Catholic) chronicler, and dying a death 'worthy of a nobler cause'.

Visit:
Leave your car in the car park and walk across the bridge. Very little of the Château remains, but the whole place is really atmospheric, with narrow, cobbled streets and old stone

houses. The 11th century church of St Etienne is interesting; its altar dedicated to St Rustique has an inscription dating it as 456AD, which makes it one of the oldest of Christian monuments. Because of vandalism, you can only visit the church by applying to the Tourist Office (invariably closed when I have been there in recent years). Near the church is a modern sculpture in tribute to the Cathar martyrs and in rue des Martyrs you can visit the Hurepel Museum which depicts in model form the main events of the Crusade.

Where to eat:
There are 2 pleasant café-restaurants in the town near the bridge or a delightful picnic site reached by driving right down into the valley, taking the little road just beyond the bridge.

For your return journey, go back to the D607 and follow it back to Narbonne, if you are staying there.
If you are staying near Carcassonne, follow the route Narbonne-Ensérune-Béziers-Minerve outlined above, but in reverse order.

Excursion 4: Rennes-le-Château

To put you in the picture:
To see the village today – on a hilltop at the end of a steep, narrow road, with only 80 or so inhabitants – you would hardly imagine that it had once been a strategic Visigoth fortress (500-700AD), capital of its region. Claimed over the centuries by various rulers, it was devastated by the plague and sank into oblivion, only to gain notoriety in the late 19th century through its priest, Bérenger Saunière.
Saunière arrived as priest in 1885 to find the church in urgent need of repair, but without the funds to do anything about it. The next year he was given 3000 francs by the countess of Chambord: just the sum needed for the most urgent repairs to his church, which he duly undertook. Not only did he repair and redecorate the church but he continued spending enormous sums to build the sumptuous Villa Bethania and the Tour Magdala, in which he created a rich library, as well as

living for 20 years a life of luxury, all far beyond the usual means of a village priest.

There are many theories as to how Saunière achieved this, but the priest *did* discover ancient parchments hidden in a hollow Visigoth pillar that supported the altar in his church. He was supposedly seen digging in the church and graveyard by night, which gave rise, as you may imagine, to rumours of his discovery of some fabulous treasure. Some said it was the Cathar treasure, brought there at the fall of Montségur (see Excursion 5), or the Templar treasure (though they were never in the region), or even the treasure of Jerusalem, brought to Rennes after the sack of Rome.

It was this treasure that of course would have paid for all his costly activities.

Among the more plausible theories is that these centuries old parchments he found brought into question the legitimacy of the Hapsburg dynasty and Saunière *was* a strong royalist sympathiser. This could explain the gift from the countess of Chambord, who was the niece of the Hapsburg Emperor Franz-Joseph and widow of the last of the Bourbons. He styled himself Count of Chambord and nearly became King Henri V in 1873 (You can see his intended coronation coach at the Château of Chambord in the Loire Valley – Tour 6). The Hapsburgs could then be the source of the money Saunière received over the years, enabling him to continue his extraordinary programme of building. Another possibility is that the parchments revealed a secret that would harm the Catholic Church, such as the theory about Christ and Mary Magdalene proposed in the *da Vinci Code*. The Hapsburgs, staunch protectors of Rome, would be keen that such a story should not be divulged. In either case they might have been prepared to thank Saunière generously.

At all events, Saunière took the secret to his grave in 1917.

Another thing:
Saunière's activities sparked off the still unsolved mystery of 'the treasure of Rennes-le-Château'. This has spawned scores of books, a BBC TV film and brings each year thousands of tourists to the village.
The name of the priest? Yes, do make the connection with characters in the *da Vinci Code*, especially as a local peak is called Le Bézu).

Visit:
The Bérenger Saunière Centre is a short distance down the road from the car park at the top of the village. Start in the Presbytery where the various rooms tell the story of Bérenger Saunière. Then go through the gardens to the Tour Magdala, enjoy the magnificent views from the belvedere, then exit via the Villa Bethania. You will be given a useful plan at the ticket office. It is a good idea to check that the church will still be open when you have finished in the houses and garden and time your visit accordingly.
Saunière's somewhat garish restoration is unexpected in a small village church. He is supposed to have modeled it on the style of St Sulpice in Paris, but some features have only added to the Saunière mystery. The porch with its decoration of roses and crosses is seen as a reference to the 17th century secret society, the Rosicrucians. Then the inscription above the door TERRIBILIS EST LOCUS ISTE has been thought to have occult connotations, especially when you see, just inside, the holy water stoup supported by a grimacing devil. Odd too is the figure in a kilt in the Stations of the Cross.
However, if you translate TERRIBILIS as awesome, as it is used in Solomon's dedication of the first temple of Jerusalem, then this is a perfectly proper description of the House of God as an awesome place, while the explanation of the stoup in the guide leaflet is equally understandable: 'the Devil conquered by the sign of the cross'.

In the boutique there is a selection of books about Rennes and Saunière. For a wider selection of books, videos etc that will satisfy any amount of hunger to solve the mystery the visit has given you, go to the bookshop further down the village street. However, please heed the notice at the entrance to the village: no digging for treasure.

The Bérenger Saunière Centre is open: July to 15th September, 10am-7.15pm; May, June, 16th-30th September, 10am-6.15pm; October to April, 10am-1pm, 2pm-5.15pm

Where to eat:
My preference is a picnic on the grassed area next to the car park, with its stunning views over the Pyrenees, but there is a snack bar in the gardens of the Villa Bethania.

How to get there:
From Carcassonne take the D118 to Limoux and Couiza. (From Narbonne go to Carcassonne first). In the middle of Couiza turn left onto the narrow, winding road up to Rennes-le-Château. NB Do not take the road signposted to Serres and Rennes-les-Bains. The turning you want is a little further on.

It is only 45kms to Rennes-le-Château from Carcassonne, but it is a winding, uphill road, particularly after Limoux, so allow a good hour for the journey. Allow another hour if you are coming from Narbonne (by the N113). The return should be a bit quicker (it's downhill), so you might like to stop in Limoux to taste the local speciality: Blanquette de Limoux, an excellent – and cheaper – alternative to champagne. Just look for the appropriate signs along the road.

Excursion 5: Carcassonne

To put you in the picture:
Its name: Legend has it that the city was under siege by Charlemagne (8th century), but the siege was effectively ended by a cunning ruse executed by Carcas, widow of the Saracen lord of the city. Supplies were low, as was the morale of the inhabitants, but she had their one remaining pig fattened

up and thrown over the ramparts to the besieging forces to show that they were not short of food. At the same time she had dummy soldiers made and, by dint of running round the walls with these dummies, showering the enemy with arrows, she gave the impression that there was still a strong garrison inside. Charlemagne's troops were duly deceived on both counts and marched away. Carcas could not resist following them in triumph, sounding her trumpet. The emperor was told 'Sire, Carcas sonne', hence the name....
In fact, the Romans already knew the place as Carcasum, which rather destroys a colourful legend – pity!

The Albigensian crusade: Once they had captured Béziers (see excursion 3) the crusading army laid siege to Carcassonne, where Raimond-Roger Trencavel had taken refuge. After two weeks, a shortage of water, the *point faible* of towns under siege in hot weather, made Trencavel decide to come out to negotiate. He was treacherously captured and so, without its leader, the city was easily taken. By the rules of the crusade his lands and title were forfeit and offered to a crusading knight. There was some reluctance among the crusaders to accept, since the circumstances of his capture were less than honorable, but the title was finally accepted by a minor lord from the Paris region, a certain Simon de Montfort. Over the next few years, until his death in 1218 – slain it is said by a stone catapulted by a woman during the siege of Toulouse – Simon de Montfort was to be the scourge of the Cathars.

In 1240 King Louis IX (St Louis) banished the inhabitants of the Cité as punishment for their heretical role, strengthened its fortifications to be a frontier fortress, along with the *fils de Carcassonne* (see Excursion 1) against Spain and built the *ville basse* (lower town) on the other bank of the river Aude.

Once the Spanish border was established further south in the 17th century, Carcassonne went into decline. The town refused to put up the funds for the engineering needed to bring the Canal du Midi through Carcassonne when it was being built in 1673. The canal originally passed by to the north and Carcassonne had to wait until the early 19th century for it to be rerouted through the town, bringing much needed trade revenue.

Another thing:
Simon de Montfort was the grandfather of the Simon de Montfort, Earl of Leicester, who is regarded as the founder of the first modern English parliament.

Viollet-le-Duc:
The walled city you see today – the largest in Europe- is thanks to the 19th century restoration of a very run-down place by the architect Eugène Viollet-le-Duc. This man was responsible for the restoration of a good number of other mediaeval monuments throughout France, including Notre-Dame, where he has included a statue of himself among those that adorn the spire on the south side.

The best views of the *cité* are from the A61 motorway or from the N113 east of the *ville basse*. Viollet-le-Duc has been criticized for getting some things wrong, eg some of the turrets along the ramparts have a slate roof, whereas the local style has always been red tiles and the slate is now gradually being replaced. However, had it not been for him, Carcassonne would not exist as it does today.

Visit:
It has to be said that the interior of the *cité* does not altogether match up to the romantic impression of a mediaeval fortress you get from outside the walls: there is the usual rash of souvenir shops and probably the best time to visit is in the early morning or late afternoon when the tourists have mostly

left and you can get a real 'feel' of the mediaeval atmosphere of the place. However, even if that is not possible, you can't leave the region without seeing the *cité*.

From the main car park enter the *cité* by the Porte Narbonnaise. Before you cross the drawbridge look for the commemorative plaque to Dame Carcas and on your left you get a good view of the *lices* (lists) that go round the *cité* between the outer and inner ramparts.Once through the gate, make your way up the narrow street, lined with the inevitable tourist shops, to the Place du Château. The château itself is frankly not worth a visit if you are only spending a morning in Carcassonne, but the wooden palisades (*les hourds*) that run round the top of the walls are an interesting piece of military architecture.

Rue St Louis will bring you to the basilica of St Nazaire, which certainly is worth visiting. The earliest church on the site dates back to the 6th century, but the present building is a mixture of Romanesque and Gothic, which actually works very well. The Romanesque church, of which the nave remains, was due for demolition and rebuilding in the northern (Gothic) style when Louis IX incorporated the County of Toulouse into the French kingdom on the death of Raimond VII (1249). The dimensions of the Gothic chancel and transept were intended for a grander edifice than the existing church, but then money ran out and the architect had to blend the old Romanesque nave with the new Gothic elements. The result is a building of contrasting styles and considerable elegance.

Look in particular at the statues on the columns round the chancel: they are carved into the columns themselves, which is very rare. In the Holy Cross chapel there is a beautiful 13th century window of the tree of life and in the south transept a tombstone, said to be that of Simon de Montfort who was buried here before being moved to the family estate by his son. The son, Amaury, took over command of the crusade on the death of his father, but was not the military strategist his father was. He lost all the territory gained by Simon de Montfort and was forced to abandon the crusade and return home to the north after himself being besieged in Carcassonne in 1224.

On the outside there is a fine Romanesque porch and the crenellations at the west end are the work of Viollet-le-Duc, who thought, wrongly, that St Nazaire had once been a fortified church.

Where to eat:
Follow rue du Plô back towards the Porte Narbonnaise. Take your choice of the *bistrots* in place Marcou, where you can sit outside in the attractive, shady square. Just before you reach place Marcou you pass a small photo/picture gallery: upstairs they have an excellent display of views of Cathar castles you may recognize, although I have found it unexpectedly shut on occasion.
Leave yourself time to explore the other areas of the city, including a walk along parts of the walls.

How to get there:
From Floure take the N113 (direction Carcassonne). As you approach Carcassonne follow signs to La Cité. The car park is opposite the Porte Narbonnaise.
From Narbonne you can take the motorway A61, coming off at junction 24 (Carcassonne). Join the N113 and pick up signs for La Cité. Park as indicated above.
Journey time: from Floure, 10 minutes; from Narbonne, 40 minutes.
Allow 1½ hours for your visit, excluding lunch.
After lunch, an hour's drive will bring you to the spectacular site of the château de Montségur, the talismanic stronghold of Cathar resistance.

To put you in the picture about Montségur:
Right from the start of the Crusade the fortress gave shelter to Cathars, and outside its walls, but still up at the top of the hill, a Cathar community, with its bishop and priest, became established, gaining renown and attracting pilgrimages; a real thorn in the flesh of the Catholic Church.
In 1242, 11 members of the inquisition were brutally massacred at Avignonet (between Toulouse and Carcassonne) in a well planned raid by a 'commando' force from Montségur. Possibly the real purpose of the raid was to destroy incriminating records kept by the inquisitors. At all events the news brought widespread joy, but also prompted a real effort

by the king and the Church to put an end to the powerful resistance of Montségur, recognized as the 'Holy See' of the Cathar belief. In May 1243 a force of about 3000 men began to lay siege to the fortress, but it was not until December that the Royal forces established a foothold up the mountain, finding a suitable route, probably by bribery.
Gradually they were able to wear down the garrison, although even up to the last minute the defenders were expecting the count of Toulouse to bring an army to their rescue. He did not, and on the 16th March 1244, the fortress surrendered, resulting in 225 Cathars going more or less willingly to their death, in a huge funeral pyre set up at the foot of the hill in the place now known as the *camp des cremats* ('field of the burnt' in Occitan).
Although Quéribus (see Excursion 1) did not surrender for another 11 years, the *bûcher de Montségur* (funeral pyre of Montségur) brought the end of the organized Cathar church in the Midi.

Visit:
From the car park it is a good hour's steep climb up to the ruined château, but the views are your reward. *Wear walking shoes and take water with you.*
You can see traces of the 'Cathar village', just below the fortress itself. As with Quéribus and Peyrepertuse, the ruins you see are of the fortress built *after* the crusade, albeit on the site of the earlier one. Like the other castles, Montségur served as an effective frontier post until the 17th century. It is still the subject of all sorts of theories concerning the elusive 'Cathar treasure', but unromantic modern thinking questions the very existence of any such treasure.
The village, at the foot of the *pog* ('mountain' in Occitan, like ***Puy*** de Dôme in the Massif Central) has a museum in the Mairie, with 13th century artefacts and literature on the Cathars.

How to get there:
Take the D119 from Carcassonne via Fanjeau and Mirepoix. At Mirepoix take the D625 to Lavalanet and after about 2kms

on the D117 (direction Foix), turn onto the scenic D9 to Montségur.
Journey time: 1 hour
The château is open from February to December, but during winter months it may be closed in bad weather.
Opening times: April to June and September, 10am-6.30pm. Entry 4,50€ and free commentary on Saturday and Sunday at 2 and 3pm. In July and August: 9am-7.30pm. Entry 4,50€ and free commentary daily at 11am, 1,3,4.30pm Entry includes the museum in the village

The central square in Mirepoix is a pleasant stop for an afternoon drink. It's 13th to 15th century arcades have some fine figures carved into the wooden beams and pillars.

Another thing:
There are impressive ruins of Cathar châteaux at **Lastours**, best seen from the viewpoint on the hill opposite, where in July and August there is a *son et lumière* show.
Take the D101 north of Carcassonne via Conques –sur-Orbiel.

*The Benedictine Abbey of **Lagrasse**, in a lovely position in the Orbieu valley, and the beautiful Cistercian Abbey of **Fontfroide**, are definitely worth visiting if you are staying on longer. The Abbot of Fontfroide, Jacques Fournier, became Pope Benedict XII at Avignon.*
For Lagrasse, take the N113 east from Carcassonne and then, at Trèbes, the winding D3 to Lagrasse.
For Fontfroide take the N113 west from Narbonne and after a few kms take the D613 until you see the sign for Fontfroide.

Further reading:
Le Bûcher de Montségur, by Zoe Oldenbourg. (In French. A detailed account)
(English version: *Massacre at Montségur*, a history of the Albigensian Crusade)
Histoire des Cathares, by Michel Roquebert. (In French. A detailed account)
La Croisade contre les Cathares Edition: Terres du Sud No 27)

Minerve Cité Cathare Edition: Terres du Sud No 30 (Both in French. Useful pocket guides)
Rennes-le-Château, le trésor de l'abbé Saunière, by Vinciane Denis. (In French. Useful factually and some interesting ideas.)
Labyrinth, by Kate Mosse (Fiction, but gives a good feel of mediaeval Carcassonne)

2 In the Footsteps of Cézanne and Pagnol

To put you in the picture:
Provence, and in particular the country round Aix-en-Provence and Aubagne, was the region most dear to the painter Paul Cézanne and the writer and film-maker Marcel Pagnol. The Montagne Ste Victoire just to the east of Aix is the subject of many paintings by Cézanne (44 oil and 43 watercolours); the wild and hilly area between Aubagne and Marseille dominated by the Massif du Garlaban is the setting for a number of Pagnol's books and films.
While Cézanne's name is a household word, Pagnol is probably best known outside France for the films *Jean de Florette* and *Manon des Sources*.

This tour is in its way a pilgrimage to places dear to the two artists. For Cézanne: La Montagne Ste Victoire, the Trois Sautets bridge, Le Tholonet, Gardanne, the Bibémus quarry, le Jas de Bouffan and his studio at Les Lauves. For Pagnol: his birthplace Aubagne, Le Garlaban and La Treille. In addition, a walk round old Aix, including the musée Granet, is a must, as is a visit to the Basilica of St-Maximin-la-Ste-Baume, traditional burial place of Mary Magdalene.

Where to stay:
Aix is a vibrant university town and an appropriate place to stay for you to explore this region and discover why it so attracted both these artists.
In Aix itself *Le Pigonnet* is an oasis of calm within walking distance of the town centre – parking in Aix is not always easy. Better still, it is on the right side of town (the south) for your excursions.
About 15kms out of Aix, at Fuveau (again on the south side), is the *Château l'Arc*. This hotel is well placed for your visits and has views over Cézanne's Montagne Ste Victoire.
Both are 4 star hotels in the *Châteaux and Hôtels de France* guide.

How to get there:
Le Pigonnet: Leave the motorway A8 at junction 30 (Aix Pont de l'Arc). Go towards the town centre. At the 3rd traffic lights turn left into Avenue du Pigonnet.
Le Château l'Arc: Leave the A8 at junction 32 (Fuveau Trets). Follow the N7 (direction Trets – ZI Rousset, briefly), then D6 (direction Trets). After about 2kms you reach a roundabout and level crossing. The hotel is on the right just beyond this.

Excursions: 1 *Cézanne trail*
                        2 *Old Aix and the Musée Granet*
                        3 *Bibémus, le Jas de Bouffan and les Lauves*
                        4 *Aubagne and St-Maximin*
                        5 *Pagnol trail*

To put you in the picture about Cézanne:
Paul Cézanne (1839-1906) was born and brought up in Aix. At school he became friends with Emile Zola, the future novelist, famous also for his newspaper article on the Dreyfus affair, with its headline *'J'Accuse...!'*. Cézanne's father, a banker, put pressure on his son to study law in spite of his preference for painting. However, he was eventually allowed to study art in Paris, where he made little progress. He came back home and joined his father's bank, but only managed to stick it for a year, before returning to Paris to study art – with his father's consent and an all important allowance. It is said that Cézanne

convinced his father of his talent by painting on the walls of the drawing room of the family home, le Jas (pronounced *jazz*) de Bouffan. He did exhibit in the 1863 *salon des refusés* (an exhibition of works turned down by the official salon), but, though he submitted paintings regularly to the official salon, the only time his work was accepted was in 1882. In the intervening years he did exhibit on two occasions with the impressionists – who were also having trouble getting recognition.

Artistically during these years his main mentor was Camille Pissarro, who encouraged Cézanne to lighten the colours of his palette, which had tended to be rather sombre. It is very interesting to compare the work of these two painters who often painted scenes round Louveciennes, Pontoise and Auvers-sur-Oise, setting up their easels on the same sites. This gave rise to an excellent exhibition in 2006 of their work between 1865 and 1885. During that period Pissarro said of Cézanne: 'he will astonish many artists who have been too quick to condemn him'.

Cézanne's private life became somewhat complicated; while in Paris in 1868 he met Hortense Fiquet who became his model and mistress. Because Cézanne was afraid his father would disapprove and cut off his allowance, he didn't tell him about Hortense, even when they moved back to Provence so that Cézanne could avoid being called up to fight in the Franco-Prussian war (1870). After the war Cézanne divided his time between Provence and Paris, still without revealing anything about Hortense or their son, also Paul, who was born in 1872. Cézanne's father found out by accident about his grandson, through a letter to him in which an enquiry was made about the boy's health – the boy was by then about six years old. Father was not best pleased and threatened to cut off his son's allowance, but eventually, in 1886, Cézanne married Hortense with his father's consent. When his father died shortly afterwards he left Cézanne his fortune and the artist was freed from financial worries for the rest of his life.

He was now beginning to be noticed and other impressionists were enthusiastic about his work. In the early 1890s comments such as: 'his painting has an original nature' and 'he is some kind of precursor of a new art' were being made about

Cézanne in the art world. However it was not until 1895 that the Parisian art dealer Ambroise Vollard held an exhibition of 150 of Cézanne's paintings. Only then could you say, in Pissarro's words, that 'this curious fellow from Provence' was really discovered.

Many of his works, especially of the later years, were painted at the family home le Jas de Bouffan, or at the Château Noir, or the Bibémus quarries, where he rented a little house to store his equipment, and many included the Montagne Ste Victoire either as the main subject or in the background. In 1901 he bought a small property in the country above Aix on the hill called les Lauves and had it made into a studio. He used to go some 2kms up the road from his studio to a spot where he had good views of the Ste Victoire. A garden has been created at the chemin de Marguerite where he painted, with panels reproducing some of the paintings of the mountain he did from there. You can still more or less see the same views that Cézanne had.

He painted to the end, dying from pleurisy a few days after being caught out in a storm while painting above les Lauves.

Another thing:
His longstanding friendship with the writer Emile Zola came to a bitter end when Cézanne recognised himself as the failed artist Claude Lantier in Zola's novel *L'Oeuvre* (1886).

Excursion 1: Cézanne Trail

From Aix itself, get onto boulevard du Roi René and then bd Carnot. Turn right onto bd des Poilus.
From outside Aix, Cours Gambetta leads onto bd des Poilus, which is the road to le Tholonet (D17). This is signposted 'Route de Cézanne'.

About 1km along this pretty, winding road you get glimpses of the Montagne Ste Victoire, passing on your left the Château Noir, where Cézanne rented two rooms to store his equipment and be near one of his favourite *motifs* (subjects). You can't really see this 19th century building, which is not black at all, though the owner did paint it with some black pigment to protect the stonework. Unfortunately for him, the rain washed it off, leaving the original sandy colour of the Bibémus quarry stone.

The restaurant now called le Relais Cézanne in Le Tholonet was a place where Cézanne often came to eat and apparently even carved a sketch on one of the tables. It is a pleasant place to stop for a coffee, even if you can't find a table with a genuine Cézanne engraved on it. As you leave the village you see on your left a windmill – one of Cézanne's favourite places to set up his easel. The views of the mountain that Cézanne had are now obscured by mature trees, but just by the windmill is a discreet monument erected by the Mayor of the village in 1939 to honour the centenary of the painter's birth. If you decide to stop here, pop into the windmill; sometimes they hold interesting little art exhibitions there.

As you continue along the D17 to St Antonin-sur-Bayon you will see that the landscape on your left hand side is dominated by the Montagne Ste Victoire. On its summit you can see a cross. This is the Croix de Provence, erected in the 19th century and surprisingly is some 17m high. Also surprising is that it doesn't feature in any of Cézanne's paintings of the mountain. At 945m altitude the cross rises above the 17th century priory of Notre-Dame-de-Ste-Victoire, which was inhabited until the Revolution. The chapel still stands and there are the remains of the cloister too. The view from here is magnificent, but the 3 hour or so climb on foot is not for the faint hearted.

After St Antonin turn onto the D56C towards Rousset. With lovely views over the wild Provençal countryside this road leads you across the Plateau du Cengle down to the valley of the river Arc and the village of Rousset, which is an appropriate place to stop for lunch.

Where to eat:
In Rousset the unpretentious *Déjeunez sous l'Arbre* will provide a reasonable light lunch to set you up for a gentle afternoon's trip to Gardanne.

Journey time to Rousset, including stops to admire the view along your route and for coffee at Le Tholonet: 1½ hours at most.

After lunch, continue on the D56 from Rousset, go across the A8 motorway in the direction of Peynier and continue as far as the junction with the D6. This will take you into Gardanne.

Here it becomes a bit complicated: follow signs to the town centre (*centre ville*) and station (*gare*). Go under the railway bridge and at the first roundabout take the 2nd exit onto a dual carriageway which, at the next roundabout, becomes Boulevard Cézanne. On your right you pass a wooded hillside which is your Cézannian destination.

However, to get to it, you should continue to the *next* roundabout, go all the way round it and take the little road that leads off it up the hill. Park when the road doubles back on itself and walk up a path through the wood, which is called the Colline des Frères and has been laid out as an open air museum relating to Cézanne's time in Gardanne. It was still a village at that time; the industrial development that makes the place rather unprepossessing now - though they *are* making an effort to brighten it up - did not come until the 1890s.

A series of panels reproduce his paintings of the old town and remarkably the views have changed little except for the towers of the 1950s power station which now dominate the horizon. Painters of Cézanne's time were fascinated by industrial developments, eg Monet's *Gare St Lazare* and Paul Signet's *Factories on the Seine*. Cézanne painted the factory chimneys at l'Estaque and he would surely have been happy to paint the Gardanne towers, representing modernity, if they had been there.

To put you in the picture about Cézanne and Gardanne:
From August 1885 to October 1886 Cézanne rented a room at 27 cours Forbin and lived there with his mistress Hortense Fiquet and their son Paul. A plaque now marks the house.

In all there are known to be 10 oils, 4 watercolours and 4 drawings of Gardanne by 'the master'. He would also go out to paint in the countryside nearby, his equipment loaded onto a little donkey cart. However, if he was not happy with what he did, Cézanne would just tear up the canvass and leave the bits on the ground. Regarding one oil he painted near Meyreuil (D58, direction Aix) he spoke of 'this still life of roofs and cubes of houses standing out from the cliff face of the Sainte Victoire'. The reproductions on the Colline des Frères clearly show his interest in a geometric structure in his landscapes, marking his break with the impressionist style. The town now proudly claims that 'cubism was born in Gardanne', Braque, Picasso and Derain being inspired by Cézanne's Gardanne paintings.

Another thing:
When he married Hortense in April 1886, two of his witnesses were from Gardanne and his letter ending his friendship with Zola was written from Gardanne.

From Gardanne return to Aix via Meyreuil and Le Pont des Trois Sautets. You have pleasant views along the D58, particularly on the Aix side of Meyreuil, but I haven't been able to pick out the one Cézanne painted from there with the Montagne Ste Victoire in the background, nor have I found any bits of his discarded canvasses....

To put you in the picture about Cézanne and the Pont des Trois Sautets:
It's worth a brief stop here - park on the grass verge just before you reach the bridge. No need to clamber down to the water, just walk onto the bridge and look, but watch out for traffic as the bridge is narrow.

There is only one arch, but the name refers to three boulders by which you could leap across the river Arc. (In French *sauter* means to leap or jump).
There is nothing particularly Cézannian to see, but it was an inspirational place for the artist. It was a favourite bathing spot for the young Cézanne and his friend Zola and in the summer before he died, Cézanne wrote to his son ' I am waiting for the carriage at 4 o'clock to take me down to the river, to the Pont des Trois Sautets. The air is fresher there'. (Aix in high summer can be stifling).
He painted one oil and two watercolours of the bridge itself but, more importantly, the bathers there gave him the inspiration for his research into integrating nudes into the landscape, resulting in his major work *Les Grandes Baigneuses*.
Journey time: Rousset to Gardanne 30 minutes. Gardanne to Aix (via Meyreuil and le Pont des Trois Sautets), 20 minutes.

Excursion 2: Old Aix and the Musée Granet:

To put you in the picture about Aix, city of water and art:
Aix, city of water:
In 124 BC the Roman consul Sextius captured the celto-ligurian capital, Entremont. The remains of this fortified town can be seen up the hill on the northern outskirts of modern Aix, off the road to Puyricard (D14). In 122 BC Sextius established the Roman colony lower down near the hot springs and it became known in Latin as Aquae Sextius (the waters of Sextius), the two Latin words evolving over the centuries into the single French word Aix. Provence is a region where its scarcity makes water a precious commodity - the powerful story of Marcel Pagnol's *Jean de Florette and Manon des Sources* hinges on the presence or otherwise of a spring, the original story being called *L'Eau des Collines* (The Water of the Hills) - and the population of Aquae Sextius grew rapidly because of the presence of its many thermal springs.
In the main boulevard, le cours Mirabeau, there are four fountains and about forty all told throughout Aix. Even so, it was the completion of the Zola dam and canal in the second

part of the 19th century that brought a really abundant supply of water to the town.

Aix, city of art:

The counts of Provence established their court in Aix towards the end of the 12th century and in 1409 Louis II of Anjou, count of Provence, created a university here. The most famous of the counts of Provence to be associated with Aix was his son René, who, as well as being duke of Anjou, and count of Provence, was titular king of Naples and Sicily and known popularly as *le bon roi René* (good King René), ruling from 1434 to1480. He was quite a strong influence at the French court and resided mainly at Angers (in the Loire Valley - see Tour 6). However, when his nephew Louis XI of France seized the Anjou region in 1474, René moved permanently to Provence, dividing his time between Aix, Gardanne and Marseille.

Le bon roi René was a man of culture, spoke several languages, wrote music and poetry, and illuminated manuscripts. His court at Aix became a cultural and artistic centre. One masterpiece, the 'burning bush' triptych, was painted for him in about 1476 by the French painter Nicolas Froment and can be seen in the St Sauveur cathedral. The side panels depict René and his wife Jeanne de Laval. René was an efficient administrator and encouraged commerce and agriculture, introducing the muscat grape to Provence. He improved sanitation in the town and created public medical services. On the down side though, his coinage was not thought particularly reliable.

A year after René's death Louis XI annexed Provence to the kingdom of France and Aix grew in fits and starts. Great architectural expansion in the 17th century saw the well-to-do move out of the old town into the new Mazarin quarter, south of the old town wall which was demolished to make a carriageway later named *cours Mirabeau*, after a famous citizen of Aix. The 18th century saw more architectural changes: broad avenues, squares, fountains, elegant buildings like the Palais de Justice.

However, the town missed out on the industrial revolution of the 19th century, mainly due to the development of Marseille, and it remained in the doldrums really until the creation in

1948 of the international festival of lyric art and music. This started out with the idea to offer a new approach to Mozart and popularise modern music, but as it has progressed, particularly since 1988, the festival - held in July - has expanded its repertoire and can justly be considered one of the top music festivals in Europe. In fact, whichever month you choose to come to Aix, you will find musical and cultural activity, ranging from contemporary ballet, jazz and film in some stunning indoor and open air settings to free concerts in the streets.

A walk round old Aix:
To get the feel of Aix-en-Provence you must begin with the cours Mirabeau. This plane tree lined boulevard was named after one of the town's famous, or perhaps notorious sons, the count of Mirabeau, who was a colourful figure in the French Revolution.

To put you in the picture about Mirabeau and Aix:
Although Gabriel Honoré de Riquetti, Count of Mirabeau was a rather ugly man, women were attracted to him. He caused something of a scandal with the local nobility by seducing the rich and much sought-after Marquise de Marignane, openly leaving his carriage outside her house when he spent the night there (No 12 rue Mazarine, but it's not really worth making a detour to see it). Marriage was the only answer, but the lady's father showed his disapproval by cutting off her allowance. Mirabeau, undeterred, ran up vast debts with local tradesmen and was put in prison, but on his release, he seduced another beautiful woman - already married this time - and ran off with her to Holland. He returned to Aix some years later, in 1783, to contest his wife's suit for divorce, pleading his case so powerfully that his wife's lawyer fainted under his verbal onslaught. He lost in the end, but in 1789 surprised everyone by standing for parliament, not to represent the nobility but the Tiers Etat (the commons). His rhetoric got him elected and thus began his spectacular career in the Revolutionary council along with Danton, Marat and Robespierre until his death in the usual way in 1791.

The walk:
Start from place du Général de Gaulle at the west end of cours Mirabeau. In the centre of the roundabout, known as la Rotonde, is the imposing fountain of the same name. Built in 1860, its three statues reflect the main activities of Aix: Justice (facing the cours Mirabeau), Agriculture (facing south towards Marseille), Fine Arts (Facing north towards Avignon). When it was built, the Rotonde fountain was a symbol of entry into an open town, replacing the gate of the enclosed mediaeval city. Now that Aix has greatly expanded, it stands, a bit like Eros in Piccadilly Circus, in the symbolic heart of the town.

Although both sides of the cours Mirabeau are part of the 'old town', they are not the same. If you look at a town plan - *available from the Tourist Office in the place du Général de Gaulle* - you see that the old, 'historic' part is ringed by broad boulevards, starting and ending at la Rotonde. The 17th century 'quartier Mazarin', on the south side of the *cours*, is set out in a grid and has a very different character from that of older part of Aix, with its narrow streets to the north of the cours Mirabeau and within the city walls until the 17th century.

On the 'quartier Mazarin' side are the elegant 17th and early 18th century former private residences, now banks and offices. No.10 (corner of rue Laroque), and no.20 (corner of rue Cabassol) have good wrought-iron balconies, but it is more interesting to walk up the left side of the *cours* and there is more shade from the trees too.

 This is where you feel the real atmosphere of Aix, especially in hot weather, so allow yourself to be tempted to sit on the terrace of one of the many cafés along the *cours* and enjoy the leisurely pace of life. If you like the idea of 'following in the footsteps....', Cézanne frequented the café Oriental (no.13 - now the Bistro Romain), or the café Clément (no.44 - ground floor of the hotel Gassendi) or the café des Deux Garçons (no. 53, ground floor of the hotel Gantes). Les Deux Garçons is supposedly *the* café to be seen in. Its name, or nickname Les 2 G, goes back to the two waiters, Guerini and Guidoni, who bought it in 1840. Over the years it has been frequented by many a celebrity, including of course Cézanne and Zola. In Aix it is something of an institution, but you may be a little disappointed by the décor, which is not quite as striking as it once was, and be prepared to wait, as elsewhere in Aix, since the service is a bit slow. Wherever you choose, you are likely to see many young people. Aix is a university town and, as well as the cafés and restaurants of the cours Mirabeau, there are bookshops too.

Another notable feature of the *cours* is its fountains. Level with rue Nazareth is the 1691 fontaine des Neuf Canons (nine cannons), built to replace the old watering trough for animals in the time before the *cours* was created. Further up, level with rue Clémenceau, the 1741 fontaine d'Eau Chaude (hot water) is fed by the water of the original thermal spring, known for its curative powers since Roman times. The heat of the water, a constant 34', has encouraged the thick growth of moss, so that the fountain is familiarly known as *la fontaine Moussue.* At the top of the *cours* is the 19th century fontaine du Roi René, appropriately enough by David d'Angers. Again appropriately, the statue shows the king holding a bunch of grapes. Just beyond is the early 18th century Hôtel du Poet whose richly decorated façade and balcony are well worth a look (*hôtel* in this context means private residence).

Now, for the old town with its elegant Baroque and Italian Renaissance buildings here and there along your route, take rue Fabrot (by the café des Deux Garçons). At the end, turn left into place St Honoré (another fountain) and then into rue Espariat, where No 6 houses the Natural History museum. It is worth stopping to look at the imposing Baroque façade, carriage entrance and courtyard of the building itself, the hotel Boyer d'Eguilles, built in 1672, even if you do not visit the museum. The museum's chief claim to fame is its collection of dinosaur eggs and an impressive skeleton discovered in the valley below the Montagne Ste Victoire. Close by is place d'Albertas, a delightful little square with more good examples of Baroque façades. It is a wonderful setting for the open air concerts that are held here in summer. The square came into being in 1745 when the wealthy and influential Marquis d'Albertas had the houses opposite his own demolished, the better to set off his own residence at No.10. The fountain - which really 'makes' the square - only came in the 1800s. It leaked and was replaced in 1912 by an identical one made by the students of the Aix Arts and Crafts College.

Turn right into rue Aude. This leads into rue du Maréchal Foch and to the attractive place de l'Hôtel de Ville (Town Hall square), especially lively on market days (Tuesday, Thursday, Saturday). Notice the Italian style façade, sculpted doors and interior courtyard of the present town hall, built between 1655 and 1678. The Tour de l'Horloge (Clock Tower) was the old town gate from the 12th century, rebuilt in the 16th century to house the town archives. The only part of its astronomical clock of the same period that is left are the four figures representing the four seasons. On the south side of the square stands the Corn Exchange. This was erected in the 18th century in the same place as the corn market had been held, its size and permanence reflecting the importance of taxes on cereals as a source of revenue to Aix. The sculpture on the pediment represents two rivers, the Rhône and the Durance, two essential elements for the prosperity of farming in the region.

By going through the Tour de l'Horloge you move into the Bourg St Sauveur (town of St Sauveur), which in the Middle Ages was separated by ramparts from the inner city, the Cité Comtale (city of the Counts). The gargoyles on the fountain are by the sculptor who decorated the Corn Exchange, while the column is from Roman times and the water too comes from an ancient spring. The Bourg St Sauveur is named after the cathedral and was itself built on the site of the Roman town, which extended from the Tour de l'Horloge up to the cathedral. Walk along the lively, part pedestrianised rue Gaston de Saporta. This was one of the main roads in the mediaeval town, where the houses were on small, usually rectangular plots. In the 1600s and 1700s the well-off citizens of Aix moved out here, building their opulent residences. Look particularly at No.17, now the Museum of Old Aix. The tall fluted pilasters of the late 17th century façade are imposing, while inside you can see some of the original painted ceilings and friezes. The museum's best exhibits are wooden puppets from a crib and from a *Fête-Dieu* ceremony. No.19 has a superb *trompe l'oeil* staircase - as you look up, a young 17th century man looks down on you. Louis XIV stayed here on his tour round Provence in 1660.

Now you come to the cathedral complex. The St Sauveur cathedral was built on top of the Roman forum and takes you on an architectural journey through the ages. The façade is made up of a small Provençal Romanesque entrance on the right, late (Flamboyant) Gothic in the middle and a Gothic bell tower on the left.

Inside, the octagonal baptistry dates back to the 5th century, several of its columns coming from a temple in the forum. Strangely, the columns support a Renaissance dome (because this was rebuilt in the 16th century). Traces of the Roman north /south road (cardo) can be seen in the baptistry. The ribbed arches and the pillars show that the nave adjacent to the cloister is in the typical Provençal Romanesque style and the charming cloister also dates from the 12th century. Its twin columns and sculpted capitals give it a certain elegance, even though much of the sculpture is damaged. The capital of one corner pillar has a fine sculpture of St Peter. In the huge Gothic central nave is the burning bush Triptych (*see above: Aix city of art*). The third nave is Baroque. A fine series of early 16th century tapestries adorn the chancel. They were designed by the Flemish painter Quentin Metsys and were orginally intended for Canterbury cathedral. St Sauveur's gain is Canterbury's loss.

The Archbishop's Palace, which adjoins the cathedral, was rebuilt between 1650 and 1730. Its grandeur reflects the ecclesiastical and political importance of the archbishops of Aix at that time. The first floor now houses the Tapestry museum, and since its inception in 1948, the Palace has been home to the main events of the Festival of Lyric Art each July.

The Espeluque fountain - Espeluco means cave in Provençal - is the oldest in Aix, and was for a long time the only water source in the Bourg St Sauveur. It was moved several times before the present version was installed in the newly created archbishop's square in 1756.

Now make your way back towards cours Mirabeau for lunch.

Where to eat:
The *cours* itself is good for atmosphere and people watching. The *Bistro Romain* does a variety of reasonably priced dishes, or try any other place that caught your eye as you walked along the *cours* earlier. If you turn right and walk down rue Espariat past the Eglise St Esprit - where Mirabeau got married to Mlle de Marignane - you will come across a number of little restaurants or *brasseries* offering a wide variety of lunch menus.

Another thing:
There is of course a Cézanne trail round Aix, available at the Tourist Office, but it may be easier to look out for the places on it as they coincide with your own route rather than make it the basis for your visit. There is also a 'literary walk' for Cézanne's contemporary and friend (see introduction above) the writer Emile Zola. He created a fictional town, *Plassans,* based very closely on Aix where he was brought up. *Plassans* and its environs were the setting for five of his novels of a family saga. Read the 'literary walk' booklet (only available in French) for the genesis of the work and for the extracts from Zola's novels describing different places in and around the town. The novels themselves are rather more challenging.
Time for the morning's visit: about 2 hours, at a very leisurely pace, but excluding a coffee break.

After lunch go to the Musée Granet via the Mazarin quarter.

To put you in the picture about the Mazarin quarter:
This was created between 1646 and 1651 by Archbishop Michel Mazarin, brother of the famous Cardinal Mazarin, one of the most influential statesmen in France in the 17th century. Within the constraints of preserving the area round the Eglise St Jean de Malte at the east end and the Benedictine convent (now gone) to the west, the whole quarter was set out in grid form, rue du 4-Septembre and rue Cardinale being the main axes. Over the next hundred years the grand houses with their enclosed gardens became the homes of the well-to-do of Aix.

Visit:

From the Moussue fountain in the cours Mirabeau, walk down rue du 4-Septembre to where it crosses rue Cardinale. This central point of the Mazarin quarter is marked by the fontaine des Quatre Dauphins (four dolphins) in the middle of the small square. The fountain, installed in 1667, is not only a charming feature but also adds a harmony to the place by its four water spouts echoing the intersecting roads.

Turn left along rue Cardinale to place St Jean de Malte (another fountain). The fortified church here was built in the 13th century outside the ramparts. It is the first known Gothic church in Provence and is named after the Hospitalers of St John. The 17th century building next to it was originally the Priory of the Knights of Malta. It became a museum in 1838 and was subsequently named in honour of the painter François Granet (1775-1849). He was a native of Aix who had great success as a painter in France and Europe. Before his death he left his collections to the museum, which has a good range of works of the 16th to 19th centuries by French painters: Le Nain, Van Loo, Géricault, David, Ingres (*portrait of Granet*). Provençal painters are represented, notably Granet himself. There are works too by Rubens and the school of Rembrandt. Unfortunately there are only eight paintings by Cézanne, of which *Portrait de Mme Cézanne (1885)* and *Les Baigneuses (1895)* are perhaps the best known subjects.

Take time to visit the Archaeology section which has objects, mainly statues, from excavations at Entremont (see introduction above) and the Roman town of Aquae Sextius.

The musée Granet is open: June to September, 11am-7pm; October to May, 12 noon-6pm; closed on Monday and 1st May Entry: 4€

Allow 1½ hours for your walk and museum visit.

Another thing:
The small number of works by Cézanne, is perhaps accounted for because they didn't start collecting them until 1984, and it is a shame there are none of the Montagne Ste Victoire, which was the subject he painted the most. It is really only since 1984 that Aix has woken up to the value of Cézanne as an attraction, and only since 2006 - the centenary of his death - have some of the principal Cézanne sites, such as the family home le Jas de Bouffan, been open to the public.

Excursion 3: Bibémus, Le Jas de Bouffan, Les Lauves

The Bibémus quarry, le Jas de Bouffan and the studio at les Lauves are iconic sites in the art of Paul Cézanne. The studio has been open to the public for some twenty years, while the quarry and the family home have been open since the Cézanne centenary in 2006, but only by reservation.

To put you in the picture:
Bibémus Quarry:
It is not for nothing that Cézanne has been called the father of cubism. He was obsessed by spheres, cylinders, cubes, geometrical shapes and the disused quarry on the Bibémus plateau between Aix and the Montagne Ste Victoire must have seemed like paradise to the artist. John Rewald, co-founder of the Cézanne Memorial Committee in 1952, said of the quarry: 'it is a vast field of seemingly accidental forms'. Having provided stone for Aix from ancient times until the 18th century it had not been in use for many years and had become overgrown. In the 11 oils and 16 watercolours Cézanne painted on site you can see his attraction to the shapes and colours, particularly the strong ochres of the stone that stand out against the greenery. He also painted the Ste Victoire from the terrace of the *cabanon* ('hut', but it is actually a small stone house, probably a quarryman's) he rented there for several years from the mid 1890s. He used it to store all his painting equipment and it was big enough for him to stay overnight if he wished.

Le Jas de Bouffan:

Cezanne's father bought this Provençal manor house with its 14 hectares (34 acres) of land in 1859. At the time it was in the country, with open views of the Ste Victoire, which is hard to imagine today, surrounded as it is by busy roads and not far from the town centre. Nonetheless it is still something of an oasis of calm and the features of some of the 39 oils and 17 watercolours Cézanne painted there are still recognisable, e.g. the outbuilding which was the setting for *The Card Players* (he used estate workers to pose for this picture). Unfortunately you can't see perhaps the most remarkable feature: the 12 pictures painted directly onto the walls of the drawing room by the young Cézanne, who was trying to prove to his father that he was good enough for him to subsidise his son's art studies, rather than train for the law as his father wished. The paintings were removed in about 1912, though the light effects on the guided tour try to make amends. The artist's father later converted part of the attic into a studio and after he died, Cézanne inherited the estate with his two sisters. He lived and painted there until 1899, when the sisters decided that the property had to be sold. There is some mystery about the sale. Cézanne was reluctant – for him it was the family home – and he could certainly have afforded to buy his sisters out (French law requires property to be divided equally). Perhaps this remark by Renoir who cut short his visit in 1888 'due to the dark miserliness that fills the house' explains why he did not, but there is also a theory that the money from the sale was needed to pay off the debts of his sister Rose's husband.

Eventually, in 1994, the estate became the property of the town of Aix.

Another thing:
The word 'Jas' in Provençal means sheep barn, which may have been a name used in jest for this substantial house.

The studio at les Lauves:
Cézanne had tried without success to buy le Château Noir where he rented a room for some years to be nearer the subject that fascinated him, the Montagne Ste Victoire. In 1901 he bought the plot of land on the les Lauves hill to the north of Aix, pulled down the existing hut and had a purpose-designed studio built. Like le Jas de Bouffan, the garden of the studio is still an island of calm in an Aix suburb.

Going up the stairs and into the studio you can almost feel Cézanne's presence. It seems 'lived in', as indeed it was; he spent every day of the last four years of his life working here. He would leave his flat in Aix to start work at the studio by about 6.30am, return to Aix for lunch, then come back up and work until about 5pm. When the weather was fine he would walk up the hill to the chemin de Marguerite to paint his favourite mountain. If it was wet or too cold he stayed in the studio working, often on a still life.

In the studio his easel, some canvasses, clothes and various objects he liked to have around him are the genuine article, except the fruit – although when I was last there the apples were decidedly mouldy. This would fit with Cézanne's character, for he tended to accumulate stale food and rubbish and disliked anyone 'tidying him up'. A specialist feature is the tall, narrow opening in one corner of the room. This was put in so that his large canvasses could be taken in and out – he painted his last version of *les Grandes Baigneuses* (the Big Bathers) in this studio.

After his death the studio remained shut up for 15 years. Then, in 1921, the academician Marcel Provence bought it from Cézanne's son in order to preserve 'a precious heritage, a spiritual treasure attached to these walls and to this garden'. He founded the first Cézanne society in 1923 and continued to own the studio until he died in 1951. To prevent it falling into the hands of building developers, two Americans, James Lord and John Rewald, founded the 'Cézanne Memorial Committee'. They raised the money to buy the studio and presented it to the University of Aix-Marseille. It was opened to the public in 1954 and given by the university to the town of Aix in 1969.

Another thing:
Among the multitude of visitors to the studio over the years was Marilyn Monroe, who wrote 'a wonderful visit' in the visitors book in 1955.
Maybe an understatement about the Cézanne site above all others that gives the visitor a real feel for the great painter.

Visit:
The visit to the studio – not guided – takes 30-45 minutes, but allow another 30 minutes to visit the site further up the road at chemin de Marguerite – now a commemorative garden called the Terrain des Peintres- where Cézanne painted 18 views of the Montagne Ste Victoire. There are plaques with reproductions of 10 of the paintings and you can still see some of Cézanne's views.
The guided visit to the Bibémus quarry lasts about 1 hour and le Jas de Bouffan – also guided - 45 minutes.
With these timings in mind you should reserve entry times to all three sites at the Tourist Office as early in your stay as possible. They are open daily from June to September, although during that period the only visit to the Bibémus quarry is at 9.45am because of fire restrictions. So I suggest going to Bibémus and le Jas de Bouffan in the morning, having lunch in the cours Mirabeau area before visiting les Lauves, which is a little out of town.

How to get there:
Bibémus quarry: pick up the transport as indicated by the Tourist Office.
Le Jas de Bouffan: from the Tourist Office, take avenue Bonaparte which leads into boulevard de la République, then turn left into cours des Minimes (dual carriageway). This leads into route de Galice. Go under the railway bridge and le Jas de Bouffan is on the left before the motorway junction. Continue over the motorway as far as the next roundabout. Go round it and come back so that you can park in front of le Jas de Bouffan, or nearby, on the right hand side of the road.
Les Lauves: from the town centre you have to follow the one way system via boulevard du Roi René, boulevard Carnot, cours St Louis, boulevard Aristide Briand. This takes you three

quarters of the way round Aix via some notable names in French history, but there is no other easy way of doing it, even with a town map – which is essential anyway. Where boulevard Aristide Briand becomes boulevard Jean Jaurès, turn right into avenue Pasteur (the studio is signposted from here) and after two blocks turn right into avenue Paul Cézanne. The studio is up the hill, on the left, but take the first on the right after the studio, park in the road or in front of the block of flats, and walk back down to the studio.
Terrain des Peintres: continue up the hill and park on the road before the next roundabout. Walk up through the park which is on your left.

Excursion 4: Aubagne and St Maximin

To put you in the picture about Marcel Pagnol:
He was born in 1895 at 16, cours Barthelémy in Aubagne, where his father was a schoolteacher. In 1900 the family moved to Marseille, whose port area was the setting for Pagnol's famous play and film trilogy: *Marius, Fanny* and *César.*
Four years later the family took their first holiday at La Treille (pronounced *La Tray*) a village in the hills above Aubagne. The series of family holidays there, always at the same house, la Bastide-Neuve, were the start of Pagnol's lifelong love affair with the wild countryside dominated by the Massif du Garlaban, for he set a number of his novels in the area and actually built sets there for his films.
With his degree in English, he taught in a number of schools in the 1920s, but was more interested in his own literary production, which included founding a periodical called Fortunio.
The breakthrough that allowed him to give up teaching to become a full-time writer came in 1928 with his play *Topaze*. This comedy was such a success in Paris that the following year it was also performed in London, Berlin, Rome and Bucharest and was in rehearsal in Moscow, Copenhagen, and Zagreb. Clearly the subject – corruption in business and

politics - struck chords well beyond France. A 1960s English film version starred Peter Sellers.

His plays and film scripts had great success. In 1938 Pagnol created his own film company and studios in Marseille. He sold it to Gaumont in 1942, becoming their production director. In 1946 he received the accolade of being elected to the Académie Française.

By the late 1950s he had turned from mainly making films to writing. His childhood memories (*Souvenirs d'Enfance*) and the novel *L'Eau des Collines* (The Water of the Hills) are best known to us through the films that were made after Pagnol's death in 1974. *La Gloire de mon Père* and *Le Château de ma Mère* are delightful evocations of Pagnol's holidays at La Treille, while *Jean de Florette* and *Manon des Sources* poignantly depict rivalries and vendettas in village life, stemming from the overriding need for water in the parched hills of Provence. All four films have as their setting the wild and beautiful scenery of the Massif du Garlaban.

Pagnol has been criticised as being a lightweight writer. He said 'I write for the public and I am pleased if the public goes to see my plays or films'. Often human weakness and tragedy lie beneath the humour of his writing and what gives Pagnol more substance than his critics give him credit for is the universality of his themes, portrayed nearly always through brilliantly observed Provençal characters. Translation of his works into seven languages, their lasting popularity and the 200 hundred or so schools named after him as well as countless roads, libraries, cinemas are facts that perhaps outweigh the criticism.

Another thing:

When his first novel was rejected his publisher offered him work updating a phrasebook for English visitors to France. Pagnol never completed it, though this gem survives: 'Shofer, conduizy moua a la plass Peeguell'

Visit: Aubagne

The two places to visit in Aubagne are La Maison Pagnol (his birthplace) and Le Petit Monde de Marcel Pagnol, a museum illustrating scenes and characters from Pagnol's stories by means of clay figurines called *santons*.

Pagnol's father, Joseph, was a teacher in the Ecole Lakanal, then the only primary school in Aubagne and now housing a faculty of the University of Provence. At first he lived in a flat above the schoolrooms, but when he married he moved to a bigger flat on the third floor of the house where his famous son was born. In fact Marcel was very nearly not born there or indeed in Aubagne. His mother, Augustine, had intended to have her baby in La Ciotat and be looked after by her sister-in-law who lived there. She set out for La Ciotat in a buggy driven by a neighbour, but suddenly changed her mind and got back home just in time.

The whole house at 16, cours Barthelémy is a museum to Marcel Pagnol, relating his career, with all sorts of memorabilia, and the family flat has been sympathetically restored and furnished to recreate its 1890s atmosphere. It makes a good start to your acquaintance with this prolific and talented man of letters, giving greater meaning to the visit to La Treille and le Garlaban (Excursion 5).

Pagnol's birthplace is open daily in July, August, 9am-6pm; April, May, June it is open daily, 9am-12.30pm, 2.30-6pm (closed on 1st May); September to March, 9am-12.30pm, 2.30-5.30pm (closed on Monday).

Le Petit Monde de Marcel Pagnol is housed in what used to be a bandstand in the Esplanade de Gaulle (avenue Antide Boyer). It represents in miniature the hills and valleys behind Aubagne where Pagnol found much of his inspiration. There are over 200 figurines *(santons)* made by local potters, representing the best known scenes and characters from his films and plays. The *santons* are sculpted in the likenesses of the actors who played the parts. You may recognise Gérard Depardieu, Yves Montand, Emmanuelle Béart, Daniel Auteuil from the films *Jean de Florette* and *Manon des Sources.* Others, from earlier productions, are legends of French cinema or theatre.

The staff are friendly and can explain some of the scenes to you, if they are not overwhelmed by a rush of visitors at the time. Do ask about the card game from the film *Marius* with its famous play on the word *coeur* (heart).

To put you in the picture about santons:
The emergence of *santons* came about because churches were closed by the by the anti-clerical and anti-monarchy revolutionaries of 1789. A certain Jean-Louis Lagnel from Marseille, who moulded statues for churches, had the idea of making inexpensive little clay figures of the Nativity so that people could have a Nativity scene in their own home, as it was no longer possible to see them in church at Christmas. The word *santon* comes from the Italian word for little saint. The scenes traditionally consisted of the Holy Family, the Kings, the shepherds and their sheep, but soon figures from all aspects of Provençal life came to be represented. The first part of the 19th century was the heyday for *santons* with Aubagne and Marseille the main centres of production. *Santon* making is very much a Provençal tradition, but nowadays they are still collected – and can be quite expensive – throughout France and beyond.
Le Petit Monde de Marcel Pagnol is open daily, 9am-12.30pm, 2.30-6pm and is free.

Another thing:
The Cigale (cicada), the ceramic emblem of Provence that is known around the world was created in 1895 by Louis Sicard in his workshop in Aubagne.

How to get there:
From Aix, take the N7 (towards Nice) and after about 10kms turn onto the N96 to Roquevaire and Aubagne. Alternatively you could use the motorways (A8, then A52), which run parallel to the N roads.
From Fuveau, pick up the N96 to Roquevaire and Aubagne.
When you reach Aubagne, follow signs to the town centre (centre ville). At place Pasteur, turn into cours Barthelémy. Pagnol's house is a little way up on the right hand side, but park in either of the two car parks signposted just beyond the far end of cours Barthelémy. You can leave your car there

while you visit Pagnol's house, the Petit Monde and have lunch.
At Pagnol's house they will be happy to give you a town plan or direct you to Le Petit Monde, which is only a few streets away and there are opportunities en route to stop for a coffee and look at possible lunch menus.

Where to eat:
I suggest one of the little cafes by place Pasteur, where you can sit outside and watch the world go by.

At either Pagnol's house, Le Petit Monde or the Tourist Office (just beyond Le Petit Monde) please pick up leaflets giving details of the various walks in the hills to visit sites associated with Pagnol.
These will be a help for my Pagnol Trail in Excursion 5.
For this, take the **Circuit Marcel Pagnol-Spécial Individuels** *which has a written itinerary on one side and a map on the other. It covers the itinerary for Excursion 5 and involves easy walking. For more exacting walks – wearing suitable shoes – the* **7 balades dans les collines de Pagnol (7 walks in Pagnol's hills)** *is what you want, but be aware that access to the hills is forbidden from the first Saturday in July to the second Saturday in September because of fire risk.*

Journey time from Aix to Aubagne: about 40 minutes. From Fuveau: about 20 minutes.

Saint-Maximin-la-Sainte-Baume

To put you in the picture:
You can't miss the huge basilica of St Maximin that dominates the little town of the same name. The basilica owes its existence to 13th century Charles d'Anjou, count of Provence, who had a dream in which Mary Magdalene herself indicated that her tomb was to be found *là même où se trouverait une plante de fenouil toute verdoyante* (at the very place where a verdant fennel plant was to be found).
Searching in the crypt of the existing church Charles unearthed several sarcophagi, one of which gave off a sweet perfume and

when opened revealed a jumble of bones including a skull with a shoot of fennel, still green, growing out of the tongue. Charles concluded that this was confirmation of his dream and the remains were officially recognised in 1295 by Pope Boniface VIII as those of Mary Magdalene. Charles therefore had this grand basilica built on the site of the old church to house the relics of the Saint, along with an adjoining convent for the Dominicans charged with looking after the pilgrims who now started flocking to Mary Magdalene's tomb.

This was a great coup for Charles, as pilgrims had hitherto venerated Mary Magdalene's supposed relics at Vézelay (in Burgundy), and it made the basilica one of the most popular places of pilgrimage in Christendom.

The Sainte-Baume part of the rather complex name of the town refers to the grotto (*baoumo* means cave in Provençal) where Mary Magdalene spent the last thirty-three years of her life in prayer and contemplation. This, after she had miraculously been washed up, according to legend, at Les Saintes Maries de la Mer after fleeing the Holy Land in a boat without a sail, accompanied by Lazarus, Martha, Sarah, Mary Jacoby and Mary Salome (hence the plural **Les Saintes Maries de la Mer**).

The grotto is 946m (about 3000 ft) up in the Massif de la Sainte-Baume that rises abruptly between the town of Saint-Maximin and the sea, the highest of the Provence mountain ranges. A crevice in the wall behind the altar is where she supposedly did her penance, in the only dry spot in the grotto. A recumbent statue of the saint shows you what it was like. However, she had some relief, as seven times a day she was transported by angels to the summit where she could listen to the *concerts du Paradis*, an event commemorated in the nearby village of Nans-les-Pins (pronounce the *s* of *Nans* but not of *Pins*) by a housing estate of that name.

Before the Christian era the grotto was already a place for pilgrimages to pagan goddesses of fertility, but its importance through its association with Mary Magdalene made it an essential pilgrimage for many kings of France and several Popes as well as vast numbers of faithful of all ranks. Louis XIV made *his* pilgrimage on horseback.

Another thing:
The forest itself is unusual: the beech, lime, maple and other trees growing here tend to be found in the cooler, wetter climate of northern France. Their presence is explained by this northern slope of the massif being kept cool and moist by the shade from the cliff face that overhangs it. Where the cliff no longer shades the slopes you see the predominance of the Provençal oak again.

Visit: Basilica of Saint-Maximin
From some distance away the basilica dominates the skyline, squat and powerful. Close up, you will be struck by the unfinished stonework of the west end and the absence of a bell tower. After the initial surge, work stopped for more or less the whole of the 14th century, mainly owing to the ravages of the plague on the working population. The famous crypt housing the sarcophagi of four saints was modified in the early 15th century and further work on the basilica over the next hundred years has given the building its present appearance, but it was never really completed.

It is from the inside that you really appreciate the Gothic style of the basilica, that makes it an exception in a region where Romanesque predominates. The inside is impressive by its size, an impression increased by the height of the central nave. The three naves and absence of a transept make it reminiscent of some more northern church architecture, like the huge Gothic cathedral at Bourges. The basilica is unusual too in that it went against the more modest architectural proportions advocated by the Dominicans, who were after all a mendicant order. However, St Maximin needed to be on the grand scale to accommodate the vast number of pilgrims.

The crypt, containing the four sarcophagi dating from the 4th century, is thought to be the family vault of a late 4th - early 5th century Roman villa. As well as the tombs of the saints Mary Magdalene, Marcelle and Suzanne, Maximin and Sidonius, you can see in a 19th century reliquary the skull, venerated as that of Mary Magdalene. The church as a whole seems a bit down at heel, but the 16th century reredos in the side chapel on the north side of the apse is worth looking at. It was painted by the Venitian born Antonio Ronzen and consists of sixteen medallions round a central crucifiction. Look for the view of St Mark's, Venice in one of the medallions.

An organist friend has described the 18th century organ as a 'magnificent beast'. It is pretty much in its original condition and a historical monument in its own right. It survived the iconoclastic zeal of the St Maximin revolutionaries, thanks to Lucien, brother of Napoleon Bonapart. He had the idea of using the basilica as a food warehouse, and saved the organ by getting the organist to play the *Marseillaise* on it.

On your way out, look for the unusual graffiti on the walls and columns, just inside the entrance. These were carved by 19th century apprentice masons whose guild made an annual pilgrimage (and still does) to the grotto of the patron saint of *compagnons*, Mary Magdalene.

Another thing:
Apprentices who work with raw materials (plumbers, masons, carpenters, bakers etc) can learn their trade through their guild or society on a *Tour de France*. These *compagnons* take several years working their way round France, spending weeks or months with local craftsmen to learn local techniques, using local materials. They stay in hostels run by 'Mothers' and are given new names after their home town or region, e.g. *Breton* (from Brittany), *Bordelais* (from Bordeaux). The aggressive rivalry between guilds, that used to provoke fights, is nowadays settled on the football field. A *compagnon* who has completed this rigorous apprenticeship is the equivalent of a master craftsman.

Like all *compagnons*, Pierre Petit, known by his *compagnon* name: *Tourangeau le disciple de la lumière* (the disciple of light from Touraine) made his pilgrimage to his patron saint. As a result he created between 1977 and 1983 the seven stained glass windows in the outside wall of the grotto up in the Massif de la Ste Baume.

How to get there:
After lunch in Aubagne take the N96 to Roquevaire and then the N560 to St Maximin through delightful Provençal pinewoods dominated on your right side by the Massif de la Ste Baume. In St Maximin, park in the main square (Place

Malherbes), or in the signposted car park nearby, and walk the short distance down rue Général de Gaulle to the basilica. Don't try to drive through the old quarter to the basilica; you could get tangled up in some very narrow streets with awkward corners, though it is quite an atmospheric little area for a stroll.

The café in place Malherbes is a good place for a drink and to people watch.

Allow 1-1½ hours for your visit, including a leisurely drink.

Journey time from Aubagne to St Maximin: 30 minutes. From St Maximin to Aix by the N7: 35 minutes. From St Maximin to Fuveau by the N7 and D6: 20 minutes.

Excursion 5: Pagnol Trail

If you did not pick up a leaflet about walks in the hills above Aubagne when you visited the town (Excursion 4), you have another chance, as this excursion has Aubagne as its starting point. The Tourist Office or Le Petit Monde de Marcel Pagnol, both in avenue Antide Boyer, are on the route you want through Aubagne.

My Pagnol Trail concentrates on the places and people associated with the best known of his works set in this delightful area: *La Gloire de mon Père, le Château de ma Mère, L'Eau des Collines (Jean de Florette* and *Manon des Sources)*.

This is a day for great scenery and views; it is certainly no hardship to drive the picturesque route from Aix or Fuveau to Aubagne a second time.

Your first stop on the 'Pagnol trail' after Aubagne is the **Château de la Buzine**, the real 'Château de ma Mère'; which is the title of the second volume of *Souvenirs d'Enfance* and later a film.

In 1941 Pagnol was looking for somewhere big enough for his ambitious project to create a 'Cinema city' in Provence. He heard that this château with its 40 hectare (100 acre) park was for sale and bought it before even inspecting it. When he did go there, he realised that it was the very place where his father had had a humiliating experience, caught taking the family on a short cut through private property to the holiday house of Pagnol's childhood, above La Treille (recounted in *Le Château de ma Mère*). The angry Pagnol apparently said 'If my mother was still alive, nobody could chase her off the property' – because of course her son was now its owner.

'Cinema city' never came into being, as the château was taken over first by the Germans, then the resistance, then by units of the French army liberating Provence. Bizarrely, on a visit Pagnol made to his father, now living in the estate manager's house in the grounds of the château, he found thirty armed Senegalese soldiers sitting meekly in front of the inveterate schoolmaster, who was giving them a dictation – a staple of French language teaching until not so long ago, on both sides of the Channel.

The story of the château is rather a sad one: the soldiers left, but squatters – mainly Spanish refugees – took over the building, and when they left in about 1965, the place was more or less uninhabitable and Pagnol by this time had abandoned the cinema. A year before his death he sold out to a developer who intended to build 500 houses on the land. In the face of local opposition, the number and area were cut by half, with the City of Marseille owning the other half, fortunately the part with the original buildings. There are plans to create a Marcel Pagnol and arts centre, but for the moment this château, with its poignant associations with Pagnol's life, looks rather sorry for itself.

Now drive to **La Treille** and park on the pavement where you see the parking sign for coaches (in French *cars*), preferably on the shady side of the road. You *can* drive the ½ kilometre up to the village centre, but neither parking nor turning there is easy.

La Treille is important in the Pagnol story for being the village that featured in his boyhood holidays as the scene of his father's triumph at *boules* and the photo of the *bartavels* (rock partridges), both recounted in *La Gloire de mon Père*. The fountain in the tiny square and the village church were settings for crucial scenes in the original film of *Manon des Sources* (though not in the Claude Berri film that is more familiar to us). The description of *Les Bastides Blanches* in chapter one of the novel *Jean de Florette* is the exact description of la Treille, and it has hardly changed since 1963.

Walk up through the village towards the hamlet of Les Bellons. On your way you will see three houses, rich in their associations with Marcel Pagnol. On the left, outside la Treille, a 1930s style villa: La Pascaline. The plaque on the wall tells the passer-by something of its role in the life of the writer. Pagnol had stayed here while shooting *Manon des Sources*, and rented it again in January 1956 to escape the cold of the Paris winter and to seek some solace after the death of his three year old daughter. His walks in the hills – in the same direction you are going – brought back memories of the childhood holidays which were to be the theme of his *Souvenirs d'Enfance* trilogy. He started writing and five chapters of his *Souvenirs* appeared in *Elle* magazine in December that year. In 1957 *La Gloire de mon Père* was published, *Le Château de ma Mère* the following year and in 1960 *Le Temps des Secrets*.

Further up the road, just after Chemin le Four, is another little turning on the left leading to Lili's house. There is no need to go down the road as the house in question is almost hidden by the summer greenery. Lili was younger than Marcel, but knew every inch of the hills and very soon became the young Marcel's *petit frère des collines* (little brother of the hills). Their adventures roaming the hills together are a key part of *La Gloire de mon Père* in particular. Lili's real name was David, but when very young he had trouble with his pronunciation: people understood 'Lili' and the nickname stuck.

About 100 metres on up the chemin des Bellons is La Bastide Neuve, the house the Pagnol family rented from 1904 to 1910, when Marcel's mother died. Of his first stay at La Bastide Neuve Pagnol wrote 'Then began the best days of my life. The house was called the New Bastide, but it had been new for a good while' *(La Gloire de mon Père)*. The family made the tiring trek up from Marseille, where Marcel's father now taught, for the school holidays and later, because they loved being up in the hills, for weekends too. Pagnol twice tried to buy La Bastide Neuve. The first time, he considered the price too high and on the second occasion he was too late; it had just been sold.

Another thing:
Unfortunately you will not see the famous 'privy', target of Uncle Jules' and Joseph's (Marcel's father) shotgun practice until they ran out of ammunition and then heard the plaintive voice of the maid: 'May I come out now?' (*La Gloire de mon Père*). It withstood that assault, but succumbed to a storm in 1981.
(For an explanation of the word *bastide* see Tour 4: To put you in the picture about bastides.)

*My Pagnol trail now brings you back down to La Treille after the gentle excursion I have outlined above, but if you want a more demanding walk, the **Circuit Marcel Pagnol** and the 7 **balades** leaflets give good suggestions, with distances and timings.*

Where to eat:
After your walk you should take advantage of the food and the views offered by the restaurant *Le Cigalon*. Its name is the same as the restaurateur in a Pagnol film, who explains in mouth-watering detail his recipes and then – in the story - offers his customers…. the lovely view from the terrace of his restaurant.

After your pause for refreshment at Le Cigalon, make your way back down the hill, but before leaving La Treille, spend a few moments in the cemetery.
Look for four graves. Marcel Pagnol is buried with his mother and his three year old daughter Estelle. The inscription on his grave reads: *Fontes, amicos, uxorem dilexit* (He loved springs,

his friends, his wife). Further on down the same row, is the Pagnol family grave. Now go down the steps to the tomb of Pagnol's friend and set builder, Marius Broquier. At Pagnol's funeral he was asked why he had not put on his 'Sunday suit' rather than the white stonemason's jacket he always wore. He replied: 'But then Marcel would not have recognised me'. Nearby is the grave of Pagnol's boyhood friend Lili (David Magnan), who was killed on the Marne in 1918. A brief but moving description of his death is given in *Le Château de ma Mère* (Ch37).

How to get there:
From Aubagne (le Petit Monde and the Tourist Office) keep on the CD2 (direction Marseille), which runs parallel to the A52 motorway. After 3kms turn right up route de la Valentine and a short distance further on, at a roundabout, go straight on into the Parc des Sept Collines. The Château de la Buzine is on the right, with car parking opposite.
For La Treille, take route de la Valentine and shortly turn right on the D4A, direction Allauch (pronounced 'allo). You come to a fork in the roads with the Bar des Quatre Saisons between them. Fork right and then left at the Cross and you can park on the La Treille road as indicated above.
The Circuit Pagnol leaflet map and description are most helpful for your journey from Aubagne.
Journey time from Aubagne to La Treille, excluding stops: 20 minutes.

3 Treasures of the Riviera

This tour gives you the opportunity to discover places you might not readily have associated with this coastal strip whose climate has attracted so many artists and writers as well as royalty and those who are just wealthy.
It includes visits to three chapels associated with the artists Picasso, Matisse and Cocteau; to two very different styles of garden at Eze and Cap Ferrat; to the homes of Renoir, Baroness Rothschild and the archaeologist (among other things) Théodore Reinach; to the old quarter of Nice and the Cours Saleya with its famous flower market; and the chance to explore Villefranche, a delightfully unspoilt seaside resort.

To put you in the picture about the Riviera:
Geographically and administratively the French Riviera stretches from Toulon to the Italian border. The coast, particularly the part around Nice, was discovered by the English aristocracy in the 18th century as a place whose mild climate was somewhat preferable to that of an English winter. According to records some 300 Britons spent the winter of 1784-85 in or near Nice for health reasons and the Dukes of York and Gloucester are among those who regularly holidayed in Nice.
The Revolution put a stop to those holidays, but after 1815 many English, Germans, Italians and Russians were to be found in Nice from November to May. Most would arrive by

stage coach, which involved a 24 hour journey from Marseille. However, the opening of the Paris – Nice railway in 1864, extending to Menton five years later, really opened up the Riviera as a centre for winter holidaymakers. Some 22000 came in 1887, increasing by 1914 to 150000. Cannes had been a small fishing village, but by 1879 it had 50 hotels, numerous villas and a number of estate agents.

The new residents – mainly English – were not always popular. Prosper Mérimée (author of the short story *Carmen*, on which Bizet's opera was based) commented bitterly: *'foreigners have bought up olive groves and settled here as if in conquered territory. They have ripped up all that was there before and deserve to be impaled on the architecture they have brought with them'*. (He was also a government inspector of historic monuments).

Short story writer Guy de Maupassant said of the villas he saw from his yacht that they were *'white eggs laid during the night'*.

One of the attractions of this coastal region for the English 'colonists' was its climate, unique in France because of its geographical isolation, sheltered as it is by the Southern Alps. They were interested in the climate not only for health reasons, but for the possibilities they thought it offered for cultivation. They sought to create on the Riviera the ideal *English* garden and so for example replaced native evergreens with deciduous plants. They were obsessed with creating lawns, which the locals could not understand: lawns needed constant watering and had no practical use.

Augustus Hare, an early 20th century chronicler of the Riviera wrote: *'The hills are covered with hideous villas, chiefly built by the rich English whose main object seems to be the effacement of all the natural beauties of the place. They sow grass which will never live, import northern shrubs which cannot grow, cut down and root up all the original woods and flowers'*.

Probably the period between 1850 and 1940 was the 'golden age' of the Riviera in terms of development largely by the rich, French or foreigners, and painters found the light wonderful. Coco Chanel and the writer Colette lived here, as did Matisse and Renoir. It was also a home to exiles for political, tax and social reasons. One of these, Somerset Maugham claimed to be the first person to grow avocadoes in Europe (smuggled in from the USA in his golf bag) and he was still digging up and resowing his lawn in 1966.

Perhaps surprisingly, when we think of holidays on the Riviera today, it was not until 1931 that hotels opened for the *summer* season and Coco Chanel created the latest fashion: beach pyjamas.

Mass tourism really began once workers were given paid holidays and discovered the delights of a region hitherto the preserve of the wealthy.

Riviera or Côte d'Azur?
The word Riviera comes from the Italian for 'shore' and was used in particular to describe the Italian coast from La Spezia to the French border and then extended to include the French coast as far as Hyères. In French it is more usually known as the *Côte d'Azur*, which was the title of a book written about the region in 1887 by Stephen Liegeard. The book was so popular that its title has become the name of the region – sometimes shortened to *la Côte* - though its author has not gained the same universal renown.

Where to stay:
Villefranche-sur-Mer is a few kilometres to the east of Nice, the capital of the Riviera, which makes it a central base from which to discover some treasures of the region without having to drive too far in any direction.

The old town, with its narrow streets running steeply down to the seafront, has some hidden delights and is small enough for you to walk round and feel that you have got to know it after only a few days' stay. There are a number of decent hotels: the *Welcome*, on the seafront, is probably the one with the most character – Jean Cocteau used to stay there – but it doesn't have a pool.

I like the *Hôtel La Flore*, in the avenue Princesse Grace de Monaco, which is a continuation of the coast road from Nice. This 3 star Logis de France has a pool and its restaurant *Le Fleuron* is good value. Ask for Category 2 or 3 rooms which will give you a balcony overlooking the beautiful Villefranche bay. The restaurant is closed on Wednesdays but they have an arrangement for half-board guests to dine at the *Versailles* next door, or you can take the opportunity to sample the restaurants in the old town or along the seafront.

How to get there:
If you are coming to Villefranche having hired your car at Nice airport (their departure drop-off zone has the sign, in English, 'Kiss and Fly', suitably romantic for the Riviera I always think), follow the coast road (N98) eastwards all the way. This takes you along the Promenade des Anglais, where you cannot miss the famed Négresco hotel – look for its dome. Otherwise leave the Motorway A9 at Exit 55 (if you miss this it's a long way to the next exit and well beyond Villefranche). From Exit 55 you do have to drive through Nice, which can be a bit of a test: follow signs to the port and then along the coast road (N98 – direction Monaco and Menton). Unfortunately Villefranche does not seem to be very well signed.

Excursions: 1. Villefranche and Eze Village
  2. St-Paul-de-Vence and the Matisse chapel in Vence
  3. Picasso museum at Vallauris and Renoir's house at Cagnes
  4. Nice
  5. Cap Ferrat

Excursion 1: Villefranche and Eze Village

To put you in the picture about Villefranche:
The bay of Villefranche is a natural, deep-water harbour, protected by a ring of mountains and has served as an anchorage since Greco-Roman times. From 1945 to 1962 it was home to the American fleet and nowadays is an overnight stop for cruise liners, whose passengers are brought ashore and bussed off to spend a day in Nice or Monte Carlo.

Over the centuries Villefranche and indeed the whole county of Nice, of which Villefranche was a part, has been shunted back and forth between various rulers.

The original settlement was a *village perché* (hilltop village) called Montolivo, situated above the modern resort of Beaulieu-sur-Mer, dating back to about the 5th century AD.

In 1295 the count of Provence, Charles II of Anjou, who was aware of the strategic importance of the bay, wanted to create a settlement at sea level. He founded the town of Villefranche.

Towards the end of the 14th century Villefranche and the county of Nice were ceded to the duchy of Savoy and remained basically in the hands of the dukes of Savoy until 1793. In the 1500s the Holy Roman Emperor Charles V could not move between his lands in Italy or Austria to his Spanish possessions without going through Savoyard territory, so it was important to him to support the dukes of Savoy against the French king, François I, who wanted to reclaim the county of Nice as part of his own heritage. Charles therefore financed new 'state of the art' fortifications: the Citadelle at Villefranche and the Mont Alban fort above Nice. The newly formed Savoyard fleet was stationed in the bay, providing an added defence against attack from the sea.

From the land, however it was more vulnerable and Louis XIV occupied Nice from 1691-97 and again from 1707-13. Each time it was retaken by Savoy. By the way, the duchy of Savoy became the kingdom of Sardinia in 1718, but still ruled the county of Nice. The Villefranche citadelle and Mont Alban fort changed hands twice more during the War of the Austrian Succession in the 1740s.

The Revolution seems to have passed the region by initially, although some of the French nobility 'emigrated' to the county of Nice for obvious reasons.

In 1793, however, Nice became French – the citadelle and Mont Alban fort capitulating without a fight - only to be returned to the king of Sardinia on the abdication of Napoleon in 1814.

The final act was the return of the County of Nice to France in 1860. Napoleon III landed at Villefranche amid the proverbial scenes of joy. He is regarded as the moderniser of Villefranche: he created the coast road *(basse corniche)* from Nice to Menton, opened in 1861 and the first train arrived at Villefranche station on Christmas day 1868.

Visit:
From the Hôtel La Flore it only takes a few minutes to walk down to the sea front (a bit longer coming back, as it's uphill). Sunday morning is a good time to explore the old town as there is a *brocante* market along avenue Foch and in place Amélie Pollonnais (*brocante* basically means second hand articles not good enough to be called antiques, though prices might indicate otherwise).

Get a town plan from the hotel or from the Tourist Office in the François Binon gardens off avenue Foch. From this you will notice that the old part of town is set out in a grid system with roads running parallel to the sea front and steps going down the hill at right angles to these. This goes back to the founding of the town in 1295.

To encourage the inhabitants of Montolivo and the surrounding area to come and live in the new town. Charles II count of Provence agreed, by charter, to ensure the safety of the inhabitants with ramparts and watch towers, build a church and provide a fresh water system, give exemption from certain taxes.

This was typical of the creation of new towns all over the south of France in the 13th and 14th centuries. These are called *bastides* and there are over 600 of them. You can readily spot them by their names: Villefranche (free town), Villeneuve (new town), Châteauneuf or Castelnau (new castle), Sauveterre or Salvetat (safe place) or including the word *bastide* (Labastide-Murat).

Near the bottom of rue de l'Eglise turn into what seems to be a tunnel. This is rue Obscure, built to protect the inhabitants under attack from enemy ships – the town was easy prey to pirates and other enemies until the citadelle was built in the 16th century.

At the top end of rue Obscure you come out into a very small square, place du Conseil, with a cross and a well. This would have been the town's public meeting place, serving a similar purpose to the forum of Roman towns. In many *bastides* the square, with its cross and well, is the centre of the 'grid' design of these mediaeval 'new towns' and typically much larger. Here the lie of the land made that impossible – the essential is that a public meeting place should exist. (For further examples of *bastides*, see Tour 4).

A wander through the narrow streets of the old town will bring glimpses of attractive old doorways and house fronts, bedecked with flowers.

Down on the quayside opposite the Hôtel Welcome, you will find the tiny Chapelle St Pierre, decorated inside and out in 1957 by Jean Cocteau, writer, painter and film maker, (he died in 1963 on the same day as the singer Edith Piaf). Cocteau discovered Villefranche in 1924, staying for 2 years in room 11 of the Welcome. From his window he could see a dilapidated former chapel used as a store for fishing nets. By the 1950s Cocteau was staying on Cap Ferrat when a friend asked him to decorate the old chapel.

The result is a series of frescoes that cover the whole of the interior with graphically portrayed scenes from the life of St Peter (patron saint of fishermen) and scenes of Provençal life: homage to the fishergirls of Villefranche and to the gypsies of Les Saintes Maries de la Mer. The simple elegance of his figures is contrasted with the elaborate geometric designs of the pillars and arches: all in all a feast for the eyes. On the quayside next to the chapel is a bust of Cocteau, sculpted in 1989 to commemorate the centenary of his birth, with the inscription: *'Quand je regarde Villefranche je vois ma jeunesse. Fassent les homes qu'elle ne change jamais'* (When I look at Villefranche I see my youth. May men make sure it never changes) - a sentiment I agree with absolutely.

NB there is a museum to Jean Cocteau in Menton.

The chapel is open every day except Monday, always closed for lunch, but open until 8.30pm from June to mid September. Entry: 2€

The citadelle St Elme is close by. This was restored in 1981 and is a fine example of a 16th century fortress. Note its star shape – by breaking up the straight lines, it gave greater strength to the walls under fire from enemy cannon. Its design, and that of the Mont Alban fort which was built on the same principle, so impressed Louis XIV's military architect Vauban that both forts were spared when Louis ordered the destruction of all the defences of the County of Nice.

Nowadays the site contains the Town hall, open air theatre and three museums. In the Volti museum enjoy the voluptuous sculpted women of this local artist.

The Volti museum is free (as are the other two), but closed on Tuesdays and for lunch (12-3pm from June to September).

In the Baroque Church of St Michel (half way up rue de l'Eglise) look out for the impressively realistic 17th century figure of Christ carved from the trunk of a fig tree by a galley slave.

Where to eat:

The sea front has a whole row of restaurants and there are more in the streets of the old town. I have enjoyed eating on the terrace of the *Caravelle* (rue du Vallon), but the one I prefer is *Michel's* in place Amélie Pollonnais (the square above the Cocteau chapel), particularly for its seafood. It's always worth booking your table in advance, especially if you are thinking of having lunch there on Sunday, before going to Eze.

Another thing:

The Russians were allowed by the king of Sardinia to set up a coaling station at Villefranche for their fleet in the 1850s, which no doubt accounts to some extent for the Russian 'colony' that became established in the Nice region, and the arrangement continued after the county returned to French rule in 1860. However, as a refuelling base it became obsolete and in 1885 the building was turned into a laboratory for zoological research, funded by Russia until 1917. The French resisted demands by the Soviet government to renew their involvement and nationalised the laboratory in 1931. It continues its research under the name of Observatoire Océanographique de Villefranche.

To put you in the picture about Eze:
This rocky outcrop has been inhabited for some 2500 years. Moorish pirates who occupied the site in about 900AD built a lookout post here (the gate known as the Porte des Maures commemorates their entry). In subsequent centuries the place had the same rulers as Nice and Villefranche. The village was fortified in the 14th century. The mediaeval postern gate still has its hinges (on the right hand wall), one mounted upside down so that the gate could not be lifted off.
The château at the top of the village was destroyed in 1706 by Louis XIV and in 1860 the inhabitants voted unanimously for the county of Nice to become French.
Until the 1970s the economy of Eze depended on the cultivation of carnations (the flower of Provence) and mandarin oranges. Now it's tourism.

Another thing:
Eze owes its name, so legend says, to the temple of the goddess Isis built here by the Phoenicians. Another possibility is that it derives from a Gallo-Celtic druid divinity Hesus or Aesus, or maybe the name comes from the Celtic root word 'av', meaning high place, since the village was called Avisione before being shortened to Isia and then Eze. As a linguist I find this last explanation the most likely.

Visit:
It's a good idea to pick up a plan of Eze from the Tourist Office in the corner of the car park. This will give you an idea of the 'shape' of the village.
From the car park you have a steep walk up to the village, which you enter by the postern gate. I have been known to drive my passengers to this gate, then go down again to park the car. Once inside the village you step back in time as you climb (slowly because it's steep) up through the narrow streets and alleyways, pausing to enjoy the scent of the flowers and to notice the way the old stone houses blend into the rock. Even

those that are now art and craft or souvenir shops do not seem to intrude.

It hardly matters which way you go: as long as you keep climbing you will reach the top of the village.

On the way, in the tiny square called Le Planet, you see one of the best houses in the village. It belonged to the Riquier family, who were lords of Eze from the 13th to the 16th century.

A little further up is the 14th century Chapel of the White Penitents, a brotherhood founded to help the poor and who also took on the task of burying the dead in time of plague. The chapel is closed but through the grill notice the 13th century crucifix on the altar where Christ appears to be smiling.

To get up to the ruined château and enjoy the best view on the Riviera (orientation tables tell you what you can see) you have to pay to go through the spectacular Jardin exotique (cactus garden) – it is worth it. This garden was created in 1949, all the earth and plants being carried up by mules…and men. It contains several hundred varieties of succulents – I particularly like mother-in-law's cushion.

On your way down go via the parish church, rebuilt in the 18th century. Its sober façade is in stark contrast with its exuberant baroque interior. Perhaps over-exuberant is the somewhat grotesque arm holding a cross sticking out from the pulpit.

Another thing:

On the way up to the village there is a footpath called Le Chemin Nietzsche, leading down to the sea. Before the Moyenne Corniche road was built, this footpath was the way up to the village from the railway station. In 1883 the German philosopher Friedrich Nietzsche composed in his mind a chapter of *Thus Spake Zarathrustra* on the hard climb up. He said later: 'My muscles have always been at their most agile when my creative force is at its strongest'

Give yourself ½ hour to wander through the village and an hour to enjoy the cactus garden and views.

The garden is open all year round: November to March, 9.30am-5pm; April, 9am-6pm; May, October, 9am-6.30pm; June, September, 9am-7pm; July, August, 9am-8pm. Entry: 5€

Where to eat:
Appropriately enough, *Le Cactus*, just inside the entrance to the village, serves very tasty salads, pancakes and ice creams and could be an alternative to lunch in Villefranche. It is worth getting the hotel to reserve your table for you.

How to get there:
Follow the Basse Corniche (Lower Coast Road- N98 direction Menton) through Villefranche until you pick up a sign on your left for Eze Village (NB not Eze Bord de Mer). A narrow, steep, winding road (drivable - I have done it in a minibus - but watch out on the tight bends) brings you onto the Moyenne Corniche (Middle Coast Road, N7). Follow this about 5kms to Eze Village and park in the car park at the foot of the village. Journey time: 20 minutes.

An alternative parking place is at the Fragonard Perfume Factory at Eze, if you wish to take the guided tour of the factory as a prelude to your visit to the village (it is clearly signposted). Allow an hour for the tour and shop purchases (the hotel will have discount vouchers). The tours run every 15 minutes or so. Both tour and parking are free.

Excursion 2: St-Paul-de-Vence and the Matisse chapel in Vence

Organise this excursion according to the chapel opening times (see below), but whether you visit it in the morning or afternoon, allow an hour to walk round the 'vieille ville' (old town) of Vence (pronounced as in dance*) and its cathedral and of course give yourself enough time to enjoy*

lunch there.

A word of warning: St-Paul is one of the most visited villages in France, so you are never likely to be able to have it to yourself and parking can be a problem, especially at weekends in high season. That said, it is worth the trouble and I have always managed to park, even with a minibus.

Probably the best time to visit St-Paul is in the morning before it gets very crowded. At that time you can get a real flavour of the mediaeval village that it was, with its narrow streets and alleys, its old stone houses that are still very atmospheric in spite of the profusion of arty boutiques and ice-cream shops that now occupy them.

To put you in the picture:
St-Paul is another mediaeval hilltop village. The original fortifications were redesigned in the 16th century by François I as St-Paul assumed strategic importance as a frontier fort in opposition to the castle at Nice during his longstanding conflict with the Holy Roman Emperor. The fortress was only decommissioned in 1868 after the county of Nice ceased to be independent *(see above:* To put you in the picture about Villefranche).

In more recent times, particularly between the two World Wars, the village has become the *rendez-vous* or home for countless artists. Chagall is buried in the cemetery here, Braque, Bonnard, Léger, Miró, Modigliani, Signac all stayed in St-Paul, as did the poet Jacques Prévert and film actors Simone Signoret and Yves Montand. Nowadays it is still the home to artists not yet so well known perhaps, as you will see by the number of galleries in the rue Grande which runs from one end of the village to the other.

Another thing:
You can call it either St-Paul or St-Paul-de-Vence. The Michelin map has St-Paul, the town plan says St-Paul-de-Vence. Putting the **de** in makes it sound more chic. With names of people it indicates nobility (compare Yves Montand and Simon **de** Montfort).

Visit:
Before you walk through the impressive fortified town gate, you will have seen a smart looking hotel, La Colombe d'Or, on the corner of place De Gaulle (note the de). This is where the artists tended to stay and the *boulodrome* (boules arena) in the square is renowned for having hosted games involving many a celebrity.

Once inside the gate, get a town plan from the tourist office, immediately on your right. This gives a good visual idea of the layout of a fortified village. Turn off rue Grande up Montée de l'Eglise and up more steps into the church with its wide 13th century nave – the side aisles were added two hundred years later. At the far end of the left aisle, admire the painting of *St Catherine of Alexandria* attributed to Tintoretto.

In the right aisle is the church treasury, one of the best collections in the region. They are particularly proud of the late Renaissance ciborium, and a parchment actually signed by Henri III of France appeals to me, probably because of his bad reputation (as duke of Angoulême he was behind the St Bartholomew's Day Massacre of Protestants and as king organised the infamous murder of the duke de Guise).

In place de l'Eglise you can see the keep, all that remains of the mediaeval castle. Come back down to rue Grande and follow it to the other end of the village where from the ramparts you get a wonderful view down the valley to the sea at Cap d'Antibes.

Allow about 1¼ hours for your visit, including a stop for refreshment.

Visit: The Fondation Maeght *(pronounced Meg)*:
The foundation was set up in 1964 by Cannes art dealer Aimé Maeght and his wife Marguerite to promote the work of modern and contemporary artists. The architect José Luis Sert described his design for the building and grounds as 'installing a museum inside Nature'. In the building or in the gardens, work by many of the big names in modern art abounds. I am always rather taken by Braque's pond mosaic, Miró's *Labyrinthe*, the emaciated figures of Giacometti and an ingenious fountain by Pol Bury.

If you are keen on modern art and sculpture this is a feast for your eyes.
The museum is open daily: July to September, 10am-7pm; October-June, 10am-6pm
Entry: 11€
Allow about 1¼ hours for your visit

How to get there:
Take the road into Nice and follow signs to the motorway (junction 55). Leave at junction 48 and follow signs for Vence (D36). It is worth following this road most of the way to Vence then doubling back the 3kms or so to St-Paul on the D7. This way you have a spectacular view of the hilltop village of St-Paul silhouetted against the sky across the valley from the D36.
Journey time from Villefranche: about ¾ hour.
For the Fondation Maeght leave St-Paul by either the chemin de Ste Claire or the montée des Trious. After about 800m the entrance to the grounds of the Fondation is on your left. It is worth driving and parking there as it is quite a long walk from the village and through the grounds to the museum.
For Vence leave St-Paul by the D2. After 2kms you reach Vence. Follow signs to the old town (vieille ville) and car parks.
Journey time: 5 minutes

Visit: The old town (vieille ville) of Vence:
Walk through one of the five town gates into this bustling mediaeval town of narrow streets, lovely old houses and lively markets selling Provençal specialities.
The cathedral entrance is tucked away in a corner of the place Clémenceau. Once inside you are struck by the size of the building, compared with what you see from the outside. As striking is the mix of styles, Romanesque, Gothic, Baroque. Do not miss the 1979 Chagall mosaic in the baptistry, representing Moses rescued from the waters. Another highlight is the set of 15th century choir stalls by the Grasse sculptor Jean Bellot. He has created some quite racy misericords and armrests, one or two of the latter obviously appreciated by the clergy, to judge by their well worn state. These were originally

round the main altar, but were moved up to the gallery only 50 years after they were made, because they were too big.

Also in the gallery are some powerful 17th and early 18th century wood-carved scenes of Christ's Passion rescued from a 'Calvary' in another part of Vence.

To see the Choir stalls close up you may have to ask permission from the gallery attendant (a good idea to offer a little donation to church funds), so don't go during her lunchtime.

Where to eat:
I have lunched more than once at *Le Clémenceau* –on the corner of the place Clémenceau - and have enjoyed M. Castenetto's pizzas and salads. Eat on his terrace in the square with the bustle of the market around you.

Visit: The Matisse chapel

To put you in the picture:
The Chapel of Our Lady of the Rosary is more often called the Matisse Chapel after its designer Henri Matisse. In 1941 Matisse was diagnosed with cancer and was nursed during his recovery by Monique Bourgeois, who had answered his advert for a 'young and pretty nurse'. In addition, she posed for him and several paintings exist of her – always clothed. In 1943 Monique entered the Dominican convent in Vence, becoming Sister Jacques-Marie. They met up again when Matisse moved to Vence that year, to get away from the threat of bombardment in Nice. She told Matisse about plans to build a chapel in Vence and asked if he would help design it. Surprisingly, as Matisse was not a practising catholic, he agreed and so, with some reluctance, did the Dominican hierarchy, because of the artist's reputation.

Matisse devoted the four years between 1947 and 1951 to working on all aspects of the new chapel: the architecture, stained glass windows, murals, furnishings, priests' vestments. In a letter which was read out at the inauguration of the chapel in 1951 Matisse said 'this project is the result of all my working life'. He considered it his masterpiece but unfortunately was unable to attend the inauguration through illness.

Another thing:
It is said that Picasso wrote to Matisse expressing surprise that he had been asked to design a chapel and that a brothel might have been more appropriate. Matisse supposedly replied that he agreed, but no one had asked him.

Visit:
From the road it is an unassuming building and you are only aware of its blue and white tiled roof and the 13m high wrought iron cross decorated with crescent moons.
Inside, the overwhelming impression is of light and space and it is full of symbolism. Two naves at right angles, the smaller for the nuns, the larger for the congregation, both focus on the altar of a soft brown stone (chosen, it is said, for its resemblance to the colour of bread and symbol of the Eucharistic bread), while the intricately carved pews harmonise with the colour of the altar. Floor, ceiling and walls are predominantly white.
The real splash of colour comes from the stained glass windows, which use three vivid colours typical of the Mediterranean: yellow (sun and flowers), green (foliage), blue (sky), but the genius of Matisse is in the way the sunlight filtering through the stained glass brings colour to the floor and walls. The effect is stunning.
So is the effect of the outline figures of St Dominic and Mary and Child painted on the wall tiles. Note the way that Mary is holding the Child and yet He has His arms outstretched to embrace the world. Nor are the Stations of the Cross just seen as a procession, but as an artistic whole. Clever use of diagonals leads our eye in to the focal point: no 12, Christ crucified.
In the adjacent gallery you can see the strikingly beautiful modern vestments designed by Matisse and only taken out on big occasions – for normal services copies are worn. Also in the gallery, photos of Matisse at work give an insight into the difficulty of the undertaking. His preparatory drawings for the murals in particular make you realise that the apparent

simplicity of the final version was the result of much work and sheer artistic brilliance.

The chapel is open: mornings – Tuesday, Thursday, 10-11.30am, Sunday for Mass, 10am; afternoons - Monday, Tuesday, Wednesday, Thursday, Saturday, 2-5.30pm (also Friday 2-5.30pm during school holidays).
Entry: 3€
The visit takes about ¾ hour.

How to get there:
From the centre of (modern) Vence follow signs for St Jeannet (D2210) and the Chapelle du Rosaire, which is on the right hand side about 1km out of the town centre. Park along the road in designated areas (you may have to go beyond the chapel to find somewhere).

Excursion 3: Nice

This all-day trip really concentrates on the old part of Nice and a visit to the permanent Matisse exhibition at Cimiez (pronounced Simyay). Old Nice is a 'must' but there are of course other museums or galleries you could visit (the best of these are probably the Musée des Beaux-Arts Jules Chéret for the widest range, the Musée Marc-Chagall, the Musée d'Art moderne et d'Art contemporain).

My choice of Matisse is, like everything else in this guide, a matter of personal preference. I do like his work; Nice was his adopted home - he came in 1917, lived here, with the exception of part of the war until his death in 1954 - and his museum is situated in a very pleasant park.

Make sure you don't visit Nice on a Monday: it's the only day there is no flower market in the Cours Saleya.

To put you in the picture about Old Nice:
What is now called the 'Old Town' was until the 18th century the entire city of Nice. Since then new districts have been added, so that the city now stretches inland as far as the A9 motorway and westwards to the airport, using up, it seems, every available bit of building land (mind you, you will see

that this is typical of building development all along the coast from Cannes to Menton). Nice is France's fifth largest city.

The original 500 BC Greek colony of Nikaia probably settled on the hill above the present port, but by 200BC the Romans moved 3kms inland to another hill to found their colony Cemelenum (Cimiez). It was only in the 15th and 16th centuries AD that the civil and religious administration moved down the hill to what is now the 'Old Town'.

Many of the buildings here owe their style to the fact that Nice was not really part of France until 1860 (see: To put you in the picture about Villefranche). Baroque predominates under the Italian influence, so that, if you are used to the austerity of the interiors of English cathedrals or churches, you may find those you visit in Nice somewhat, or even over ornate. The character of the Old Town is quite Italian, from the Baroque architecture and the strong colours of 'Sardinian red' and yellow ochre on the facades of buildings to the Italian style food offered in so many of the cafés and restaurants.

Another thing:

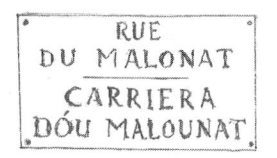

> RUE
> DU MALONAT
> CARRIERA
> DÓU MALOUNAT

You may hear local people speaking something other than French amongst themselves. This is Nissart, a local version of the Occitan language common all over the south of France until the 20th century. Italian became the official language of the county of Nice in the 16th century, superseded by French of course when the territory was returned to France in 1860. Despite all the odds Nissart survived and is now taught in schools and at the University. Look for examples of it in the street names, which are given in French and Nissart.

Visit:

Start by strolling through the flower market of the Cours Saleya (if you are lucky you will have managed to park in the underground car park there). This flower market is considered the best in France. When I took a French friend in Narbonne

flowers from here she was delighted: she had never before been given flowers from 'the famous Cours Saleya market'.
From the central square onwards it becomes a fruit and vegetable market. The stalls full of bowls of spices have a real Mediterranean, even North African flavour. This part of the market is cleared by 1pm but the flower market goes on until after 5pm and at the end of the afternoon beautiful bouquets are sold off at bargain prices.
On the corner of place Pierre-Gautier and Cours Saleya the Chapelle de la Miséricorde is the finest piece of Baroque religious architecture in Nice. It has an unusual elliptical nave and fine 19th century decoration.
At the end of the Cours Saleya, the yellow building at no1 with a backdrop of the Castle Hill is an old palace, but is better known as the home of Henri Matisse. From 1921 to 1938 he rented rooms, first on the 3rd floor, then on the 4th, both overlooking the sea.
As you reach place Charles Félix turn left into rue de la Poissonnerie. The centre piece of the first storey of No 8 is an unusual bas-relief of Adam and Eve, unusual in that they seem to be involved in a 'domestic' – have branches of the olive trees been damaged by their swinging clubs? This lively piece of story-telling is dated 1584 but its most recent restoration

was in 1986.
Further up the road on the left you come to the very simple façade of the Eglise de l'Annonciation. The mediaeval church was originally dedicated to St Giaume, rebuilt in the 17th century, rededicated - after a fire in 1834 - to the

Annunciation, which is depicted in the painting behind the altar. However, the church is more usually known as Ste Rita, who is the patron saint of desperate causes. Worship of this 15th century Augustinian nun came about after 1860 through the many Italian immigrants who put their trust in her. To judge by the number of candles and flowers that always adorn her chapel, visitors from far and wide still come to pray to her. Her chapel is the first on the left as you come in.

Go straight on and take the second on the right, rue de la Place Vieille.

Just before the steps up to the Colline du Château turn left into rue Droite (the adjective *droit/droite* means *straight* or *direct*. This street isn't straight, but, in spite of its curves, it was a direct route between two city gates). Almost immediately on your right is the Eglise St Jacques. It was built for the Jesuits (Society of Jesus) in the 17th century and doubtless for this reason is better known as the Eglise du Gesù (Jesus). The Baroque façade dates from 1825, but the interior has a single rectangular nave which would be rather austere but for its sumptuous Baroque decoration. Notice especially the frieze of angels – 164 painted and 48 sculpted – and the pulpit with its arm holding a cross (as in the church at Eze).

Another thing:
When you look at Baroque church interiors, notice the way the decoration is ordered: at the lowest level – that of man – it is quite plain; the higher it goes the richer and more intricate it becomes, the nearer it gets to heaven – represented by the vaulted ceilings.

Continue up rue Droite. On your left past the next crossroads is the Palais Lascaris at No15. Palace was the name given to homes of the nobility and rich bourgeoisie, and is taken directly from its Italian usage – another Italian influence in Nice. This was the home of the Lascaris-Vintimille family, one of the most prestigious families and residences in Nice. It was built in 1648 by Field-Marshall Jean-Baptiste Lascaris, nephew of Jean-Paul Lascaris de Castellar, Grand Master of the Order of Malta (Knights of St John, whence St John's

Ambulance brigade), which gives you an idea of the family's standing .

It was confiscated during the Revolution and turned into small flats, rapidly falling into disrepair (a similar thing happened in the Marais district in Paris). However, it was classified as a Historical Monument in 1946 and over the years has been restored to its former glory – work is still going on.

It is difficult to see the decoration of the façade, as the street is so narrow, but inside it is magnificent. Looking up at the façade, try to pick out, round the windows, masks of the ages of man: old people on the first floor, children on the second, adults under the balconies.

Now a municipal museum, it houses, somewhat incongruously it seems to me, an 18th century chemist's, acquired from Victor Hugo's birthplace in Besançon, apparently to remind us that shops often occupied the ground floor of old palaces in Nice, although they would have opened straight onto the street.

All is Baroque, from the richly decorated monumental staircase to the state rooms on the second floor (the *piano nobile*) giving onto rue Droite. The guest bedroom is particularly ornate with its caryatids and painted ceiling. On the other side of the house a chapel was converted in the 18th century into a bedchamber. All the Lascaris family furniture has disappeared and been replaced with fine contemporary pieces, but the wonderful decor of the *piano nobile* is original, though of course restored. Notice the so called 'flying' doors in all the rooms. Mounted on asymmetrical hinges, they shut automatically.

Entry to the Palais Lascaris is free, but it is closed on Mondays and for lunch, 12-2pm.

Another thing:
There are just two places in France I covet as a pied-à-terre: the Palais Lascaris is one of them, the other is 47 rue Vieille du Temple in the Marais district of Paris.

Retrace your steps down rue Droite past the Eglise du Gesù. Turn right into rue du Jésus. This brings you into place Rosetti, on the opposite side of which is the cathédrale Ste Réparate. As you approach the square you can hardly fail to see the dome of the cathedral with its 14000 glazed tiles – a landmark in the Old Town. The cathedral was built on the site of an older church in 1750, but the decoration of the façade had to wait until 1825. Again, the interior is impressively Baroque, the chapel of the Blessed Sacrament in the right transept being the most spectacular with its twisted coupled marble columns. For an idea of Nice in the 17th century look at the painting above the main altar to the right of *La Gloire de sainte Réparate.*

Another thing:
Ste Réparate, patron saint of Nice, was a 15 year old girl martyred in Palestine in the 3rd century AD. Her body was, according to legend, carried across the sea to Nice in a boat drawn by angels. This would account for the bay in which Nice lies being called La Baie des Anges, unless it was because of the abundance of angel fish found there. Take your choice.

Where to eat:
I like the restaurant *La Claire Fontaine* facing the cathedral. You sit outside and watch the bustle of the square and enjoy the local cuisine – try one of their dishes that give you a selection of local specialities.
There is also a tempting ice-cream shop a few yards away.

Your gentle morning's walk round Old Nice should take about 2 hours. Be sure to give yourself time to look in the cathedral before lunch – it tends to close at 12.30pm. It's a good idea to book your table at the restaurant before visiting the cathedral, as it can fill up quickly.

Matisse Museum, Cimiez:

To put you in the picture:
The permanent collection of Matisse's work is housed in a splendid 17th century Genoese style villa set in spacious grounds next to the remains of the baths and amphitheatre of the Roman settlement of Cemelenum.

The villa was built for Jean-Baptiste Gubernatis, consul of Nice, and completed a few years later by his grandson who was president of the Nice Senate and ambassador to the Dukes of Savoy in Spain, Portugal and Rome, all of which contributed to the grandeur and style of the place. It is not until you are really close that you realise that the decoration round the windows of the façade is all *trompe-l'oeil*.

The wealthy bourgeois Garin de Cocconato family owned the villa from 1823 until it was bought by the municipality in 1950 and renamed Villa des Arènes, because of its proximity to the amphitheatre.

The connection with Matisse?

The artist had lived since 1938 in an apartment in the Hôtel Régina on avenue de Cimiez just below the present museum. He therefore knew the area well and while convalescing after his illness in 1941 he would walk in the grounds of the villa with his nurse Monique Bourgeois. Shortly before his death in 1954, Matisse gave the town a substantial number of his works in recognition of his deep affection for Nice. So when, in their turn, Matisse's widow and children made a gift of the artist's work to create a museum, the Villa des Arènes was their choice and the museum was opened in 1963.

Visit:

The aim of the gifts made by Matisse himself, and later by his family, was that people should understand the nature of his work. Matisse's earlier choice of works for the museum of his birthplace in the north of France, Cateau-Cambrésis, already indicated his concern to show the way his work had evolved.

That is the principle of this exhibition too. As we move from room to room we see his work evolve. His first painting, a still life, *Nature morte aux livres*, was painted in 1890 in traditional style and with a signature that is a palindrome of his name. His early landscapes show his gradual discovery of colour. Matisse himself said: *'Soon I became enamoured of the brightness of pure colour. I returned from my trip (to Brittany) with a passion for the colours of the rainbow.'* His paintings in the south of France and Corsica in 1898 show the new emphasis on light, shade and colour. Compare *Village en Bretagne* with *la Cour du Moulin à Ajaccio*. A stay in Collioure in 1905 with

Derain marked the start of fauvism (in French *fauve* is 'wild beast'). His *Portrait de Mme Matisse* is an example, with its strong application of pure colour.

Light effects and colour are central to Matisse's work, which exudes a sensuality without the constraint of conventional rules. *Odalisque au coffret rouge (1927), Fenêtre à Tahiti (1935), Nu au fauteuil (1937), Fauteuil rocaille (1946), Nature morte aux grenades (1947)* are notable exhibits.

For Matisse there was an interplay between the various component parts that created the pictorial tension of the picture. Matisse often used patterns as background or to frame the picture. These patterns, which came from his love of fabrics and from the collection he was always adding to, were an integral part of the work.

This love of fabric patterns was influential in the paper cut-out work of Matisse's later years, examples of which form an important part of the exhibition. The simple elegance he achieved in these sometimes startling cut-outs is reflected in his designs for the chapel at Vence (see Excursion 2) and in his drawings which are on display.

Another thing:
Le Cateau-Cambrésis, his birthplace, was a textile town and Bohain, where Matisse grew up, was famous for the spectacular coloured silks it produced for the Paris fashion trade. Both places clearly influenced his work.

How to get there:
Make your way to place Masséna and turn right into boulevard Jean Jaures (it's one way). Keep on this street as far as the Bibliothèque Louis Nucéra. Then turn left into boulevard Carabacel, which leads into boulevard de Cimiez. By now you should be picking up signs to Cimiez and Musée Matisse. Follow boulevard de Cimiez all the way up the hill, past smart residences and roads with posh English names (avenue George V, boulevard Prince de Galles), which say something about the 20th century history of Nice. When the road forks (just after boulevard Edouard VII on the right hand side), turn right into avenue de Cimiez and right again into

avenue des Arènes de Cimiez. There is parking in front of the gardens which you walk through to reach the museum.
The museum - a very well choreographed journey through the artistic life of Matisse - is open daily, except Tuesdays, 10am-6pm (5pm between October and March). Entry: 4€
Allow a good hour for your visit.

Excursion 4: Picasso museum at Vallauris and Renoir's house at Cagnes

To put you in the picture:
Picasso visited the annual pottery fair at Vallauris in 1946 and, liking the work exhibited by the Madoura studio, asked to try his hand at pottery with them. A year later he returned to the studio and was delighted to see that they had kept his pieces from the previous year (two miniature bulls and the head of a faun). Thus began a collaboration that was to result in Picasso creating over 4000 pieces in their studio until his death in 1973.

Vallauris had been a centre for domestic pottery since Roman times, but the art side developed in the 19th and 20th centuries. However it is fair to say that it was Picasso coming to live and work there who really put it on the map. His presence attracted many famous artists and personalities to Vallauris. Ali Khan even married Rita Hayworth there. Picasso, a member of the French communist party, was made a freeman of the town by the communist town council.

Another thing:
Picasso loved bullfighting – he was born in Spain – and organised several bullfights in Vallauris. The bulls were always spared, except for his 80th birthday celebration when he invited the famous Spanish toreador Domingín and the bulls were killed. This was strictly against the law and resulted in legal proceedings against Picasso and the municipality.

Visit: National 'War and Peace' Museum and Ceramics Museum

Both museums are housed in the Château. This quite rare example of Renaissance architecture in Provence was built on the ruins of an old priory, of which only the chapel still exists. This now houses Picasso's monumental *War and Peace* paintings, which, however much you like pottery, are the main reason for coming here.

This is a unique work: panels painted in his studio and then fixed in place in the vaulted vestibule of this 12th century former chapel.

Like his painting *Guernica* this is a very political statement by Picasso, a committed communist and member of the Peace Movement. He was chairman of its meeting in Nice in 1950, when peace in Korea was very much on the agenda. The following year at the banquet given by the town to honour his 70th birthday, Picasso decided to decorate this chapel. There is reason to believe that his motivation was in part to equal the monumental projects of his fellow artists who lived in the region. Chagall had his *Message biblique* and decorated part of the cathedral in Vence, Matisse designed the Chapelle du Rosaire, also in Vence (see Excursion 2). Picasso, not a believer, doubtless enjoyed the idea of creating what he called a 'Temple of Peace', with its overtones of the French Revolution, when churches became 'Temples of Reason'.

The paintings were first exhibited in 1953 in Rome and Milan, without making the impact they have in the Vallauris chapel, which of course is where they were designed for and installed the next year, although not opened to the public until 1959.

I have deliberately not gone into the details of the paintings because, to my mind, their initial impact as you walk into the chapel with its deliberately subdued lighting is an important part of your experience. All I would say is that Picasso was worried that, after the strong images of war, his portrayal of peace might seem banal: *'I wonder what people do in peacetime, go to the office from 9 to 5, make love on Saturday and go out for a picnic on Sunday'*. His partner Françoise Gilot apparently helped him by suggesting: *'in peacetime all is possible. A child could plough the sea'*. Look for this and other incongruities as well as Françoise Gilot's face on the shield of the 'peace warrior'. The explanatory sheet, available in English at the entrance to the chapel is good and will certainly provoke discussion of the paintings as you walk round, while the *petit guide* goes into much more detail and is illustrated. It is on sale in the museum bookshop and is well worth buying if you read French.

In the ceramics museum I especially like his pieces that depict bullfighting, where the movement and confrontation between man and bull really come through.

How to get there:
Take the road into Nice and follow signs to the motorway (junction 55). Leave the motorway at junction 44 (Vallauris). Follow the D35 into Vallauris. There you will pick up signs to the Picasso museum. Park in the square facing the Château and walk round the corner to the Château entrance.
Journey time: about 50 minutes
The museums are open: 15th September to 14th June, 10am-12.15pm, 2pm-5pm (-end June, 1st-15th September, -6pm); July, August, 10am-7pm Entry: 3,25€
Allow 1 ½ hours to visit both museums

Where to eat:
There is a pleasant *brasserie* opposite the Château entrance, or try the *Gousse d'Ail* in the avenue de Grasse.

Renoir's house at Cagnes:
Renoir moved to Cagnes-sur-Mer in 1905, having already lived in Provence for some years to help combat his increasingly bad arthritis. In 1907 he had this house, 'Les Collettes', built in the delightful setting of its olive grove, with views of the old village and the sea.

While he was confined to a wheelchair, he became more and more crippled by arthritis, to the extent that his brush would have to be wedged between his fingers. Nonetheless, his paintings exuded happiness, alive with colour and light. One of the joys of this visit for me is that you can see, close up, a number of Renoir's original paintings from this period, decorating the rooms on the ground floor.

He took up sculpture too, using the hands of a young Spaniard, Richard Guino to form the sculpture according to Renoir's sketches and verbal instructions (literally: 'take a bit off there…'). You can admire several examples of this amazing collaboration and, in the garden, the impressive bronze *Venus Victrix*.

The house has a homely feel. The furniture and personal effects of 'the old master' in the studios, the knowledge that great names of the artistic world came to visit: Matisse, Bonnard, Rodin and Maillol; it all inspires a certain reverence and you can quite understand why Renoir chose to live and work in this delightful oasis of calm.

Another thing:
From the notes his fellow artists and sculptors who visited him made of their talks with Renoir we have valuable information about his ideas and we know he hated the expression 'the old master'.

How to get there:
From Vallauris take the motorway back to junction 48 (Cagnes-sur-Mer) and go through the town centre (NB You are heading away from the sea). Follow the signs to the Musée Renoir (avenue des Collettes). The museum is about 1km up on the left, but easy to miss on your first visit. When you find it, park in the road.
Journey time from Vallauris: 20minutes.
The museum is open: May to September, 10am-12 noon, 2-6pm; October, 22nd November to April,10am-12 noon, 2-5pm. Closed on Tuesday and in November Entry 3€
Visit: a good hour, including a stroll round the gardens.

Excursion 5: Cap Ferrat

To put you in the picture:
This peninsula shelters the Bay of Villefranche on its eastern side and looks pretty but pretty inaccessible. On the far side, approached from Beaulieu, there are more beaches and the small resort of St-Jean-Cap-Ferrat. Until the last decade of the

19th century, it was just a tiny fishing port, in the lee of the hilly outcrop of the headland. Then two property speculators started building and it soon became 'the' place to live to get away from the bustle of Nice and Monte Carlo. Its residents have included *entre autres* King Leopold II of Belgium, Scott Fitzgerald, Gregory Peck and Somerset Maugham. You can drive round the headland, or take the little tourist train whose commentary will tell you who lived where, but you won't see anything as all the properties are well hidden behind walls and lush greenery. However, *two* are open to the public.

Visit: La Villa Ephrussi-de-Rothschild

To put you in the picture:
The land was bought by Beatrice, Baroness Ephrussi de Rothschild in 1905, outbidding King Leopold II who wanted to extend his neighbouring property. She, backed by her Rothschild wealth and that of her banker husband, Maurice Ephrussi, started to create a place to house their vast collections of paintings, sculptures, furniture and *objets d'art,* among the richest in France.

The rocky outcrop was levelled and all the soil and water to make the garden was brought in. She even had full-scale wood and painted canvas 'mock-ups' of the house built to see how her design worked. She was so demanding that she got through more than twenty architects before the house was completed in 1912. A contemporary said of her that she was 'the sort of pretty woman whose destiny it is to thwart the stupid rules of common sense'. The villa was nicknamed the 'pink palazzo', being built in an Italian style with pink stucco rendering, but was given the name 'Ile de France' by Mme Ephrussi in memory of a cruise she took on a liner of that name.

When she died in 1934 she bequeathed the villa, complete with all its furnishings and the garden to the Institut de France so that it could become a museum that would look like a house that had been lived in, which it does, though by rather wealthy people by most standards.

Visit:

Your entrance fee allows you to visit all the rooms on the ground floor and the gardens, but it is worth paying the extra for a guided tour of the upstairs rooms.

It is also worth getting to the Villa Ephrussi when it opens at 10am so that you can explore the garden straightaway. Then you are more likely to have it to yourselves and see it at its best, as most visitors seem to do the tour of the house first.

In fact it is not just one, but a whole series of themed garden 'rooms', surrounding the central 'French' garden. The planting and landscaping reflect the style of different countries. Apart from the formal French style garden with its Temple of Love based on the Trianon at Versailles and its formal fountain (accompanied sometimes by the sound of music), my favourites are the Spanish garden whose canal and pergola are deliciously cool on a hot summer day, or the pagodas and streams in the Japanese garden (I like running water). The stone garden is a curiosity, created to house the sculptures and stonework that she had no room for in the house.

The house itself is surprising in that its inspiration is Italian, but the rooms all lead off a distinctively Spanish central 'patio', where the ceiling is painted blue to give the impression that you are outdoors looking up to the sky. Each room is furnished with period treasures: wood panels in the Louis XVI salon from the Hôtel Crillon in Paris; priceless Sèvres and Vincennes porcelain; Beauvais and Gobelins tapestries and an Aubusson rug of the period in the Louis XV salon. In Beatrice's boudoir is the piece that I would love to have: a delicately proportioned writing desk with Marie-Antoinette's monogram.

Upstairs, on the guided tour, you will see other gems including Meissen porcelain and Fragonard sketches. You will also be able to step out onto the loggia overlooking the garden which stretches out in front of you with the sea visible on both sides. It's as though you were standing on the bridge of a ship.

Another thing:
It is said that from the loggia Beatrice would stand like the captain of a ship and oversee her thirty gardeners, who she made wear sailors' berets while they worked.

Where to eat:
Where better to have lunch than in the dining room of the villa, now a restaurant and *salon de thé*. The setting is elegant and the various *formules* are not expensive. It's a good idea to book your table earlier in your visit.

How to get there:
Take the road (N98) through Villefranche towards Beaulieu. At the Beaulieu turn – traffic lights - follow signs to Villa Ephrussi. There is parking in the drive up to the villa.
Journey time: 10 minutes.
Visit of the house and garden: 2hours
NB Buy a combined ticket for the Villa Ephrussi and the Villa Kérylos, which you will visit in the afternoon.
Opening times for both places: 15th February to 1st November, 10am- 6pm (-7pm in July, August); 2nd November to 14th February, 2-6pm (weekends and school holidays, 10am-6pm)
Combined entry: 15€

Visit: Villa Kérylos

This faithful reconstruction of an ancient Greek villa is in a superb position on a little headland. The waves of the Golfe d'Eze lap at its walls and it certainly would not get planning permission today. It was the dream-come-true of Théodore Reinach, an erudite and rich French MP, one of whose hobbies was Greek archaeology. Working with a young Italian architect, Emmanuel Pontremoli, he created this luxury villa that reflects the way of life of a rich merchant from the Isle of Delos in the 2nd century BC. Built between 1902 and 1908, it nonetheless did include such modern comforts of the *Belle Epoque* as central heating and electricity…and a piano.

No expense was spared regarding the materials used to recreate the furniture and fittings, whose details were gleaned from illustrations on ancient Greek vases and mosaics.

Round three sides of the villa Reinach created a gallery at sea level to house a collection of reproductions of the most famous statues of ancient times. This atmospheric setting, where the windows open directly onto the sea, only serves to enhance the impressive array of sculptures, even if you know they are reproductions.

On his death in 1928 Reinach, as Mme Ephrussi was to do, bequeathed his unique villa to the Institut de France.

An audioguide is included in the entrance fee. It provides an excellent commentary about the ancient Greek features of the villa.

Visit: 1 hour

Another thing:
Théodore Reinach was sometimes to be seen dressed in a toga – really living the part.

How to get there:
From the Villa Ephrussi return to the turning for Beaulieu and follow the signs for Villa Kérylos. In Beaulieu, park near the seafront opposite the Casino. A little further on, turn right into rue Gustave Eiffel – he used to spend his winters in a villa here. Villa Kérylos is about 800m away at the far end of the road.

Journey time: 10 minutes

4 Bastides of the South West

The Midi-Pyénées region of South West France counts some 200 bastides, or 'mediaeval new towns'. The area covered by this tour brings extra interest to the story of the bastides, as it uncovers the machinations of politicians and the church, as well as offering fine examples of these lovely 'vieilles pierres' (old stonework).
Cordes was the first bastide to be created, while Villefranche is the 'pearl of the Rouergue'. Villeneuve d'Aveyron, Sauveterre-de-Rouergue, Najac and la Bastide l'Evêque represent different facets of this 13th century, yet incredibly modern phenomenon.
Albi, though not a bastide, is an absolute 'must' and both Monestiès and St-Antonin-Noble-Val provide unexpected attractions.

Where to stay:
I propose the *Hostellerie du Vieux Cordes*, a 3 star Logis de France in the heart of this lovely hilltop *bastide*. It has loads of charm, including its courtyard where you can have your evening meal under the shade of the two hundred year old wisteria. The hotel restaurant is run under the auspices of master chef Yves Thuriès who owns the 4 star *Le Grand Ecuyer*, also in Cordes. The food at the *Hostellerie du Vieux*

Cordes is worthy of him, but not as expensive as *Le Grand Ecuyer.*
The only way to savour fully the magic of Cordes is to be there at night.

How to get there:
From Toulouse take the A68 motorway (direction Albi). Leave at exit 9 (Gaillac). Follow the main road into and through Gaillac, picking up signs for Cordes and Villefranche-de-Rouergue (D922). As you approach Cordes you will have a good view of the bastide. 2kms outside Cordes you join the D600. In the square of the lower town (place de la Bouteillerie), turn left up the narrow road signposted Vieux Cordes.
Follow this road, which climbs steeply up the hillside, for about 2 kms. NB it is one-way. Just before the road starts to go down again turn sharp right and go through the narrow town gate. Take the left fork (it is still one-way) and 800m further up park, temporarily, in front of the Hostellerie du Vieux Cordes on your left.
If you have decided to stay at Le Grand Ecuyer, you have to turn right opposite the Hostellerie and then right again to get down to Le Grand Ecuyer. Both hotels will explain where you have to park overnight.

Excursions: 1. Villefranche-de-Rouergue, Villeneuve d'Aveyron, La Bastide l'Evêque
2. Cordes, Najac
3. Sauveterre-de-Rouergue, Monestiès
4. Albi
5. St Antonin, Gorges de l'Aveyron, Bruniquel, Castelnau-de-Montmiral.

To put you in the picture about Bastides:
Bastides fit into the wider movement of proper townships that grew up all over France from the 11th through to the 14th century. The *bastide* however was peculiar to the north of Italy, northern Spain and southern France from Aquitaine to Provence. In France the first foundation was Cordes in 1222

and the last was La Bastide-d'Anjou in the Aude department in 1373. The area most densely populated with *bastides* was the south west, in the region today called Midi-Pyrénées.

What distinguishes a *bastide* from other mediaeval towns or villages is that these were deliberate creations with specific characteristics. On their creation they were given a charter, but unfortunately most have been lost. However it is possible to recognise a *bastide* by its physical characteristics. Very often they were set out like a grid, with straight streets and regular intersections, dividing the ground into equal sized plots for the houses. They would have a main square, which would serve as a market and public meeting place. The square would in most cases have a well, a cross and be surrounded by covered arcades. This last is a feature of many southern towns, be they *bastides* or not, as a means of providing protection from the elements – mainly the sun.

Another way of recognising a bastide is from its name. Sometimes this is a giveaway, like *La Bastide-l'Evêque* (bastide of the bishop) or *La Bastide-d'Anjou* (bastide of the Anjou family), showing the name of the founder. Other tell-tale names are *Villeneuve* (new town) or *Villefranche* (free town).

However, it is not always as easy. In the 11th and 12th centuries, towns or villages given protection by the church would be called *Sauveté* (safe place) or its *Occitan* version *Salvetat*. At much the same time other towns grew up protected by a castle and were given the name Châteauneuf (new castle) or again the *Occitan* Castelnau. (pronounced *castelno*)

These then predate the foundation of actual *bastides,* but in places the *bastide* is tacked on to the existing village or replaces it, keeping the name, like *Castelnau-de-Montmiral* and *Sauveterre-de-Rouergue.*

Another thing:
From the 16th century *bastide* has is also been the name for a small country house in the south of France. Marcel Pagnol spent his childhood holidays in a house called La Bastide Neuve (see Tour 2).

Excursion 1: Villefranche-de-Rouergue, Villeneuve d'Aveyron, La Bastide l'Evêque

To put you in the picture about Villefranche-de-Rouergue:
Villefranche is situated on the Aveyron river at a crossing point of the Roman roads from Montauban to Montpellier and Cahors to Rodez. Though there is little concrete evidence, there seems to have been a settlement, on one side of the river or the other, since the time of the Gauls. Nor is there real archaeological evidence for the foundation of a township called La Peyrade on the left bank by Raimond IV, count of Toulouse in 1099.

What is certain is the creation of Villefranche on the right bank of the Aveyron in 1252 by Alphonse de Poitiers, brother of Louis IX of France (Saint Louis). The ramparts and fortified gateways have gone, but the town still retains the look of a *bastide* with its central square and rectilinear street plan. The houses are later, mainly 15th and 16th centuries, and the decoration of some bears witness to the prosperity of the town at that time. Building started on the cathedral as early as 1260, but took three hundred years to complete.

Villefranche was in a fertile area for crops and the Roman roads continued to be a trade route, which made it an important market town throughout the Middle Ages. It was also a staging post on the pilgrim route to Compostela.

Its decline set in during the Wars of Religion towards the end of the 16th century, when its support for the Protestants hindered commercial expansion. Then the town was hard hit by the outbreak of plague in 1628 and a few years later by fighting during *la Révolte des Croquants*, a series of peasant revolts against taxes.

Every cloud has its silver lining, for the tourist at least. Modern trade routes have passed it by and the decline in its prosperity has meant that Villefranche has retained its atmosphere of a small provincial town of an earlier age.

The town's creation in 1252 was a consequence of a revolt by the local lords around Najac (see Excursion 2), a fortress and administrative centre of the area further down the river Aveyron. These lords had managed to avoid attack by Simon de Montfort during the crusade against the Cathars (see Tour 1) and became rather reluctant vassals of Raimond VII of Toulouse after his loss of authority by the terms of the treaty of Meaux in 1229. Raimond, cunning politician that he was, managed to regain control of the region and make life hard for the dissident lords. On Raimond's death in 1249, his son-in-law, Alphonse de Poitiers became count of Toulouse and lord of Najac.

The local lords took advantage of the change of overlord to rise up in order to regain the lands that Raimond had appropriated from them. Alphonse put down the revolt, confiscated property and founded Villefranche in order to move the centre of his own authority away from Najac.

Visit:
From the right hand corner of place Bernard Lhez (your car park) walk towards the town centre. After two blocks turn left into place de la Fontaine. At the foot of the steps is the fine double basin *griffoul*, dating from 1336 and fed by a natural spring. Its upper basin is carved from a single sandstone block. This was the public water supply and meeting place for the inhabitants of the *bastide*. Ideally the *griffoul* would be in the main square, but in Villefranche this could not be so because the spring surfaced here.

At the top of the steps turn right into rue du Sergent Bories and head for place Notre Dame, the main square. On your left you pass the carved doorway of an early 16th century house. This rich early Renaissance decoration is an indication of the prosperity of the town in those days. At the corner of the square turn left into rue Marcellin Fabre. Immediately on your right you see another little gem of a doorway and façade of a late 15th century house. One reason why there are not more of these lovely old houses is the fire of 1497 which destroyed the richest quarter of the town at the height of its prosperity. What a shame.

Walk a few steps further on, to the next intersection. These narrow alleys at right angles to the wider thoroughfares give a very good idea of how the *bastide* was originally conceived: rectangular plots with shops or workshops on the ground floor, accommodation on the upper floors and an interior courtyard or garden. When I started coming to Villefranche in the 1980s many of these alleys were still paths of *terre battue* (mud and stones) that gave even more of an idea of how the town had been centuries before.

In the main square only a couple of houses have a particular architectural merit: on the South side, the Romanesque façade of the Maison du président Raynal and the Renaissance interior courtyard of the Maison Dardenne next door. The architecture here is worthy of the *traboules* and *miraboules* (passages and courtyards) from the same period in the old part of Lyon, designated a World Heritage Site.

It is the atmosphere of the square itself that is captivating, especially on market day (Thursday). The colour and noise might make you think you were living in another age, not least because the southern French accent mingled with *Occitan* sounds more than normally foreign. A true *bastide* square, it is bordered on all four sides by *couverts* (arcades), one named after the founder. The really unexpected feature is the imposing cathedral tower that dominates the whole square and has a roadway running under the massive pillars of its porch. You have the impression from its sheer size that it was originally intended to have a spire on top, but wars and lack of funds resulted in work coming to a halt in 1585, leaving it with its present fortress-like appearance.

The inside is in the Languedoc Gothic style: a single nave with no side aisles, and chapels built into the buttresses. It is worth sparing a moment to look at the carved capitals of two pillars near the entrance: the sacrifice of Isaac and the fairground monkey leader, both 15th century. However, the joy of this cathedral is the carving on the choir stalls, which is in real contrast with the overall sombre feel of the building. The panels and backs of the stalls are richly carved, but the misericords are a feast for the eye. They were carved between 1473 and 1487 by the master wood-carver André Sulpice.

Here you have a vision of the mediaeval world, an amazing mixture of the fantastical and everyday reality. Beautifully carved animals and hybrids abound, but I am fascinated by the scenes of domestic life and the images of carnival, the time of feasting and excess before Lent. My favourites are the woman turning the spit, being given a bath (both on the left facing the altar) and the obvious domestic discord between man and wife (front right). At the carnival: the man sleeping it off, the village idiot with his ass's ears hat (both on the right) and especially the *soufflacul* with his bellows (front left), because it refers to a somewhat unusual tradition.

It is not as rude as the name or the image implies. It is, says Gilles Bernard, author of *Le Carnaval des Miséricordes*, 'the means by which the soul, sullied by sins, is released from the human body. Just as normal life is turned upside down during carnival so the bellows are used here to *draw out* the offending air'. I am not quite sure what I make of the expression of the monkey with its hand over its mouth....

Soufflaculs still form part of the carnival procession in Lodève, Prats-de-Mollo (both in the south west) and Saint-Claude (near Geneva).

Before leaving Villefranche, walk down rue de la République to the river. Like the other main axes of the town it is not quite straight, yet all the side roads and alleys are, so you can see that the grid plan, one of the hallmarks of a *bastide,* has been applied, while fitting it to the natural lie of the land.

The bridge was built in 1321. Until the 18th century it had twin towers on the far bank and a larger tower – later a prison – built into the ramparts on the near bank. From the image of it on a 14th century official seal, it must have rivalled the splendid Pont Valentré at Cahors.

Another thing:
If you are in Villefranche on market day you may well see the label *Stockfish* on some rather unappetising desiccated product. The word and the product – dried, salted cod – come from the Dutch and Scandinavian traders who brought it in the

Middle Ages to the region via Bordeaux and up the river Lot. De-salted, it is the basis for a dish called *l'estofinade*.

Where to eat:
Dali's and *les Arcades* serve light lunches. Both have seating on the terrace overlooking the square. It is a good place to soak up the atmosphere, particularly on market day, in which case book your table early.

How to get there:
From your car park in Cordes turn right and follow the one-way road down to the main road (D600). Turn right. At the square (place de la Bouteillerie) turn left onto the D922 to Villefranche-de-Rouergue. The 13kms to Laguépie are winding but with good views of rural scenery. Climb out of Laguépie up onto the plateau and continue for 30kms along the D922. The views are good the whole way. As you go down into Villefranche you get a good view of the town too. Cross the bridge and go along boulevard Général de Gaulle past the park on your left then turn right and park in place Bernard Lhez.
Journey time: 1 hour, and allow 1 hour for your visit, excluding lunch and coffee breaks.

Visit: Villeneuve d'Aveyron

To put you in the picture about Villeneuve:
If Villefranche is an example of a *bastide* adapted to its topography, Villeneuve is one that has been tacked onto an existing town which was a *sauveté*.
The *sauveté* came into existence in a curious way. In 1053 a rich local landowner, Ozil de Morlhon, made a pilgrimage to Jerusalem. He was so marked by this that he donated his wealth to the patriarch of Jerusalem for a church and monastery to be built on his land on the Causse. The church was to look like the Basilica of the Holy Sepulchre in Jerusalem. The new town of Villeneuve that grew up round the monastery became a *sauveté* and such was the power of the clergy that the town did not even need walls.

During the Albigensian crusade Simon de Montfort took over the town, placing it under the authority of the bishop of Rodez. Now, Raimond VII of Toulouse, having been humiliated by the treaty of Meaux in 1229, urgently needed to re-establish his control, particularly over areas at the limits of his territory. As he did with the Najac lords (see above) he succeeded in obtaining, through various deals, the rights and powers of the bishop of Rodez over Villeneuve. In 1231 he began the transformation of Villeneuve the *sauveté* into Villeneuve the *bastide*.

Visit:
The *bastide* part lies to the east of the church and is built round the market square, place des Conques. You come to this square when you enter the town through the 1456 Porte Haute (upper gate), described to me by a local man as a 'magnificent monster'.
As you walk to the square, on a house wall a stone carved with the Templar cross has the Latin inscription: Ramundus comes dedit istum locum Deo e pauperibus (Count Raimond gave this place to God and the poor). The house has undergone changes - for a long time a hospital, now a private dwelling – but the plaque is still where it was put in the 13th century to commemorate the founder of the *bastide*. Another trace of the uniformity of the plan of a *bastide*, not only in its streets but in buildings too, is seen in the three identical houses said to be of Raimond VII's time. Others of the original uniform structures around this picturesque square were later embellished to suit the fashions of the times as their owners grew more prosperous. The square itself is not a regular shape, but as in Villefranche plans were adapted to fit the terrain.
Walk along rue Pavée, the cobbled main street that goes from the square to the other end of town. This will take all of five minutes, except that you will doubtless want to linger to enjoy the lovely old buildings you pass and look down the little side streets – you can see through to the old moat, now a tree-lined boulevard that encircles the town. When you reach place de l'Eglise – the church is on your left – you see that the side streets are more higgledy-piggledy. You have left the *bastide* and are now in the earlier *sauveté*, but it is all charming.

When you have seen enough, go back to the church, which has its surprises.

From the outside it looks like a Gothic church with a typical southern French octagonal bell tower. Inside, however, you understand its name, Church of the Holy Sepulchre. Four great pillars support a dome, the centre of a Greek cross, like the original basilica in Jerusalem. One of the arms of the cross has been lengthened to become the Gothic nave, added in the 13th century after Villeneuve became a bastide. This hybrid Romanesque and Gothic building is reminiscent of the basilica of St Nazaire in Carcassonne (see Tour 1, Excursion 5). The chapel on the south side of the central dome had an entrance into the cloister, but all the monastic buildings have long since gone.

The chapel on the opposite side is decorated with 14th century frescoes based on the pilgrimage to Santiago de Compostela, which indicates that Villeneuve was on the pilgrim route. Either side of the window in this chapel the frescoes depict a legend popular among pilgrims:

A couple of pilgrims and their son stopped at an inn. The innkeeper's daughter made advances to the handsome lad, who wasn't interested. Out of spite she slipped a silver goblet into his rucksack and accused him of stealing it. The son was condemned to be hanged. The parents completed their pilgrimage nonetheless and on their way back stopped at their son's gibbet to find him still hanging, but alive. St James had supported him all that time to spare him an unjust death. But the story doesn't end there. The local judge would only believe the miracle and free the boy if the chicken cooking for his dinner would crow, so St James duly obliged. The boy was declared innocent, the saint greatly revered and you can guess what happened to the girl.

Another thing:
Villeneuve is on the Causse, the chalky plateau to the north of Villefranche, characterised by outcrops of stunted oak trees. To the south is the rolling Ségala, traditionally poor land where they grew rye (seigle). With modern farming methods it is a more fertile cereal producing area.

How to get there:
From the car park in Villefranche go back down to the river, turn left and follow signs to Figeac. Once out of town, keep on the D922 (direction Figeac) to Villeneuve (10kms). At Villeneuve follow boulevard Cardalhac round the outside of the village (on the filled in moat as it happens) and park beyond the easily recognisable Porte Haute.
Journey time: 20 minutes, and allow up to 1 hour for your visit.

Visit: La Bastide l'Evêque:
This visit rounds off your day's tour of bastides in terms of both structure and politics.

Barely ten kilometres from Villefranche, this bastide was created in 1280 by the bishop of Rodez in direct political opposition to Alphonse de Poitiers' foundation, an opposition by the church to the civil authority. The problem for the bishop was that the rural population had been attracted to Villefranche for the security and exemption from taxes offered to those who chose to move there. This therefore meant a loss of revenue and manpower for the church.

However, it is uncertain whether the church really expected la Bastide l'Evêque to be an attractive rival to its near neighbour, or whether the bishops of Rodez were just 'marking their territory'. A reason for inclining towards the latter view is the bastide's position, in the poor quality land of the Ségala.

La Bastide l'Evêque has stood still in time, probably with the same number of inhabitants - about one hundred – as all those centuries ago.

The structure of the village is deliberate. Three main east/west streets intersect at right angles with narrower ones, forming blocks of buildings. The other requirements of a bastide are present too: the square, the cross, the well, and it has a charter. Even the church bell tower reminds you distinctly of Villefranche.

This little village is a living example of how bastides were an incredibly modern concept of urban living for their time, and because it has hardly changed, you feel you are stepping back into history. That is its fascination.

How to get there:
From Villeneuve go back the way you came, through Villefranche, across the river and up the hill on the D922 towards Laguépie. After 8kms turn left onto the D69. This little road winds down for 3kms to la Bastide l'Evêque. The curious entry to the village is through the narrow porch of the house adjoining the church. Park in the square.
Journey time: 30 minutes, and allow 20 minutes for your walk round the village. The church has always been closed when I have been there.

Excursion 2: Cordes and Najac

To put you in the picture about Cordes:
The death in 1218 of the commander of the king's crusade, Simon de Montfort (see Tour 1), gave back the initiative to the count of Toulouse, Raimond VI. He died in August 1222, but the new count, Raimond VII, straightaway began to strengthen defences in the north of his territory. He created Cordes in November 1222 to replace the fortress of St-Marcel, destroyed by Montfort and to give some protection to the inhabitants of the region, who had suffered badly at the hands of the crusading army. As a clever politician, the count was aware that doing this also brought him loyalty, and of course revenue.

Cordes was an immediate success, attracting merchants and craftsmen from all over the region. Unsurprisingly it also became a hotbed of Catharism. The town prospered through finance and trade, mainly in cloth and leather, and in three generations the ramparts had to be enlarged five times, to cope with a population that had risen to five thousand.

Many of the houses in the Ville Haute (upper town) date from this early period of great wealth, which continued for another two hundred years, barring attacks by the Black Death, which succeeded in wiping out a quarter of the population, and the English, who didn't succeed in capturing the hilltop fortress during the Hundred Years' War.

Cordes came under attack from both sides in the 16th century Wars of Religion, but what contributed most to the town's

economic decline was the advent, at the end of the 17th century, of the Canal du Midi, which dramatically altered traditional trade routes.
Present-day Cordes owes its relative prosperity to tourism – to people who like *vieilles pierres*, good food and good stories – and to the artists who settled in Cordes during the Second World War. Today it is still a thriving centre for artists and craftsmen.

Another thing:
Some say the name derives from Córdoba in Spain, famous for its own cloth and leather. Another theory is that for Raimond VII, the founder, it symbolised freedom regained, just as the Spanish reconquest had begun with a victory over the forces of the Caliph of Córdoba ten years earlier. In addition, he had married the daughter of one of the Spanish victors, Pedro of Aragón, who had also supported his father against the crusaders.
Rather less complicated, and to my mind just as likely, it is a corruption of an Indo-European word *corte,* meaning rocky hill. The choice is yours.
The name Cordes sur Ciel was first used in 1947 by a writer and became officially recognised by state decree in 1993. You can buy post cards of the old town bathed in sunlight above a swathe of white misty cloud, making it appear 'up in the sky'.

Visit:
Since you are staying in the Ville Haute, you have the chance to look round this bastide at leisure over the period of your stay; a good thing as there is too much to absorb in one go.
In fact it is such a charming place to be that you will probably want to wander the streets and enjoy the views more than once. *To find your way round all the nooks and crannies, pick up a town plan from the tourist office (just across from the hotel and turn right, down the main street, Grand'rue Raimond VII).*
The Halle (covered market) is the best place to begin your visit, as it is the most obvious indication that Cordes *is* a bastide. The original building was put up in 1276 in the form it still has, though the pillars have been restored several times

and it was re-roofed in the 19th century. With its cross and well, this was the main public and trading place for the bastide. The need for a *covered* market place of this size only fifty years after its foundation says much about the town's early commercial success.

The well (the stone is modern) is a mystery, however. It is over 100 metres deep, yet the 32 cubic metres of water it holds would be nowhere near enough for a population of 5,000 under siege and, in any case, there were several more efficient water sources in the town. No-one has yet come up with a convincing explanation, but the plaque on the pillar behind the cross tells of a grisly incident from the very early days. The story goes that, in 1233, the inquisitors burnt to death a woman suspected of being a Cathar. They were on the point of doing the same to a man, but this incensed the habitants so much that they threw three of the inquisitors down the well. It doesn't say much for equality of the sexes, but shows the town's fervent adherence to Catharism. It took another hundred years before Cordes officially came back into the Catholic fold.

As with Villefranche, this bastide was built to fit its site. The two main streets, Grand'rue Raimond VII and rue Saint Michel are roughly parallel and, while there are hardly any intersecting streets, you can still see here and there narrow gaps between the houses. These were firebreaks, and marked the limits of the plots allocated to the original inhabitants.

The main features of the Grand'rue are the magnificent facades of the 13th and 14th century houses on both sides. Working your way down the slope, the Maison Fonpeyrouse, so called after one of its owners, now houses the tourist office. This is a typical example of the elegant restrained 'Cordes Gothic' with its harmonious vertical and horizontal lines. Interestingly its façade neatly follows the curve of the street and the interior courtyard has a fine wooden gallery running round two sides.

Opposite, the Maison du Grand Veneur is the only four storey house in Cordes. It gets its name from the hunting frieze that adorns the second storey. Nearly all the sculptures are the originals.

You can take the graphically sculpted hunting scene at face value, but you might wonder why the people all seem so frightened, surely not of an ordinary hunt. In the context of the Cathar heresy – the builder of the house in the early 14th century was from a Cathar family - the scene could have a symbolic interpretation. The hunters of Cathars were the Dominicans, who themselves recognised the pun on their Latin name: *domini canes,* the dogs of the Lord. They are hunting the boar, representing true spirituality (in this case, of the Cathars), but they have lost the scent of the stag (Christ), as the dog is on the wrong line, looking perplexed, with its tongue lolling out. No wonder the onlookers (Cathars) are frightened of the *domini canes*, the inquisitors. Whether you go along with it or not, it is a good story. Another thought: is it pure coincidence that this building, with its possible implied criticism of the Inquisition, stares across at St Michael's - Catholic - church? Ironically, St Michael's, started in 1269, was already declared a ruin by 1345.

Further down on the left, the Maison du Grand Ecuyer is also from the early 14th century.

The Gothic façade is rich in sculptures, all original, but not always what they seem at first sight. This is the mediaeval world of the fantastic, like the misericords of Villefranche cathedral. Here are strange creatures: a winged woman with webbed feet and snake's tail; another woman with eagle claws, eating an apple; men with paws of a dog or a lion; headless dragons…and unexpectedly in this fantasy world, a bagpiper and violin player.

In a number of the grand houses along the main street you see the elegant Gothic arches of arcades at street level. These are now closed off, but at the time of construction would have been open, the entrance to shops, stores or workshops. There are many traces of this commercial architecture all over Cordes.

The town gate, Porte des Ormeaux, with its double portcullis was a formidable defence to breach, even if the enemy had managed to get through the Porte de la Jane, just below it on the outer ring of fortifications. Both formed part of the original defences of the 13th century *bastide*, as did the Portail Peint and, below it, Porte du Vainqueur at the other end of town.

Between the two gates at the top end of town, the Maison Gorsse is a good example of how the good life had returned to

Cordes after economic downturns during the Hundred Years' War. Well-off citizens could afford to modernize. The graceful Renaissance windows are the outstanding feature of the modernized Maison Gorsse, but you can still see the outline of an earlier arcade.

On the right as you go up the main street from La Halle three 14th century merchants' houses stand out. First, the Maison du Grand Fauconnier, named after its sculptures of birds of prey. It was built later than its neighbours, as indicated by the slender columns, the more pointed arcs and intricate tracery of the windows. In the courtyard: the tower of the spiral staircase and, above a doorway, the emblem of Cordes. Here the cross of the counts of Toulouse has been elongated, perhaps representing the shape of the *bastide*.

It is also worth looking at the Yves Brayer museum – he was the painter who put Cordes on the artistic map in 1940. After the fall of France he was demobbed and came to live in Cordes, bringing fellow painters with him. They formed the Cordes Academy and held exhibitions throughout the region during the war years.

Next to the Maison du Grand Fauconnier, are the Maison Prunet, with its mauve coloured stone and sculptures of faces, dogs and monkeys, and the Maison Carré-Boyer. Unfortunately, some of the Gothic arches have been replaced by rectangular windows and sculptures destroyed to accommodate the shutters. The Gothic style of these two houses is earlier, less ornate than the Grand Fauconnier.

The Maison Prunet owes its name to its 19th century owner. M. Prunet was knocking down an interior wall when he discovered a manuscript in *Occitan*. This turned out to be a 13th century collection of prophecies, the last one of which started: *'These are the prophecies of the Apostles which are never wrong'*. People came from afar to consult the Apostles of Cordes, but doubtless the document was hidden during the Inquisition, since soothsayers as well as Cathar 'heretics' were outlawed by the church. You can see a reproduction of this unique document in the Charles Portal museum near the Portail Peint.

The rue Obscure, so called from the houses built over the road, and the rue Chaude (Hot Street) are curious side streets of the mediaeval town. Oddly, the latter hardly gets any sun, but it is thought that its name derives, as in other southern towns, from the activities of the ladies of pleasure who worked here, protected by law and under the auspices of their Abbess.

The Place de la Bride, just up from your hotel, beyond the Halle, has a superb view over the valley to the north and would have been the position *par excellence* for a ballista (an ancient missile launcher), given that attackers were expected from this direction. There is no more historical proof for this than for the story of it being the spot where a mason's trowel was found, a sign from above that the new bastide should be built here. Apparently the count of Toulouse had chosen another hilltop for his fortress, but each day's building got mysteriously destroyed, so that in the end a mason threw away his trowel in frustration. It landed here and the rest, as they say, is history..... However, the site for the ballista is perhaps more credible.

Another thing:
The unusual brackets on the walls of some houses (Le Grand Veneur, Le Grand Ecuyer) are only found in Cordes and its immediate surrounds. They are thought to have been used to hang blinds to keep the sun out, as in Italian towns. However, the streets of Cordes are so narrow that this would hardly seem necessary. It has been speculated that the Gothic architecture here shows an Italian influence and these were just a decorative manifestation of that influence. Another intriguing mystery of this magical place.

For a very detailed guide to the town, I recommend Cordes sur Ciel by Jean-Gabriel Jonin, Editions OMT (in French).

Where to eat:
Your hotel serves lunch and there is a choice of *brasseries* in the Halle/Place de la Bride area. However I suggest you go to Najac for lunch, which means leaving Cordes between 11-11.30am to be in good time (see below, Where to eat in Najac, for details).

Visit: Najac

To put you in the picture about the bastide:
As you approach Najac its superb defensive position is evident. The 13th century château perched on a rocky escarpment dominates the valley of the river Aveyron. The shorter of the two keeps is from the original château, built in about 1100. After the uprising against him by the local lords (see above), Alphonse de Poitiers made it into a state of the art fortress in 1253, adding the forty metre high keep.

The village which had grown up along the ridge under the protection of the castle, was therefore a *castelnau*. Despite his differences with them, in 1255 Alphonse granted the inhabitants of Najac a charter to extend the village. A new quarter was developed in the form of a *bastide*. Just as Villeneuve was a *bastide* tacked onto a *sauveté*, Najac's *bastide* was an extension of a *castelnau*.

The village now spreads down the hillside, but in the time of Alphonse de Poitiers, Najac was, from one end to the other, little more than a village street with houses on either side, hardly the layout of a bastide.

Visit:
Park in the place du Foirail and walk through what once was a fortified gateway, pulled down in 1785. Immediately you are in the *bastide*. The whole thing is like an elongated public square, less than three hundred metres long. Part way down it does broaden out a little and has the requisites of a *bastide* square: a cross and well. The exteriors of the old houses on the south side have hardly changed since the creation of the *bastide*. The narrow gaps between them are a fire-break, and looking through, you can see the steeply sloping gardens that

made up the plots allocated to each citizen of the bastide. It is only on the south side that the houses have *couverts*, for shade. The markings on one of the stone pillars were for measuring cloth.

Pick up a guide 'Discovering the bastide' (available in English) from the tourist office under the 'couverts'.

Beyond the *griffoul* there are more treats in store for lovers of *vieilles pierres*, as you move into the earlier *castelnau*. With cars not allowed during the summer, the sense of going back in time is heightened. The 1344 Fontaine des Consuls (town councillors), made out of a single granite block has evocative carvings of those consuls and of the bishop giving his blessing. You are in the Middle Ages throughout the village. Several corbelled houses from the 13th to 15th century are particularly striking. Just beyond the Porte de la Pique, the only remaining gate of the ten that guarded Najac, is the church of St John the Evangelist.

This replaced the earlier Romanesque church of St Martin which was pulled down and rebuilt by the inhabitants between 1258 and 1269 as a punishment for having been pro Cathar. It is the oldest Gothic church in the Rouergue still standing.

If you bump into the admirable M. Guy Tourette, self appointed custodian against vandalism of the church, he will give you a comprehensive guided tour, in broken English if necessary. Just give a small donation for church upkeep.

In case you miss him, the altar and open work stained glass are 14th century, while on the left side of the nave the curious cage was made to house the *chandelle Notre-Dame* (the Paschal candle).

Another thing:
As M. Tourette will tell you, Najac is now served by the TGV (High Speed Train), giving direct communication with the capital (though you get the impression that he considers Najac the capital, rather than Paris).

The château has a great view over the village and the Aveyron valley. The arrow slits are nearly seven metres high, designed for three archers to be able to shoot at the same time. Locals claim this is a world record height for arrow slits.

Where to eat:
La Salamandre (rue du Barriou) does good salads and light lunches, as well as serving a pleasant rosé. It is a convenient place to stop after you have walked through the *bastide* and before you see the rest of Najac. In high season try to arrive for lunch by 12.30pm

How to get there:
Take the D922 from Cordes, through Laguépie, towards Villefranche (the views are worth seeing again). 15kms after Laguépie turn left onto the D39 at La Fouillade. Najac is a further 5kms.
Journey time: 45 minutes. Allow a good hour for a stroll through Najac. Add another 30 minutes if you want to see the château and another 30 minutes for a visit to the church with M. Tourette.
The château is open in April, May 10am-12.30pm, 2.30-5.30 pm; in June, July, August 10am 1pm, 3pm 7pm; in September it closes at 6pm.

Excursion 3: Sauveterre-de-Rouergue and Monestiès

To put you in the picture:
This royal *bastide* was founded in 1281 by the Seneschal of Rouergue in the name of Philippe III of France. This was a political manoeuvre by the king to strengthen his hold on an outlying region of his kingdom and weaken the power of still dissident local lords and the Church. He was mindful of the creation of la Bastide l'Evêque by the bishop of Rodez only the year before.

Sauveterre was not a great commercial success, even after the king granted it a charter in 1284, with very favourable tax exemptions and privileges to entice more people into the *bastide*. The problem was an inability to acquire enough land around the *bastide* to farm it profitably, especially as its site, like la Bastide l'Evêque, was on the poor soil of the Ségala.

So Sauveterre attracted mainly craftsmen – there were thirty blacksmiths in 1425, weavers, drapers – and became a centre of the king's administration and justice.

It was a beautifully constructed *bastide,* but in the wrong place and, despite royal input, it remained unable to break out from its original constraints, quite the opposite of Cordes.

The name suggests that a *sauveté* already existed somewhere in the locality, but there is no record of quite where. A local guide told me he thought there had been a château here belonging to the counts of Toulouse and that the bell tower of the church was built on the foundations of one of the former château towers. This might explain why it is slightly out of alignment with the perfect symmetry of the rest of the *bastide*. For here you have an archetypal *bastide* layout: nine equal sized rectangular plots, the middle one being the public square. It had originally been intended to extend the *bastide* outwards as its population grew – you can still see the intended new quarters by looking at the roads outside the walls, which continue the line of rue St Christophe, rue St Jean, rue St Vital and rue Notre Dame in particular. However, as I have said, not enough people came, so in 1327 perimeter walls were built, surrounded by a moat, to avoid incursions by bands of brigands. The walls and moat of course made it all the more difficult to enlarge the *bastide* later on and what we have today, luckily for us, is something of a time warp.

Visit:
Drive once round the village to take in the general picture and park outside the walls – on the filled in moat. All roads lead to the central square, which is the jewel in Sauveterre's crown. You will best appreciate its buildings and grandeur from the middle – it is bigger than the Villefranche square. The harmony of architectural

style gives the square its charm and makes it worth coming to Sauveterre just to admire it..

The vaulted arcades are mainly the originals from the 14th and 15th centuries. They were at the same time covered markets, public walkways and private entrances. The surface has recently been paved, like the little alleys in Villefranche, and looks a bit 'sanitized'. It would have been *terre battue*, which you can still see in an alley behind rue Notre-Dame.

It is worth walking round the *couverts* to see the stone and woodwork of the doorways, which shows that the mediaeval owners were comfortably off, even if Sauveterre could not reach the economic heights of Cordes or Villefranche. In the passageway to the inner courtyard of the tourist office, look at the sculpture of the vaulting and, in the courtyard, the trade guild frieze and the well, shared by two houses.

At the tourist office, pick up the leaflet 'Balade en Bastide' which has a useful town plan.

The *bastide* was divided into four quarters, each represented by a *consul*. The administration was highly developed, each quarter having its areas of civic responsibility: St Jean housed the salt store, communal bread oven and prison; Notre-Dame, the church and school; St-Vital, the hospital and cemetery; the top people had their residences in the Fonbougine quarter. The timbered houses in rue St-Jean and rue St-Vital are particularly attractive. In the latter, I like the low relief carving on one of them, showing Saint Valerie and her child taking a jug of water, or maybe it's wine, to her husband Saint Vital.

The two remaining town gates, at the end of rue St-Christophe and rue St-Vital have traces of their 14th century origins. The St-Christophe gate had machicolations (for tipping boiling liquid or stones onto the marauding brigands). On the St-Vital gate you can see where the huge hinges for the doors were and the fixings for the beam that was dropped into place to keep them closed. Both gates look more benign now than their counterparts at Villeneuve.

On the corner outside the St Vital quarter are the remnants of one of the four towers of the mediaeval defences, while the building on the Notre-Dame corner is the *four banal* (communal bread oven), built on the foundations of another of the mediaeval towers.

Another thing:
Consuls were elected annually from among the well off citizens. In addition to their administrative duties, they were the police, tax collectors, organised guard duty, were responsible for the church, hospital and school (by 1529 Sauveterre had a school, which was rare at that time for a place of its size in the back of beyond).

Where to eat:
La Clef des Champs (closed on Mondays) and *Les 4 Saisons* (open daily in July, August and September) are both in the main square and serve light lunches, including a variety of salads. – try a *salade rouergate*)

How to get there:
From Cordes take the D600 to Albi. Avoiding the town centre, follow signs to Rodez (N88). After about 35 kms, at Naucelle Gare, take the D997 to Naucelle and keep on the D997 as it winds another 5kms through the countryside to Sauveterre. Journey time: 1 hour. Allow 1 hour for your visit to Sauveterre, excluding lunch.

Visit: Monestiès
Monestiès (pronounced *Monest-yes*) could hardly be more different from the rigorous design of Sauveterre. It is a sleepy mediaeval village that nestles in a loop of the river Cérou. The river formed a natural defence, especially as it was prone to sudden and violent flooding. The streets twist and turn, allowing the tourist to discover, by chance, old corbelled houses (rue de l'Eglise, rue Jean-Jaurès), an *échoppe* (rue Jean-Jaurès – what is now the window sill was the shop counter), carved stones on the façades of houses in rue de la Treille, the few remaining *couverts*, traces of the windows of an earlier Romanesque church in the wall of the 16th century Gothic bell tower, the wayside cross in the church porch. This cross has two carvings: Christ on the Cross and on the other side the Virgin and child. It used to pivot, the idea being that you turned the Virgin to face approaching storm clouds and she would ward off damage to the crops. At the western end of the village, the graceful 12th - 13th century bridge (le pont de

Candèze) was on the Roman road from Rodez to Toulouse. A cornerstone of a house on the left just before the bridge marks the worst floods.

The village itself merits a visit, but the real point of coming here is to see the chapelle St Jacques (St James' chapel) just up the rue du Barry, opposite the *griffoul*.

To put you in the picture:
There used to be a little one room hospital here on the pilgrim route from Rodez to Compostela until 1761, when it received a holy relic: a fragment of the true cross. It was decided to transform the building into a chapel to house the relic. The same year, the bishop of Albi decided to give up his summer residence, the château de Combéfa, just outside Monestiès. The château was pulled down and a set of twenty statues from the chapel were dumped outside along with other fittings, where they lay rotting for thirteen years.

In 1774 the inhabitants of Monestiès asked the church authorities for permission to bring these life size statues, sculpted from limestone in 1490, to their new chapel. It took 31 men 3 days, with 14 carts drawn by 28 oxen, to transport the statues, each of which weighed 400 kilos. The chapel wasn't high enough to fit the statues in properly, so their effect was lost. The place was damp too and the statues deteriorated further. It needed a rescue operation in 1992 to restore the statues, during which the restorers discovered the original colours beneath other layers of paint. At the same time proper temperature control was installed and the ceiling raised, so the statues could be placed as originally intended.

Visit: La chapelle St Jacques
Walking into the chapel and seeing these statues for the first time takes the breath away. For me it does each time. The first thing to do is to sit down and drink in the whole scene: the Crucifixion at the upper level; below that, the Pietà; at floor level, the Entombment. The colours are delicate blues, greens, rusts. There seem to be two styles of sculpture: Italian Renaissance (the curls and drapes of Mary Magdalene and St John) and Gothic (Mary Salomé). The attitudes and

expressions of the mourners outweigh any conventionality in the scene and really give it life.

When you go up and look closely you see a remarkable attention to detail, from the muscles and veins of the dead Christ to the hairpins in Mary Cleophas' veil. Note too the furrowed brow and missing tooth of the bishop of Albi, Louis d'Amboise, who commissioned these sculptures. He dispensed with convention by giving himself the prime position next to Jesus, holding the shroud instead of Joseph of Arimathaea.

This set of sculptures may well be unique, is certainly an unexpected find in a little village, and a masterpiece that has real 'wow factor'.

Another thing:
The choir stalls also came from the château de Combéfa at the same time and were made for the bishop of Albi in 1468. If you look carefully you can see several carvings of a 'green man' with vine tendrils coming out of his mouth.

The plaque with the sinister skull and crossbones and two tears, outside on the wall next to the chapel, marks the cemetery of the former hospital. The inscription, dedicated to those who didn't make it to Compostela, reads: 'passers by, whoever you are, pray to God for the dead'.

How to get there:
From Sauveterre, rejoin the N88, direction Carmaux. At the beginning of the by-pass follow signs to Carmaux town centre. Then follow signs for Cordes (D91). Monestiès is some 8kms along this winding road that follows the river Cérou. Afterwards continue on the D91 to Cordes (15kms)

Journey time: Sauveterre to Monestiès, 40minutes. Monestiès to Cordes, 20minutes. Allow ½ hour to wander round Monestiès and ¾ hour for the chapel.

Chapel opening times: daily 10am-12.30 pm, 2-6.30 pm in summer. Mid March – mid June, mid September – mid October: daily 10 am–12 noon, 2–6 pm. Mid October – mid December: daily 10 am –12 noon, 2–5 pm. Winter: Monday–Friday, 2–5 pm; weekends, 10 am–12 noon, 2–5 pm.

Entry: 3€

Excursion 4: Albi

To put you in the picture:
Albi lies at the crossroads between the fertile Toulouse plain to the south and the beginnings of the less hospitable Massif Central, and the Ségala to the north. On the way up from Toulouse you will see a sign announcing the Pays de Cocagne (land of milk and honey). This refers to the great period of prosperity for the cities of Toulouse and Albi through cultivation of the pastel plant for making much prized blue dyes (woad).
Toulouse, Cahors, Montauban and Albi are the main *villes roses* (pink towns) because so much of the building was in brick rather than stone.

As you approach Albi from Cordes, the road sweeps down to the river Tarn and your first sight of Albi is the brick built Cathédrale Sainte Cécile which dominates the town. With its windows that resemble arrow slits, it looks more like a fortress, an impression which sits well with the timing of its construction in 1281. Less than forty years after the fall of the Cathar stronghold of Montségur (see Tour 1 Excursion 5), the 'heresy' was still active, though less openly so in the face of the inquisition. The construction of this fortress-cathedral was

a powerful statement of the might of the Catholic church, a clear warning to dissenters, even though it took another two hundred years to complete. Next to it, the brick Palais de la Berbie (Bishop's Palace), was deliberately built as a fortress. An impressive construction, its *donjon* (keep) rises four square above the river Tarn and yet is dwarfed by the cathedral.
The cathedral and the Palais de Berbie, which is home to the Toulouse-Lautrec museum, are the two places to see in Albi.

Another thing:
Berbie is a corruption of the *Occitan 'bisbie'* (bishop). This has produced the French slang word *bisbille* – a squabble or tiff, obviously a comment on what people thought of the sort of disputes bishops indulged in.
The crusade against the Cathars is also known as the Albigensian crusade. Not that Albi was a particular hotbed of Catharism. On the contrary the town blew hot and cold in its support for the so called heretics. Probably the association came from the chilly reception given to the papal legate in 1145 or from the Council of Lombers (near Albi) in 1165, the last attempt at reconciliation between Catholics and Cathars.

Visit: Cathédrale Sainte Cécile
When you walk through the archway and up the steps to the entrance on the south side, the first thing that strikes you is the porch. The extravagant decoration of this 1520 addition is in complete contrast to the sober brick of the rest of the outside. But this is nothing compared to the inside.
You are almost overwhelmed by the rich colours of the walls and the gold ribbed vaulting of the ceiling of this vast nave. This is the work of Italian artists, done between 1509 and 1512. Some side chapels are painted with geometric patterns, others in *trompe l'oeil*. But there is more to come in this unique building.
Dominating the west wall is the huge late 15th century mural of the Last Judgement, the work of French artists and the largest ever painted in the Middle Ages. The central panel - Christ in judgement and, below, the sin of sloth - was destroyed in 1693 by the creation of a chapel beneath the organ. It is still awesome from a distance and on the bottom

level the punishments for the deadly sins would surely have struck dread into the hearts of those who looked more closely, as of course they were meant to. For those who could actually read, the written descriptions of these punishments are equally graphic, the word *puant* (stinking) cropping up frequently.

From the west end, look back towards the rood screen, another remarkable feature of this remarkable building. This dates from the same period as the entrance porch, both commissioned by bishop Louis d'Amboise. The superb craftsmanship is so delicate that it is often compared to lacework. Nearly all the statues were destroyed in the Revolution, but you can still see a rather coquettish Eve, that Adam, opposite, could hardly resist.

You have to pay to go into the chancel, but you should go in. Sit down in this 'Holy of Holies' and shrug off the strain of looking up at the wonderful vaulting. The leaflet that goes with your entry explains all the imagery, although I enjoy just looking at it all as a thing of great beauty, which, remarkably, has needed no restoration.

Continue round the apse, leaflet in hand to know which saint is which. Judith, Isiah, Jerome, and Esther in particular are considered masterpieces of mediaeval art. Look carefully at the side chapels as you walk round: on some walls a cheeky face peeps out from the painted foliage – the artists secretly having a visual joke.

When I am walking round the apse, I always pause to say a quiet thank you in front of the plaque on the wall of the chancel at the east end. This commemorates M. Maries, an engineer who managed to persuade the minister of the Revolutionary Council in 1792 not to demolish the rood screen and chancel, which had been designated a grain store. Without his intelligent intervention we would not be able to enjoy and admire this amazing work of art.

Another thing:

You unexpectedly see the high altar in front of the Last Judgement, whereas it is normally at the east end of a church. For centuries mass was celebrated in the enclosed chancel, the congregation not taking an active part. The church moved the altar so that mass could be seen as well as heard.

Outside, you see that the top of the walls is a lighter brick colour than the rest, because this level was added in the 19th century.

Visit: Palais de la Berbie

To put you in the picture about Henri de Toulouse-Lautrec (1864-1901):
Born in the Château du Bosc, near Albi, he was a descendant of the younger branch of the counts of Toulouse who ruled the Languedoc in the Middle Ages. His parents were first cousins and his father was eccentric to say the least, so perhaps it is not so surprising that Henri had congenital problems. His bones were fragile and breaking both legs in his early teens stopped their growth. He developed the torso of an adult, but with a child's legs. After his two accidents he was never again able to walk properly. As he grew up Henri knew his infirmity made him a disappointment to his father, a great riding enthusiast who said: *'in our family we baptise them straightaway, then put them on a horse'*. Henri had at least inherited one family trait, the ability to paint. To try to please his father who had seemingly lost interest in him, Henri painted all the time, mostly horses.

Aged eighteen he went to study painting in Montmartre, the artistic heart of Paris. He discovered the 'marginal' lifestyle of this bohemian area of the capital, even living for a while in a brothel. The subjects of his paintings and sketches were those familiar to him: brothels, horse races, the circus, night clubs. By 1891 his fame as an artist began to spread, his posters advertising shows soon appearing all over Paris. However, the excesses of drink and his lifestyle led him to spend several months in a sanatorium in 1899. When he left his health had improved, but he soon took up his old habits and died only two years later from the effects of alcoholism and syphilis.

In some twenty years he produced the prodigious number of 737 oils, 275 watercolours, 363 prints or posters, 5084 drawings.

Another thing:
His staunchly royalist parents christened him Henri in honour of the count of Chambord, last of the Bourbon line, who was campaigning to become Henri V of France (see Tour 1, Excursion 4 and Tour 6, Excursion 5).
His eccentric father, about whom Henri's dying words were allegedly *le vieux con* (the old fool), liked dressing up....as a crusader, cowboy, or Scottish highlander.

Visit: Musée Toulouse-Lautrec
This, the largest collection of the artist's works in the world, was donated to the city of Albi in 1922 by his mother the Countess Adèle de Toulouse-Lautrec. The galleries have been recently refurbished, with the works now displayed in well lit rooms.
Each area relates to a different theme. The most familiar will doubtless be the pictures of nightclub performers. Seemingly all Paris nightlife is here, for he is known as the 'chronicler of the Belle Epoque' (the 1890s). What is astonishing about Lautrec's work is the way he captures his subject with such movement and yet such economy, so that even his sketches are often as good as the finished article. Some of the performers are caricatural, but, perhaps because of his own problems, he portrays the inhabitants of the *maisons closes* (brothels) and ordinary working girls with real sympathy, such as: *La modiste* (milliner), *Au Salon de la rue des Moulins* (girls in the brothel sitting around waiting), the sketch of *Gueule de bois* (hangover). For sheer economy of line and great effect, the sketch of *Femme tirant son bas* (woman pulling on her stocking) is better to my mind than the finished painting in the Musée d'Orsay, Paris.
Upstairs many of the nightclub posters are well known, but I like the little joke in the advert for Simpson cycles, whose director is a certain LB Spoke.
His circus sketches are remarkable for being done entirely from memory while he was interned in the sanatorium.
Less well known are Lautrec's youthful paintings of horses, which exude life and movement. The lady I overheard say: *'yes, but he hasn't got the fetlock right'* probably missed the point. In his portraits of his mother he catches her air of

resigned melancholy, while in his *Cheval de trait à Céleyran* (mother's family home) you really feel for the weary carthorse.

When he was on holiday at Céleyran he would sketch anything and everything, paying the estate workers a few *sous* to pose for him. Some of my favourites, for their sensitivity and sureness of touch, are his series of studies of *Le Jeune Routy*.

Another thing:
Lautrec signed his work in a number of ways. As well as his name or initials, he used Monfa (he was viscount of Montfa, a commune in the Tarn departement) and Treclau (anagram of Lautrec).

Where to eat:
Nowhere better than *La Berbie*, in the place Ste-Cécile. I suggest you have their excellent light lunch in between your visit to the cathedral and the Toulouse-Lautrec museum.

How to get there:
Take the D600 from Cordes to Albi. After the bridge over the Tarn there are several car parks along the road you are on, the Lices Georges Pompidou, or at the far end by the coach park. Follow the signs and take the nearest one available. Albi will be more crowded on Saturday, market day. From any car park it is a 5-10 minute walk. Aim at the cathedral tower.
Journey time: 30 minutes.
Cathedral Chancel opening times: June-September 9am-6.30pm; otherwise 9am-12 noon, 2.30-6.30pm. Entry: 1€.
Musée Toulouse-Lautrec: July, August 9am-6pm; April, May, June, September 9am-12noon, 2-6pm (closed 1st May); October-March 10am-12noon 2-5pm, (closed on Tuesdays and 1st November). Entry: 5€.
Allow 1½ hours for the cathedral and 2 hours for the museum.

Excursion 5: St Antonin Noble Val, Gorges de l'Aveyron, Bruniquel, Castelnau de Montmiral

To put you in the picture about St Antonin:
The name is derived from two sources: Noble Val (exceptional valley), from the Gallo-Roman settlement that recognized the qualities of the site by the river, and St Antonin, an early Christian who converted the region. He then decided to convert his native Pamiers (in the foothills of the Pyrenees), but was beheaded and thrown in the river by the unconvinced citizens. However, angels placed the venerable remains in a boat, which floated, guided by white eagles, down the rivers Ariège and Garonne, then up the Tarn and Aveyron to alight here.
After such a miraculous journey an abbey was built on the site to honour the martyred saint, and the town that sprang up took his name. Situated on an important river crossing, it prospered in the Middle Ages, through its cloth and leather trade and revenue from tolls that it levied as a crossing point.

Visit:
To get the still mediaeval feel of St Antonin, turn right out of place du Bessarel (the car park) and walk along rue de la Treille. On the corner of the little place de la Jougario (Jews) the so called Maison du Roy (King's House) has a good façade. Turn left into rue des Grandes Boucheries and at place du Timple, turn right into place de Payrols and from there, left into rue Guilhem Peyre, which has a couple of fine 13th-15th century houses. You reach the square by passing under the tower of the 12th century home of the viscount, one of the oldest examples of civil architecture in France. The decorations of the façade are particularly good, including Adam and Eve with the serpent, and the capitals of twin columns carved as monsters. In 1845 the building was classified as an ancient monument, but why Viollet-le-Duc then had to add a belfry with an Italian style loggia in his restoration is a mystery to me. While in the square, look at the racquet shaped 14th century cross in the Halle (covered

market). It is an unusual design, being sculpted on both sides and probably originally stood in the centre of the cemetery.

Beyond the viscount's house turn left into rue Droite. The romantic names now attributed to two houses in this street come from their carved keystones: the Maison du Repentir (house of regret), where a man and a woman have turned away from each other, whereas, further on at the Maison de l'Amour (house of love), they are back together, their love sealed with a kiss. (Unless you approach from the opposite direction, in which case the story is not so romantic.)

In between the two houses, the picturesque little canal running along rue Rive Valat was dug in the Middle Ages to supply water – and act as drainage – for the tanneries in that street, so maybe was not so picturesque.

After the Maison de l'Amour, turn left into rue du Pont des Vierges, which brings you back to the car park.

Without much effort, the narrow, winding streets, little side alleys and old houses of St Antonin transport you back to the Middle Ages, or even the German Occupation.

Another thing:
St Antonin was the setting for the 2001 film *Charlotte Gray*, a story of WW2 resistance, with Cate Blanchett. In the film the square is definitely recognisable and the proprietor of the café will show you his photo album if you ask. For some months the filming brought unaccustomed life to this sleepy town.

Where to eat:
Try either the *Beffroi Tentation*, off rue Guilhem Peyre, just before the main square, or *L'Olivier* in place du Buoc, past the Halle.

How to get there:
Take the scenic D600 from Cordes (direction St Antonin). After18kms join the D115. St Antonin is a further 13kms. At St Antonin cross the river and bear left along boulevard des Thermes, which leads into boulevard de la Condamine. Turn right at the first crossroads into avenue des Anciens Combattants and park in place du Bessarel.
Journey time: ½ hour.

If you want a really scenic route over the Causse, take the D600 and after 5kms turn onto the very winding D91 and then D19 down into St Antonin. Shorter distance, but longer in time.

Allow 1 hour for a leisurely tour of St Antonin, excluding lunch.

Visit: Gorges de l'Aveyron, Bruniquel, Castelnau de Montmiral

This circuit takes you through the spectacular Aveyron gorges to the mediaeval village of Bruniquel, on to the hilltop *bastide* of Castelnau de Montmiral and back to Cordes.

Leave St Antonin by the bridge over the Aveyron and take the D115 (direction Montauban). After 3kms turn left onto the D115bis. This is the old road. It is narrow and winds, but you get the best views of the rugged river valley below. (The modern section is straighter, but lower). For more spectacular views, cross the river after about 5kms onto the D173. Rejoin the D115 (main road) shortly before Penne, whose mediaeval fortress is silhouetted against the skyline. After 6 kms turn onto the D964 and follow the signs for Bruniquel.

Visit:

Park just outside the entrance to the village and pick up a plan of the village from the tourist office on the corner.

The church on the opposite corner has a *clocher mur* (bell tower wall), rather than the traditional tower. This is also a feature of churches in the Toulouse region.

It is now a steady climb through the streets of this very picturesque village, dominated by the keep of the so called 'old' castle (13th century) and the 'new' one (15-17th).

At the top of rue de l'Hôpital, the Porte Mejane was the middle gate into the old village, a warren of streets and squares with evocative names: rue Trotte-Garces (a shopping street frequented by the women of Bruniquel), rue du Trauc (Hole St), rue Bombe-Cul (Fat Bottom St). At the end of rue Henri Ramey, off rue du Mazel, the Maison Payrol was the residence of the Payrol family, wealthy merchants who governed Bruniquel after the Albigensian crusade. It houses a regional museum, but of special interest are its 13th century painted walls, a rare example of mediaeval decoration.

Another thing:
The name of the village comes from Brunehaut, who supposedly founded the first fortress in the 6th century. This unfortunate daughter of the king of the Visigoths was captured in battle in 613AD, attached to the tail of a wild horse which trampled her to death.
Rue Trotte-Garces: nowadays *garce* has a pejorative meaning. When the street was given its name, *garce* was just the female equivalent of *garcon* (boy).
Rue Bombe-Cul: According to the Mayor, in olden times villagers riding up the street on their carts bumped up and down so much on the uneven cobbles that their bottoms became fattened from the repeated bouncing.

Maison Payrol: April-September, daily 10am-6.30pm; March and October, weekends, 10am-5.30pm. Entry: 3€
Allow ¾-1 hour for your tour of the village.
Journey time from St Antonin to Bruniquel: 45minutes

Visit: Castelnau de Montmiral
Rejoin the D964 (direction Gaillac). After driving 30kms through delightful scenery you come upon Castelnau de Montmiral perched on its rocky spur. Drive up the hill and park as near as you can to the *bastide*.
Castelnau de Montmiral was founded by Raimond VII de Toulouse in 1222, shortly after Cordes, as part of his move to strengthen the northern reaches of his territory against invasion. Walk the short distance to the central square, the delightful place des Arcades, which has beautifully preserved all the elements you expect in a *bastide*: *couverts*, well, cross. This *place* is justifiably the jewel of Castelnau de Montmiral. *A town plan from the tourist office in the square shows how the layout of the bastide was adapted to its topography.* The 14th century church just off the square unusually has a human head carved over the entrance and, inside, on the left of the chancel, the cross of the counts of Armagnac. This cross, known as the

cross of Montmiral, is studded with precious stones, a masterpiece of 13th century religious jewellery.

The area round the church is the most interesting part of the bastide, apart from the square. There are some fine old houses and the Porte des Garrics (the only one of four town gates remaining) is a good example of the original defences of the *bastide*.

Allow ¾ hour for your visit.

Another thing:
In a corner of the square the pillory not only had the traditional use of punishing adulterous women and thieves, but was also used to tether animals before they were due to be butchered.

Journey time from Bruniquel to Castlnau de Montmiral: 30minutes
Return to Cordes by continuing on the D964 (direction Gaillac), then cut across to Cordes on the D115A to Cahuzac, where you join the D922 to Cordes.
Journey time: 30 minutes
For a really detailed study of the subject: Histoire des bastides de Midi-Pyrénées by Jacques Dubourg, Editions Sud Ouest (in French)

5 The Heart of France

This tour is built round literary and historical characters associated with the region: Alain-Fournier, George Sand, Jacques Coeur, the Stuarts and Tintin. It explores the historic old quarter of Bourges, takes you through the villages and peaceful countryside of the Sologne to the Château de Cheverny, visits some of the places along the route Jacques Coeur, discovers the home at Nohant of George Sand and the charm of the surrounding country that she called the 'Vallée Noire'

Excursions: 1. Château d'Angillon, Henrichemont and
　　　　　　　Ménetou-Salon
　　　　　　2. Aubigny-sur-Nère and La Verrerie
　　　　　　3. Nohant and the surrounding country
　　　　　　4. Bourges
　　　　　　5. Cheverny and the Sologne

To put you in the picture:
What better place than Bourges as the base for your holiday in this region. Bourges lies geographically right at the heart of the *hexagone* (the name the French give to their country because of its shape), and to the north it gives you easy access to the Sologne, a region of lakes where local

people say 'land, water and sky fuse together'.
To the south you are in the Berry, the setting for many of the novels of George Sand. Linking the two is the 'Route Jacques Coeur', a tourist route created to take you to some fascinating places that are a little off the beaten track in this delightful and still relatively unknown region. And of course Bourges itself has over two thousand years of history and its *centre historique* has lots of charm.

Where to stay:
The *Best Western Hôtel d'Angleterre*, Place des Quatre-Piliers, is the only hotel in the centre of the old town. The building has character and the service is very friendly. They only serve breakfast, but they do have a locked garage. It used to be called the Hôtel du Commerce, but 'Angleterre' was thought more up market after the future King Edward VIII stayed there. In fact he may even have insisted on the change of name.
The places you will want to see in Bourges are all within walking distance of the hotel, as are a number of good, very reasonably priced restaurants. You can get a town plan at the hotel reception.
The hotel and *centre historique* are well signposted from the outskirts of Bourges.

Excursion 1 Château d'Angillon, Henrichemont and Ménetou-Salon

To put you in the picture:
The château is in village of La Chapelle d'Angillon, which owes its name to a linguistic confusion. The story goes that it was originally the site of the tomb and later a *chapel* dedicated to the 9th century hermit St Jacques de Saxeau who had made his home there. What is fact is that in about 1060 a certain *Gilon* de Sully built a small fortress here. The village that grew up around it became 'the *chapel* of *Gilon*', pronunciation and spelling changing over time to bring about its present name.
By strange coincidence, nearly 600 years later the Château was bought by a descendent of Gilon: the first minister of

King Henri IV, Maximilien de Béthune-Sully, known as 'Le Grand Sully'.

Visit: Le Château d'Angillon
The château retains the original keep–one of the oldest in the region- though it was much rebuilt in the 15th and 16th centuries and has a fine Renaissance gallery known as the *jeu de paume* (tennis court). When he heard of the improvements Sully was making, especially to the gardens, his king was so impressed that he gave him 6000 écus 'pour vous aider à faire quelque chose de beau' (to help you make something beautiful).
The château now houses a museum to the writer Alain-Fournier (1886-1914), who was born in the village and killed in action in the first weeks of the war. He is known for his great romantic novel, *Le Grand Meaulnes* (pronounced *moan*), set in the Sologne countryside. A classic in France and beyond, it is a work of fiction, but, to a considerable degree, is a disguised autobiography of Alain-Fournier's own schooldays and youthful love.
The hero, Augustin Meaulnes – a big teenage boy, hence the title 'Big Meaulnes' - joins the village school where the narrator's father is the teacher. The somewhat timid, law-abiding narrator, François Seurel and the daring Meaulnes can be taken as illustrating different sides of Alain-Fournier's character and some scenes in the story are, word for word, scenes from the author's own life. Shortly after his arrival at the school, Meaulnes is entrusted with taking the pony and trap to the station some miles away, gets lost and only returns three days later. He recounts his adventure his friend François, the narrator: he has fallen in love with a beautiful girl, Yvonne de Galais, at a fancy-dress party *(la fête étrange)* in a mysterious château, and must find it and her again. All sorts of innocent schoolboy adventures ensue, although Meaulnes is unsuccessful in his quest. He leaves school to continue his studies in Paris, still hoping he will find Yvonne, whose family home is there. Eventually, through François, now a teacher himself, Meaulnes does meet up again with Yvonne, they marry, but Meaulnes leaves the very next day to fulfil some mysterious obligation.

I shall not spoil the ending, but the photography in the 1967 film by Jean-Gabriel Albicocco really manages to capture the romantic atmosphere of the story and the particular beauty of the Sologne. In his book Alain-Fournier mentions the village, but calls it *La Ferté d'Angillon*, perhaps because of the still rather fortress-like aspect of the château.

The current owner, Count Jean d'Ogny gives the guided tours himself and will tell you in excellent English about the history of the château. In the chapel admire the *Virgin with child* by della Robia and the *St Stephen* by Murillo.

The count is a friend of the pretender to the throne of Albania, which explains the presence in the château of a museum of the history of the Albanian royal family. Since 1983 the château has been the HQ in France of the Royal Albanian Foundation, dedicated to the restoration of the monarchy in that country.

In the *jeu de paume* the count will be happy to explain the origins of the scoring system for tennis. Tennis terminology comes mainly from its French forerunner, the *'jeu de paume'*. The name itself is a corruption of *'Tenez'* (take this), called out by the server, as he was about to serve. 'Deuce' is from *'à deux le jeu'* (two points for the game), while 'love' is thought to derive from *'l'oeuf'* (egg), a symbol for 'nothing.' The count has interesting explanations for 15, 30, 40, but I have never quite mastered them.

If you have read *'Le Grand Meaulnes'* or are intrigued by the story having seen the Alain-Fournier museum, a few minutes' drive away (D940 towards Bourges, then D168) you can see from the road the now rather sad looking Abbaye de Loroy, setting for the *fête étrange* that is a central part of the story. The abbey is privately owned and you should not try to get a closer look.

The guided visit to the château is by appointment. Telephone le Comte d'Ogny, or get the hotel to do so, on 0248734110.
Entry: 8€
The château boutique has of course a selection of material about Alain-Fournier.

Another thing:
Alain-Fournier's real name was Henri Alban Fournier. When his first work – an essay *Le Corps de la Femme* - was published in 1907 there were two well-known Frenchmen

called Henri Fournier, an admiral and a racing cyclist, so, rather than compete with their fame, he decided on the *nom-de-plume* 'Alain-Fournier'.

The family home was in La Chapelle d'Angillon, but his father's school, where Alain-Fournier grew up, is south of Bourges in the village of Epineuil-le-Fleuriel, which also has an Alain-Fournier museum, and nearby is another village, called Meaulne-les-Alliers.

Visit: Henrichemont

Henrichemont was once the capital of the sovereign principality of Boisbelle. This pocket-handkerchief 'state within a state' was given in 1606 to le Grand Sully by his king, Henri IV. It remained a principality until returned to the state by the last of the Sully family in 1771, minting its own coins and having the prerogatives of an independent state. Henrichemont (Henricis Mons or an anagram – nearly – of 'Mon cher Henri': take your choice), was designed in tribute to the monarch, with roads radiating out from a central square whose buildings imitate, but on a rather smaller scale, the Place des Vosges in Paris, itself designed by Henri IV. Unfortunately the fall from grace of Sully – for misappropriation of funds - and the assassination soon after of the king meant that this project for a 'model' town was never completed, but enough remains to make it an architectural curiosity.

Ménetou-Salon, along with Quincy (pronounced *can-see*) and Reuilly (pronounced *ro-*as in rotund-*yee*), produces wine (mainly white, sauvignon blanc) less well known than Sancerre and Pouilly (pronounced *poo yee*). They make a red too, light but worth a try. For a friendly atmosphere and tasting try the Domaine Chavet in the village. They supply wine to the 'Jacques Coeur' restaurant in Bourges.

Where to eat:
On a warm day there I like to picnic by the lake overlooking the Château d'Angillon.

Otherwise, go on to Henrichemont and try *La Fontaine* in the square or *Le Soleil Levan*t, off the square in rue de Bourgogne (NB it is closed on Monday).

How to get there:
La Chapelle d'Angillon is 30 kms north of Bourges on the D940 (direction Gien). In the village the château is signposted off to the right.
Journey time: It always seems to take time to get out of Bourges, so allow 45minutes to reach La Chapelle d'Angillon and a good hour for the guided visit to the Château (NB closed from 12 to 2pm)
For Henrichemont, take the D12 eastwards from la Chapelle d'Angillon and park in the square (Place Henri IV).
Journey time: 20 minutes through pleasant countryside. Allow however long you wish for lunch, which is the main purpose of your visit. You will certainly have enough time to take in Sully's architecture and plan of the town as you go to lunch.
For Ménetou-Salon, leave Henrichemont, going south on the D11.
Journey time: 15 minutes. You will have plenty of time for 'tasting' at Ménetou-Salon, which is the point of coming here.
Return to Bourges on the D11 which joins the D940 just outside Bourges).
Journey time: 30 minutes.

Excursion 2: Aubigny-sur-Nère and la Verrerie

To put you in the picture:
In 1423 Aubigny was given by the Dauphin, the future Charles VII, to John Stuart, count of Darnley, in gratitude to the 7000 strong Scottish force led by Darnley which came to France to the aid of Charles. This army defeated the English at the battle of Baugé in 1421. So grateful was the French King that he gave the Stuarts the right to incorporate the *fleur-de-lys* into their coat of arms.
Subsequently 11 generations of Stuarts ruled in Aubigny and the surrounding lands that they acquired over the years. When Charles Stuart died in 1672 without a male heir, a little

problem arose. The only male who could succeed him was his cousin Charles who was descended from a Stuart, a certain Henry Darnley, lover and then husband of the unfortunate Mary Queen of Scots. However, this cousin Charles happened to be Charles II, king of England, and it would have been just a bit awkward for him, as lord of Aubigny, to vow his allegiance to the king of France, as the terms of the original gift required.

A diplomatic compromise was reached: Charles II would give Aubigny to his mistress the Duchess of Portsmouth. She was in fact French, Louise de Kéroualle, sometime mistress of Louis XIV and sent by him to infiltrate the English court. She obviously did this rather well, for in addition to becoming Charles II's mistress she produced an illegitimate son for him, the Duke of Richmond, who would inherit Aubigny on the death of the duchess. Thus the Richmonds administered Aubigny until the Revolution inevitably changed things.

However, Aubigny is very proud of its Scottish connection, to the extent that it is known as 'the city of the Stuarts'.

Visit: La Verrerie

NB. Visit La Verrerie in the morning as the museum in Aubigny is only open in the afternoon, except in July and August.

La Verrerie is one of the châteaux that used to belong to the Stuarts of Aubigny. The name means 'glassworks', which was one of the two main economic activities of the Stuarts of Aubigny – the other was weaving.

The drive through the park, past the lake with its reflection of the château, gives the impression of peaceful elegance. This impression is reinforced by the lovely Renaissance gallery through which you enter the château itself. Some commentators consider La Verrerie to be the setting for the *fête étrange* in Le Grand Meaulnes (see Excursion 1). I don't, but it is certainly a setting worthy of that romantic episode.

La Verrerie has been in the hands of the de Vogüé family (pronounced *Vogway*) since 1841. The pride of the château's collection are 4 of the set of 40 *pleurants*, 15th century alabaster statues of mourners made for the tomb of the duc de Berry (several more can be seen at the Hermitage in St Petersburg). Unfortunately the ones you actually see are reproductions, as the originals would be too expensive to insure for display here, the count says. Still the visit is worthwhile just for the personal reminiscences – in English - of the present Count Béraud de Vogüé, who conducts the guided tour, which lasts about 45 minutes.
The guided visit is by appointment. Telephone 0248815160, or get the hotel to do so. The château is open from April to October.

Visit: Aubigny

The château was built by Robert Stuart in the 16th century. When a fire practically destroyed the town in 1512, he allowed the citizens to take wood from his forests to rebuild their houses, helping bring prosperity back to the town. It is thanks to his generosity that you can see splendid timbered houses on a stroll round the town, especially in rue de l'Eglise and the adjacent rue du Bourg-Coutant. *For your stroll, pick up a plan of Aubigny at the Tourist Office, next to the church, in rue de l'Eglise.* The château, which doubles as the Town Hall, now houses a very well presented museum 'Le Mémorial de l'Auld Alliance' recounting the history of the Stuarts of Aubigny and the Scottish connection.

Another thing:

Diana Princess of Wales belonged to the Richmond family and was therefore a descendent of Louise de Kéroualle....

Where to eat:

Have lunch at *l'Auberge de la Maison d'Hélène* in the grounds of the château de la Verrerie (closed on Tuesday), or *Le Bien Aller*, opposite the Tourist Office in Aubigny

How to get there:
For La Verrerie, take the D940 from Bourges to La Chapelle d'Angillon and then the D12 towards Henrichemont. At Ivoy-le-Pré turn left onto the D39 and follow signs to La Verrerie.
Allow about an hour for this journey.
Aubigny is some 15kms further up the D940, so, from La Verrerie go back to La Chapelle d'Angillon and rejoin the D940, going north.
Journey time: about 30 minutes.
The museum of the 'Auld Alliance' in Aubigny: July, August 10am-12.30pm, 3-7pm. Easter to June, September, October 2.30-6pm. Closed from November to Easter.
Entry 2€.

Excursion 3: Château de Nohant and surrounding country

To put you in the picture:
A visit to the château de Nohant, home of the 19th century writer George Sand (pronounced *Sond*) takes you into a different world. She was born Aurore Dupin in 1804 and by her marriage became Baroness Dudevant. The lifestyle of this remarkable woman caused a furore in Parisian literary and political circles. She dressed as a man, smoked a pipe, was a fervent republican and had affairs with the poet Musset and the composer Chopin.

Why *George Sand*? Her first novel (5 volumes) was written in collaboration with Jules Sandeau, a young journalist and her current lover. They used the *nom-de-plume* '*Jules Sand*' for this collective enterprise. She wrote the next one herself and expected to publish it in the same way, but Jules honourably declined to put their joint signature to the work, saying that it would be unworthy of him to accept the credit for it. Because of the scandal she was causing in Paris for her uninhibited lifestyle, her family was strongly against her using her real name, so she had to find a suitable pseudonym to be able to publish. She already had Sand and it happened to be St George's day....She wrote: 'In Paris Mme Dudevant is dead, but George Sand is a fellow who is full of life'.

The novel, *Indiana*, tells the passionate story of the eponymous beautiful Creole heroine's escape from her sadistic husband to join her lover. A serial seducer, he jilts her, but she is saved by her English cousin 'Sir' Brown. They decide to commit suicide together, but at the last moment they recognise their love for each other....and live happily ever after. This romantic, at times racy novel took 1830s Paris by storm.

George Sand was a prolific and successful writer of romantic novels, many set in the country around Nohant where she grew up and came back to live. Great literary figures of the time, Balzac, Flaubert, Hugo, Gautier, Dumas the younger considered her as their equal and spent time with her at Nohant, which is where she wrote most of her novels.

The 18th century château remains much as it was when she died there in 1876. The visit gives an insight into her many-faceted life, and includes the theatre where plays were written by George, performed by family and friends, accompanied on the piano by Chopin....

In the grounds, make sure you see the little cemetery where George Sand and members of her family are buried. There was talk that the bicentenary of her birth (2004) should be the occasion to honour her memory by transferring her tomb to the Panthéon in Paris (burial place for the great and the good). There was, however, local opposition to the thought of losing *la bonne dame de Nohant* (the good lady of Nohant).

If you are, like me, fascinated by the life and achievements of this extraordinary woman, there is a well stocked bookshop where you buy your tickets for the guided visit, which lasts an hour.

The château is open all day in July and August, but closes between 12 and 2pm at other times of the year. It is closed on May 1st and November 1st and 11th.

Entry (by guided visit only): 7€. Free to members of the E.U. aged under 26.

How to get there:
For Nohant take the N144 south from Bourges to Levet, then the D940 to Lignières. Some 16kms beyond Lignières, at the village of Thévet-St-Julien turn right onto the little country road (D69) to Verneuil-sur-Igneraie and St-Chartier. These

8kms begin to give you an idea of why George Sand loved the area. At St-Chartier join the D918 (direction La Châtre). Nohant is 3km further on, just after you meet the D943.
Vic is just north of Nohant on the D943.
Allow 1½ hours for this journey.

The charming country around Nohant readily evokes the settings George Sand used in her novels: Take the D51 from Nohant to Sarzay. The 14th century building still has the air of a fortress well able to resist, as it did, many assaults down the years. It originally had 38 towers and 3 drawbridges. In her novel *Le Meunier d'Angibault* it becomes the 'Château de Blanchemont', which she describes as *'un castel assez élégant'*.

Now take the D41 to Montipouret and the Moulin d'Angibault is signposted. This old mill, still in working order, is the setting for *Le Meunier d'Angibault* (1845), a novel of country life where obstacles to true love are overcome by timely events. George Sand called the place a *'coin de paradis sauvage'* (a wild corner of paradise – in French wild flowers are *fleurs sauvages*) when she came across it, walking in the country with her children the year before.

From Montipouret the D38 will bring you to Mers-sur-Indre and the lake referred to in the title of her novel *La Mare au Diable* (1846). A young widowed farmer sets off for the next village with one of his children and a village girl Marie, he to meet an eligible widow, she to her first post as servant. They lose their way in the mist near the reputedly enchanted lake of the title, and have to spend the night there as best they can. Marie's cheerful good sense endears her to the widower, making him think he could do worse for a wife. They both find their intended situations unacceptable – he dislikes the widow, while Marie flees from the evil intentions of her employer. You will have guessed how the story develops and it ends with their traditional country wedding.

Simone de Beauvoir described George Sand as a 'sentimental feminist'.

Return by the D69 and D943 to Vic.
This circuit will take you about 1½ -2 hours with stops.

Another thing:
Drop in to the little church at Vic to see the frescoes, intensely dramatic paintings by 12th century monks, rediscovered in 1839 under layers of plaster by the village priest. Through the efforts of George Sand they became classified as a historical monument. The lower parts of some of the frescoes were damaged by unfortunate attempts at restoration in the 1930s, but the *Last Supper* and the *Kiss of Judas* are particularly powerful.

Where to eat:
For a tasty lunch, or afternoon tea, try the restaurant *(La Bergerie)* adjacent to George Sand's home. There is also a pleasant picnic site down the lane from the house.

Return to Bourges by the same route. It is a little quicker to go via La Châtre instead of the country road. For more about George Sand you could drop into the museum there, but unless there is time for both I much prefer her home at Nohant.

Excursion 4: Bourges

You will need a good 2 days to do justice to this place that is so rich in history.

To put you in the picture:
The name comes from the Celtic tribe, the Bituriges whose home it was until they were defeated by Julius Caesar (according to him the whole population of 40,000 was massacred). However, under the Romans the city grew and prospered, as archaeological digs have revealed. In Roman times it was called Avaricum and was the capital of the province of Aquitaine.

During the Hundred Years' war, Paris fell into English hands and Bourges effectively became the capital of France from 1422 to 1437 (Charles VII was derisively known as the King of Bourges). The royal presence and the founding of a university (Calvin came to study here) brought prosperity and renown.

The many buildings of the 15th and 16th centuries that remain and have been very sympathetically restored are a testimony to the glory years of Bourges. The town suffers from 20th century urban and commercial sprawl, but the historic old quarter has been well restored, so don't be put off by the outskirts.

Visit:

A walk round the old town is a good introduction as it gives a real sense of its history. *NB Wear comfortable shoes because some of the streets are cobbled.*

Walk up to the cathedral and follow part of the town trail with its explanatory panels. *A leaflet for the full trail is available from the Tourist office near the Cathedral.*

Try going along rue des 3 Maillets, then down rue des Remparts, where you can see how some of the houses are built into the mediaeval ramparts. Then up the steps (formerly called Passage Casse-cou (breakneck) – readily understood if you go *down* them). At the top, turn right into rue de l'Hôtel Lallemant.

It's worth walking into the Cour d'Honneur of the Hôtel Lallemant and looking around at its architecture of the 15th (mullioned windows and arcades), 16th (doorways and bays over the passage) and 17th centuries (frescoes). At some stage too, visit the Musée des Arts Décoratifs which it houses.

Cross place Gordaine (look for the stone where Calvin is supposed to have stood to preach) and take rue Mirebeau, then turn into rue Pelvoysin. Follow this along to rue des Arènes where the Musée du Berry in the Hôtel Cujas has some interesting collections showing the history of Bourges and its region (look for the 15th century statue of a mourner from the tomb of the duc de Berry – see Excursion 2: la Verrerie).

Finally, go up the steps at the side of the Palais Jacques Coeur. If you decide to do this walk on the day of your arrival, you will appreciate all the more a meal in the restaurant Jacques Coeur (just opposite the Palace), which is a fitting introduction to the gastronomic pleasures of Bourges.

Visit: Le Palais Jacques Coeur

To put you in the picture about Jacques Coeur:
This palace is the material legacy in his home town of a fur trader's son who rose to become King Charles VII's Minister of Finance in 1439. Clearly an astute businessman, Jacques Coeur's travels to the Middle East and his trading with Genoese and Venetian merchants as well as his favoured position with the king had enabled him to amass a vast fortune.

So, at this high point in his career, he began in 1442 the construction of a residence that would reflect his success and status. It is one of the most magnificent Gothic residential buildings in France. His wealth allowed him to fulfil his liking for comfort, modernity and beauty, so that what we see today is a magnificent Gothic building yet with signs of Renaissance elegance. A self-made man, he was not afraid to show off his ownership of this sumptuous palace: carvings of scallop shells and hearts abound: i.e. his name in images, the scallop being the symbol of St Jacques and seen on buildings along the pilgrim route to Santiago, while the French word for heart is *coeur*. Nonetheless, the *fleur-de-lys* motif of the chapel window and banqueting hall doorway clearly shows his reverence for his king.

Jacques Coeur never lived in the palace he had created, for the inevitable happened and he, like other finance ministers in France (Sully: see Excursion 1, and Fouquet under Louis XIV), was disgraced in 1450. His property was confiscated, he was given a heavy fine and condemned to life imprisonment. Though he never lived in the palace, he lived up to his motto (*to brave hearts nothing is impossible*) for he escaped from prison and sought the protection in Rome of the Pope, who gave him command of a crusade against the Turks on the island of Chios. He never returned to France, but in 1456 died from illness on his crusading expedition.

Visit:
You can get a combined ticket for the palace and the cathedral crypt and north tower- which is good value (see below).
The palace can only be visited by guided tour, lasting 1 hour, during which you will have the chance to see close up the rich sculpture that adorns walls, windows, fireplaces and doorways, giving the palace its elegance tinged with the ostentation characteristic of Jacques Coeur.

Visit: La Cathédrale St Etienne
The silhouette of this vast edifice dominates the skyline and can be seen from miles away as you approach Bourges. Building was started in 1195 by the archbishop of Bourges, Henri de Sully, on the site of the existing cathedral, but of that building only the south and north doors remain. It is one of the largest Gothic cathedrals in France. Its height and length, along with the absence of a transept increase the impression of size and of its architectural unity.
The alternate levels of galleries and windows in the double side aisles create an unusual effect of light and dark. It is worth visiting this great cathedral just to see the 13th century stained glass of the apse – some of the best in France - where biblical stories are graphically portrayed in beautiful colours. All the windows are superb, though the *Good Samaritan* and the *Last Judgement* are my favourites. They are supposedly seen at their best in the late morning sun, but are stunning at any time.
The cathedral was so big that the apse extended out beyond the city ramparts and had to be supported by a crypt. You can only see the fascinating collection of sculptures in the crypt with a guide. This is well worth doing, using the combined ticket that gives you entry to the crypt, the Palais Jacques Coeur and the 16th century north tower.
Once you have made it up the 396 steps of the spiral staircase, the tower affords a panoramic view over Bourges (best on a sunny day).
The cathedral is open daily: April to September: 8.30am-7.15pm (-9pm in July, August); October to March, 9am-5.45pm.

The crypt closes at lunchtime, Sunday morning and 6pm in high season. Last entry in the morning, 11am; in the afternoon, 5pm (4pm in winter)
The Palais Jacques Coeur is open: May, June, 9.30-12noon, 2-6.15pm; July, August, 9.30am-12.30pm, 2-6.30pm; September to April, 9.30-12 noon, 2-5.45pm
Combined entry to the cathedral, crypt, tower and the Palais Jacques Coeur: 9€, free to members of the E.U. aged under 26

The Tourist Office has a good selection of books about the city and the cathedral. For a clear pictorial explanation of how to follow the stories told in the stained glass windows: Les grands Vitraux de Bourges, by Hervé Benoit, FAC-éditions (in French).

Another thing:
The brother of Henri de Sully was also archbishop – of Paris – and, a few years earlier, had started his own cathedral-building project: Notre-Dame.

Where to eat:
Le Jacques Coeur, 3 Place Jacques Coeur (opposite the Palais Jacques Coeur) I like to eat here on the first *and* last nights of my stay.
Le Bourbonnoux, 44 rue Bourbonnoux
Le Sénat, 8 rue de la Poissonnerie
Les Beaux Arts, 1 place Cujas
L'Abbaye St-Ambroix, 60 avenue Jean-Jaurès (further away, possibly a car ride)

Excursion 5: Cheverny and the Sologne

The stopping places on your drive through the Sologne are only open in the afternoon so I suggest you visit Cheverny in the morning .

To put you in the picture about Cheverny:
Cheverny is unusual among the châteaux of the Loire valley where many were built during the 16th century Renaissance

period. Cheverny is pure 17th century and has remained much the same since its construction, mainly because it has always been owned by the same family.

However it was not the first castle on the site and, so the story goes, owes its construction to a tragic event. Its owner, Henri Hurault, was governor of Blois and faithful servant of Henri IV. Hurault was rather traditional in his views on marriage and kept his young wife at home, well out of the public eye so that she would not fall for the charms of other men. (cf Molière's *Ecole des Femmes)*. One day the king mocked him by making the well-known gesture of cuckoldry behind Hurault's head. Unfortunately Hurault spotted this in a mirror and in high dudgeon rode off to Cheverny, where of course he found his wife entangled with a page. Hurault stabbed him to death, gave his wife the choice of the same fate or of taking poison. An hour later she was dead, but the king was not best pleased and condemned Hurault to house arrest. After the death of the king, Hurault married a woman he felt less likely to cause him the same problem as his first wife. No doubt to erase the memory of the earlier tragedy, he demolished the old fortress, leaving his wife to oversee the building of the new château – which is what you see today. She was clearly a lady of taste and refinement.

Visit:

Louis XIV's cousin, the Duchess of Montpensier, known as *La Grande Mademoiselle,* who as a guest at Cheverny wrote 'there is nothing more romantic….more superb than the interior'. As well as the beauty and elegance of the staircase, ceilings, Flanders tapestries and furniture, homage is paid to the hunting tradition of the region in the Trophy room, next door to the kennels of the Cheverny hounds that have featured on many a poster of the château.

Devotees of the cartoon character *Tintin* by Hergé will notice that Cheverny bears a remarkable resemblance to Moulinsart. Driving past the château while on holiday, Hergé was struck by its classic lines and decided to use it as his model for Captain Haddock's ancestral home. In 2001 a permanent exhibition, the 'Secrets of Moulinsart', was created where Hergé's characters relive their exploits.

The grounds are lovely and can be enjoyed on foot, or by electric car. You can also have a restful boat ride on the canal that runs through the grounds.

Various ticket combinations allow you to take in all or some of these attractions.

Cheverny is open daily: April, May, June, September, 9.15am-6.15pm; July, August, 9.15am-6.45pm; October, 9.45am-5.30pm

Basic entry to the château and grounds: 7€

Where to eat:
In Cour-Cheverny, the *Trois Marchands* and the *St Hubert* both offer good lunch menus.

How to get there:
For this excursion, I suggest you take the motorway A71 to Vierzon, then the A85 to Romorantin, and then the D765 (direction Blois) to Cour-Cheverny. On the outskirts of Cour-Cheverny the Château de Cheverny is signposted.
Journey time: about an hour.

The Sologne:
St Viâtre (Lakes museum), Chaon (Poaching museum), Vouzeron (Hunting and Nature museum)

To put you in the picture:
Part of the joy of visiting this part of France is the opportunity to drive through beautiful but not grandiose countryside, along roads pleasantly free of heavy traffic. My suggested route uses very minor roads at times but the distances are short and the surfaces good.

This afternoon's leisurely journey takes you to 3 places that are representative of the history and traditions of the region. The Sologne boasts over 2800 lakes (*étangs,* which actually means ponds, though many are larger than a size I normally associate with the word - for you to judge), which account for 10% of all lakes in France, big and small. The region constitutes a 'wet continental area' of particular interest for its aquatic birds (various species of duck, grebe, heron, bittern, snipe, curlew).

St Viâtre:
The little ecomuseum (La Maison des Etangs) explains the biological richness of the region and you can spend a pleasant moment wandering round the nearby Etang de la Ville, seeing things for yourself.

How to get there:
From Cheverny take the D765 back towards Romorantin. Before Romorantin turn left onto the D122 to Millançay, cross the D922 and continue another 8kms to Marcilly-en-Gault. There take the D49 to St Viâtre.
Journey time: about 40 minutes.

Chaon:
The Poaching museum (la Maison du Braconnage) recounts the history of poaching, an activity particularly dear to the hearts of the men of this region. The eponymous hero of Maurice Genevoix' novel, *Raboliot,* is a native of the Sologne and master poacher relentlessly pursued by the local

gendarme. The book, with its fine descriptions of the men and countryside of the Sologne, won the Prix Goncourt in 1925.

How to get there:
From St Viâtre follow the D93 over the Motorway to Nouan-le-Fuzelier, then the D44 via Les Rouches until you meet the D923. At this junction take the D55 northward towards Chaon. After about 3kms turn right onto the D29 for the remaining 5kms to Chaon.
Journey time: about 20 minutes.

Vouzeron:
The hunting and nature museum (Maison de la Chasse et de la Nature) is in an 18th century Sologne farmhouse. As the guide says, 'being so near to Alain-Fournier country, it was natural to recreate a magical place where reality fuses with the imaginary'. The guided tour takes you on a virtual journey through the myths and forest of the Vouzeron countryside.

How to get there:
From Chaon the quickest way is to take the D29 to Lamotte-Beuvron; from there the N20 to Salbris, where you turn onto the D944 to Neuvy-sur-Barangeon (15kms via Nançay). From Neuvy a further 6kms on the D30 will bring you to Vouzeron.
The D104 takes you the 20kms back to Bourges.
Journey time from Chaon to Vouzeron: about 45 minutes, and from Vouzeron to Bourges: 30 minutes.

Should you find time too short to include all 3 visits in this afternoon's excursion - lunch can be a lengthy pleasure in France - you might prefer to incorporate Vouzeron into your Bourges sightseeing itinerary.

Another thing:
Lamotte-Beuvron is the reputed home of the famous French dessert *tarte tatin*. The Tatin sisters, Stephanie and Caroline, ran the hotel there. One Sunday in 1898 (some say 1889) the restaurant was particularly busy and Stephanie became flustered. In her hurry she apparently forgot to line the base of the tin with pastry for her apple tart, but just put in the slices of

apple to cook in the oven. When she realised her mistake she tried to rescue the situation by cooking the pastry on top of the caramelised apple, turning it upside down to serve. The customers were delighted with this new dish and refused to believe that it could have been a mistake. It soon became a 'signature dish' of the restaurant and its fame spread, especially when the owner of the Paris restaurant Maxim's tasted it and put it on his own menu.

You will see the hotel Tatin on the road through Lamotte-Beuvron.

6 The Valley of the Kings

The Loire Valley was a favourite residence and hunting ground for kings of France from Charles VII to Louis XIV, which is a reason for the many magnificent châteaux in this fertile valley, the 'garden of France'.

There is a wealth of wonderful places to visit here, more than in any other region of France, so the destinations on this tour, like all those in this book, are my personal favourites.

Blois, Chambord, and Chenonceau, 'the pearl of the Loire Valley', are worth the visit for their architectural beauty, let alone their associations with French monarchy.

Azay-le-Rideau and Villandry are not royal châteaux, but in their past they have had their contacts with monarchs of France.... and England.

Azay was described by the writer Honoré de Balzac as 'a facetted diamond set in the Indre' and Villandry owes its renown to its unique gardens.

Although the château at Angers does have royal connections, the highlight of a visit there is the amazing Tapestry of the Apocalypse.

The abbey of Fontevraud has had a chequered history, being at one time a prison, but it is also a royal burial place, notably of Henry II of England and his son Richard Lionheart.

Amboise and le Clos-Lucé both figured in royal history, as did Chaumont, although this tour focuses on its international garden festival.

Where to stay:
To cut down on travel, I recommend the *Hôtel Abbaye Royale de Fontevraud* as your base for visits to Angers, Azay-le-Rideau, Villandry and of course Fontevraud abbey. This hotel is in the abbey grounds, in the former hospital, le Prieuré St Lazare. The style of furnishing and the fact that you dine in the cloister give an appropriately monastic feel to your stay, although the fare is anything but monastic. Another pleasure of staying here is that you are free to enjoy the abbey grounds out of normal opening times.

For your visits to Blois, Chambord, Chaumont, Chenonceau and Le Clos-Lucé, stay at *Le Bon Laboureur* in Chenonceaux. This atmospheric 18th century coaching inn well merits its 4 star status for its food, comfort and really excellent service. After an outing on a hot summer day, the hotel pool is most welcoming too.

How to get there:
For the Abbaye Royale de Fontevraud, leave the A85 motorway at junction 3 (Saumur), take the N147 into Saumur, cross the river and turn onto the D947 (direction Montsoreau, Chinon). At Montsoreau follow the D947 to Fontevraud (3kms).
In the village turn left into rue St Jean, which leads to the hotel.
For le Bon Laboureur, see directions to Chenonceau (Excursion 3)

Excursions: 1 Angers and Fontevraud
*   2 Azay-le-Rideau and Villandry*
*   3 Chenonceau, via Château de la Grille*
*   4 Amboise, le Clos-Lucé and Chaumont garden festival*
*   5 Blois and Chambord*

Excursion 1: Angers and Fontevraud

To put you in the picture about Angers:
Nowadays Angers (pronounced *Onjay*) is a city of well over 200,000 inhabitants, astride the river Maine just upstream from its confluence with the Loire. Regarded by some as one of the most beautiful cities in France, the oldest part, stretching round the château and across the river to the district called La Doutre (literally: the other side), has an intimate feel about it. This is the area that will be the focus of this visit.

The imposing walls and towers (there are seventeen of them) of the château dominate the city, especially from downstream, so you can readily see why the château was never captured. The sombre and powerful appearance of the fortress contrasts strongly with the pretty gardens planted in the moat, with deer roaming in parts of them. In fact the moat was never filled with water as it is way above the river level. The fortress as it is now, follows the outline of the one built in the 13th century by Blanche de Castille, regent in the minority of her son Louis IX (the future Saint Louis). The site had already been home to the early bishops of Angers until the Norman invasions of the 9th century, but, after they were driven out, the Foulques dynasty became counts of Anjou.

The most famous, Foulques III, called Nerra (the black), had put Anjou on the map in the 11th century by his ferocious conquests throughout the region. He built castles at Langeais and Loches, and fortified Saumur and Angers, though virtually nothing remains of his castle here.

Later, another Count Foulques married his young son Geoffroy to the grand-daughter of William the Conqueror. As count, Geoffroy used to sport a sprig of broom in his hat, which earned him the nickname *Plante-à-genêt.* Their son Henry became king of England (Henry II), founding the House of Plantagenêt. His kingdom of course incorporated Anjou (through birth), Aquitaine (through marriage to Eleanor of Aquitaine), Normandy and other regions of France (through inheritance and conquest).

After Henry's death in 1189, his French territories were lost bit by bit. Angers became French again in 1204, though the region was fought over by the two nations until the end of the Hundred Years' War.

By 1360 it had been elevated from county to duchy, and it was Duke Louis I who commissioned the famous tapestry in 1375. Eventually the duchy lost its independent status and was brought under direct control of the king of France in 1474 during the rule of the last duke, known as *le bon roi René* (good king René – he was also king of Sicily. (See Tour 2 for his connection to Aix-en-Provence). It was under the auspices of Duke René that culture and learning flourished in Angers. Again in the Renaissance, learning and building were the hallmarks of the town, to the extent that it was called 'the Athens of the West'.

In the 17th and 18th centuries sail and rope making were Angers' principal industries, but after that went out of fashion economic decline set in until well into the 20th century. Light industry, wine, fruit and flowers sustain the town now, though the ubiquitous *rosé d'Anjou* of my youth has certainly been overtaken by drier Provençal *rosés*.

Another thing:
Louis XI, the king who rather sneakily took over Angers from le bon roi René was actually the good man's nephew. Louis pretended to pay a courtesy visit to his unsuspecting uncle and then proceeded to set up a garrison of his soldiers in the city. Aged sixty-five, René decided it was not worth the effort of waging war against his king, so he gave in and went to do good things in Aix-en-Provence.

Visit: the château
The most impressive aspect of this château, apart from the tapestry, is its walls. With their great round towers they are almost forty metres high and look pretty forbidding. *Look at them from the outside to get the best views.* When built in the 13th century the towers were much higher and topped in traditional 'pepper-pot' style. During the 16th century Wars of Religion, Henri III was pressured by the Catholic faction 'la Ligue' (league) into demolishing the castle. The governor deliberately took his time to execute the king's order, and had only partly completed the job when the king died and the

Protestant Henri IV took over, effectively saving the château. In fact, by levelling everything off it was now easier to manoeuvre artillery pieces round the walls and doubtless this helped republican Angers repel the advance of the Vendée royalist army during the Revolution.

The 15th century château buildings are attractive, as are the gardens, which make up the largest part of the precinct. The interest here is not the gardens themselves, but imagining what this area would have looked like in le bon roi René's time. For he, alongside his love of music, reading, poetry and prose writing, created a *ménagerie* of domestic and exotic animals in the grounds of the château.

The Crusades had really started the fashion for private zoos and while the Papal legate had banned the one belonging to Notre-Dame in Paris as 'harmful, useless and ridiculous', the Papacy in Avignon had one of its own, like all great European courts in the late Middle Ages. René's was one of the biggest in France, the animals mostly being gifts from other nobles. For example, in 1450 the duke of Brittany gave him a lion and lioness, the king of Portugal sent an elephant, white monkeys and 'other beasts from the Indies'. Exotic birds were usually bought – in Angers traders had their own street, *rue de l'Oisellerie* (bird selling street).

An excellent little book on the subject, La ménagerie du roi René, *produced by the Natural history museum of Angers, is available in the château bookshop (in French).*

The book has a plan of the grounds showing where the various animals are thought to have been kept: the moat was home to wild boar, pigs, deer, swans and wild geese – a little less tranquil perhaps than today's scene.

Another thing:

René's accounts show the considerable cost of keeping his *ménagerie,* especially in food. An Angers butcher supplied him with 600 sheep a year – the lions required half a sheep daily and the leopards a quarter. But that was not the only cost: records show that on April 3rd 1463 one of the keepers was killed *estranglé par l'un des lyepars* (strangled by one of the leopards).

Visit: The Tapestry of the Apocalypse

To put you in the picture:
The history is almost as remarkable as the work itself. Charles V of France lent his brother, Louis I, duke of Anjou, an illuminated manuscript of the Book of Revelations to 'make his beautiful tapestry'. Louis' accounts from 1377 show payments for its manufacture and it is thought to have been completed by about 1382. It was used for ceremonial occasions like the wedding of Louis' son in 1400. This took place in Arles (in the south of France), so the logistical problems of getting it there must have been enormous, for the original tapestry was 140m long x 6m high (albeit in six sections of over 23m in length).

From the start it was recognised as a masterpiece in its portrayal of St John's vision and for the quality of its weaving. There is absolutely no difference between the front and the reverse side: no leftover threads, or threads that 'jump' from one area to another – except where it has been restored.

René donated the tapestry to Angers cathedral, where it continued to be exhibited at religious festivals until late in the 18th century. Then the horror story begins. The cathedral authorities tried to sell it because tapestries were no longer in fashion, but, probably for that reason, they could not find a buyer. So they threw this great but unfashionable work of art away or made use of bits of it. It was cut up and used to protect fruit in greenhouses against frost, as floor covering when a ceiling was being painted, as rugs or tablecloths and even nailed in strips to stalls in the bishop's stables to stop the horses bruising themselves.

Fortunately, in 1843, Canon Joubert of Angers cathedral discovered what had happened and bought all the pieces he could. Thanks to his and subsequent careful restoration, the tapestry was finally given back to the château in 1954. Some parts were inevitably lost, but the 103m that remain still make it the largest extant mediaeval tapestry.

Visit:
The short introductory film will prepare you to an extent, but you will nonetheless be awestruck by the sheer size and beauty

of the tapestry that stretches away as far as you can see in this specially built gallery.

Each of the six sections is introduced by a full height scene (now 4,5m) of a figure reading, seated under a high canopy. Two are missing, but it would appear that the figures are inviting us to meditate on the scenes that follow. These are in two rows, one above the other, and are meant to be 'read' from left to right, upper row first.

The tapestry is a biblical account, but it has contemporary (ie 14th century) overtones. The banners above each of the readers' canopies display the coat of arms of Anjou, which makes you wonder if any of the figures (they are not the same man) is the duke who commissioned the work. This was of course during the Hundred Years' War, so look out for the beast on horseback come to make war, conquer and kill (Revelations11:7-8). He has the form of an English king and the country he has come from looks suspiciously like England. Again, the dragon gives his power, his throne and his great authority to the beast (Revelations13:1-2). The symbol of power that he hands over is the *fleur-de-lys,* emblem of the French monarchy, which didn't begin to regain its authority in France until the time of Joan of Arc, fifty years after the tapestry was woven. It is no doubt a contemporary comment too that the New Jerusalem is a 'state of the art' mediaeval castle.

The tapestry is so beautiful and the imagery so powerful that it is an idea to read St John's apocalyptic vision before you see it, as his are probably the only words that do it justice.

The château is open daily (except 1st May): 5th September to 30th April, 10am-5.30pm; 2nd May to 4th September, 9.30am-6.30pm
Entry (including the tapestry): 6€
There are guided visits (in French, lasting 1hour) at 11.15am, 3.15pm weekdays; 11.15am, 2.15pm, 3.30pm weekends
Audio-guides are available in English: 4,50€
*Make sure you visit other château buildings **before** you see the Tapestry of the Apocalypse, as all you will want to do afterwards is to reflect on what you have seen and, I suggest, relax in the gardens, where you will be able to have lunch.*

Allow 1½ hours for your visit, excluding lunch.

Where to eat:
In the pleasant setting of the château grounds the restaurant *Le Logis du Château* offers various *formules*.

After lunch, make your way back to your car via the cathedral, which is definitely worth seeing. To get the best views of it as you approach, turn left out of the château and go to the end of the road, amusingly named promenade du Bout du Monde (far end of the world). Here you get a great view over the river to the la Doutre area. The names of the bridge downstream (Pont de la Basse-Chaîne) and of the second bridge you see upstream (Pont de la Haute-Chaîne) refer to mediaeval times when chains were stretched across the river at those points to stop enemy ships.

Now go along to the montée St-Maurice, whose steps lead up to the cathedral. The construction marks a transition between Romanesque and Gothic. The unusually narrow façade is striking: the lower level dates from the 12th century, the two side towers from the 15th and the central one was added a century later. Inside, the nave is the oldest part, 12th century and wide for a Romanesque building, with no side aisles. The ribbed vaulting is in a very local style known as the Plantagenêt or Angevin vault.

Another fine feature of the cathedral is its stained glass windows. On the north side of the nave they are 12th century, while the lovely windows in the chancel date mainly from the 13th.

Remembering that the Apocalypse tapestry once hung here it is perhaps not surprising to find the walls hung with others, mostly mediaeval, from the cathedral's large collection. On the south side of the nave notice the Last Supper, with its fourteenth person. In the south transept, the tapestries of St John the Evangelist in boiling oil and the beheading of John the Baptist echo the powerful imagery of the Apocalypse tapestry.

In the street behind the cathedral apse, the 16th century half-timbered house on the corner is considered the most beautiful of all the houses in old Angers and is known as the Maison d'Adam, either because of the statues of Adam and Eve that adorned it, or, more simply, because of its 18th century owner, Michel Adam. Details of the profusion of carved figures repay careful scrutiny.

Another thing:
Famous sons of Angers include the sculptor David d'Angers (1788-1856), best known for the pediment of the Panthéon in Paris. You may see his marble figure of St Cecilia in the chancel of the cathedral. David based it on a girl he fell in love with in Rome, who became a nun.
René Bazin and his nephew Hervé Bazin were both writers. I have enjoyed reading Hervé Bazin's novels about a dysfunctional family. His first – and probably his best - *Vipère au Poing* (Viper in the Fist - 1948), recounts the escapades of three children, in revolt against their tyrannical mother, whom he nicknames Folcoche (mad pig) and who is based on his own mother. The novel was a great success and the film not bad either. English translations (there are two) may be difficult to find.

How to get there:
From Fontevraud, take the D947 to Montsoreau, then follow the river to Saumur. There, cross the river and take the D952 into Angers, where you follow signs for the cathedral and château.
Journey time: 45 minutes
Parking close to the château will be difficult until the tramway is completed (2010/2011), so the best bet is the Parking République near the cathedral in rue Plantagenêt and then walking through the streets of the old town to the château, 10 minutes' walk via rue Millet and rue Donadieu-de-Puycharic, with a little detour to rue St-Aignan, which runs parallel to it.
Between the cathedral and the château you can see some fine 16th and 17th century residences (rue Donadieu-de-Puycharic) and late middle ages architecture (rue St-Aignan).

Visit: the Abbaye de Fontevraud
The advantage of staying at the Prieuré St Lazare in the grounds of the abbey is that you can visit the different parts of it at your leisure over the two days of your stay.

To put you in the picture about the abbey:
Fontevraud was founded in the early 12th century by an itinerant preacher Robert d'Arbrissel. His preaching attracted a great following wherever he went, of all classes and of both sexes. The presence of women in his unconventional, unkempt community, sleeping rough alongside the men, caused a scandal with the church authorities, who considered there was as much opportunity for sin as for following the word of the Lord. However, when they eventually settled in the forest by a spring near the Loire and created what was to become the greatest monastic complex in the western Christian world, women were to play the leading role. Arbrissel founded a dual order, monks and nuns working together, but both under the authority of a woman, a remarkable concept for the time.

From the start Fontevraud had five distinct priories in its complex, each with its chapel and cloister, refectory and dormitory. These were the Prieuré Ste-Marie (aka Grand Moutier), for contemplative nuns; the Prieuré de la Madeleine, for repentant prostitutes; the Prieuré St-Jean, for monks; the Prieuré St-Lazare for lepers; the Prieuré St-Benoît was the hospital.

Things were not always easy in this female-run institution. Arbrissel deemed that proximity to women would better overcome carnal desires and told the monks that submission to the sisters was 'for the salvation of their souls'. Monks did not always take kindly to female rule and in his lifetime Arbrissel was forced to restore discipline on several occasions at Fontevraud and its dependent priories. However, for the next seven hundred years, thirty six abbesses, half of them of royal blood, governed Fontevraud.

At the time of the Revolution Fontevraud was still a rich and active community, but in 1792, the government closed down religious houses. After the monks and nuns had left, the whole place was ransacked: two of the priories were demolished for their stone, the bells were melted down (proceeds to state funds), tombs broken open and statues smashed.

The place, now in very poor repair, was eventually designated a state prison by Napoleon in 1804, but it took another ten years before it actually opened. At the start there over 400 inmates: men, women and children as young as 8. Subsequently numbers varied between 1400 and 1800. During World War Two it housed captured members of the resistance and, in 1945, collaborators.

The prison was closed in 1962, but when I first visited Fontevraud in the '70s one former inmate had apparently decided to stay on and was working as a gardener.

Another thing:
The fact that both monks and nuns were under the authority of the abbess produced an instance of more than equal rights for women. At mealtimes nuns were allowed ½ litre of wine, while monks were only allowed ¼ litre. No wonder some monks complained.

Visit:
Restoration of parts of the abbey buildings began as early as the 1900s, with the nave of the abbey church and the great Romanesque kitchen. I remember it as all looking pretty shabby when I first came, a far cry from today, though restoration work still continues.

As you walk round you will see that there is no one style of architecture. The main body of the buildings was erected in the early days of the foundation, but right up to the 18th century successive abbesses made their own changes.

There is so much to see that I recommend you take a guided tour or audio-guide (see details below)

The most impressive building is certainly the abbey church. The chancel was the first part to be built, soberly Romanesque, but with tall, elegant pillars that give it a majestic appearance. The nave was added fifty years later, with heavier, square pillars. Its vaulted roof is in the same Plantagenêt style as Angers cathedral.

The Plantagenêts gave great financial support to the abbey and Henry II, his wife Eleanor of Aquitaine, their son Richard

Lionheart and Isabelle d'Angoulême, wife of their other son John Lackland, were buried here, as well as the hearts of John Lackland and Henry III. Jeanne of England, wife of Raimond VI of Toulouse and their son Raimond VII of Toulouse (see Tour 1) were also buried here.

Henry died at nearby Chinon, Eleanor spent the last years of her life in the nunnery here and Richard Lionheart, at odds with his father for much of his life, was in repentant mood at his father's funeral, stating that he wished to be buried near his father.

This important slice of English history is captured here in the four magnificent painted recumbent tomb statues (*gisants*) of Henry, Eleanor, Richard and Isabelle, displayed in the church.

It is hard to imagine now that during its time as a prison in the 19th century, the nave was partitioned into four levels of dormitories and workshops. The refectory suffered a similar fate.

The cloister was rebuilt in the 16th century by two royal abbesses, Renée and Louise de Bourbon. You can see their arms and monograms on the columns and in particular in the richly decorated chapter house. Here the biblical paintings contain portraits of nuns, all from the noble Bourbon and Rochechouart families, some of whom were superimposed on previous ones because there was no other room for them. Look around you for the letters RB and L (Renée and Louise).

The most unusual building and the one that has been subject to most speculation is the Romanesque kitchen. In fact it looks somewhat Bysantine with all its turrets and 'fish scale' roof. Inside, the design is equally complicated: octagonal, then square, then octagonal again as it goes up.

Another thing:
Even in the 1800s legend had it that the 'kitchen' was the tower of a bandit called Evraud, converted by Robert d'Arbrissel. Scholars then thought it variously a funeral chapel or baptistry. Only much later was it discovered by looking at a 17th century book of plans, *Monasticon Gallicanum* (Gallic monasteries), that other Loire Valley abbeys had similar constructions, and that it was a kitchen or smoke-house, part of the original abbey. These other kitchens had eight fireplaces

going round in the form of the apse of a church. What makes the Fontevraud one unique in France is that only stone was used in its construction, even the roof 'tiles'.

The abbey is open: January to March, November, December; 10am-5pm. Entry 7€
April to June, September, October, 10am-6pm; July, August, 10am-7pm. Entry 8,40€
By staying at the hotel in the grounds you benefit from half price entry to the abbey buildings.
It's a good idea to find out on your arrival the times of guided tours, so you can join one to suit your programme, or take an audio-guide (4€).
The guided tour lasts about 75 minutes. Spend as much time as you like in the gardens.

In your hotel, don't miss the Plantagenêt style chapel and the elegant 17th century stairway

Excursion 2: Azay-le-Rideau and Villandry

To put you in the picture about Azay-le-Rideau:
The name of the château and the village comes from its 12th century lord, Hugues Ridel. There was already a fortress on the island site, defending a crossing point on the river Indre on the route between Chinon and Tours.
Later the village's name became Azay-le-Brûlé (the burnt) as a result, it is said, of the wrath of the future Charles VII. In 1418, during the Hundred Years' War, he was insulted by soldiers garrisoned at the castle, who taunted Charles for having lost his capital (Paris was occupied by the English). Charles ordered the whole place to be burnt down and the three hundred soldiers executed for their temerity.
The mediaeval fortress was rebuilt and in the early 16th century Gilles Bertholot inherited the château from his father. Bertholot, who rose to become treasurer to François I, pulled down the old fortress, except for the main tower, and work began on the new château in 1518. The accounts books that have survived tell us that a huge workforce was involved,

draining the lake to drive in the foundation piles, working day and night, no expense spared.

François I paid a visit in 1524, which accounts for the salamander and ermine motif above the entrance (salamander for the king and ermine for the queen).

However, as happened to a number of those involved with state finances over the centuries, Bertholot was accused of 'financial mismanagement' by his king and fled the country to avoid the fatal noose. His goods were confiscated, the château given to a captain of the king's guard and Bertholot died in exile. His wife tried for several years to hang on to Azay, but eventually lost her case in 1535.
It stayed in the possession of the same family until the Revolution. It was then bought by the marquis de Biencourt, a noble with revolutionary tendencies, whose descendents kept it for the next hundred years, before it was bought by the state in 1905.

Another thing:
As Bertholot's state duties often took him away for long periods, his wife became the site manager, as did Catherine Briçonnet at Chenonceau and the second wife of Philippe Hurault at Cheverny (see Tour 5, Excursion 5). Each of these lovely châteaux certainly has 'the feminine touch'.
During the Franco-Prussian War of 1870, Prince Frederick-Charles of Prussia, a general in the invading army, was billeted at Azay when a light fitting fell on the table where he was dining. He thought it was an assassination attempt, and threatened to destroy the château – which would have been the second time.

Visit:
This château, built in the early 16th century, is a combination of the new Renaissance and the traditional fortress look. It has the corner towers, turrets, machicolations and moat of a fortress, but here they are purely decorative. The windows and delicate decoration of the façades reveal the Italian influence, which was becoming very popular in France at that period. The real innovation was, however, the monumental staircase. The château at Blois has a remarkable exterior spiral staircase, but here and at Chenonceau, both built just that bit later, the stairs are inside and straight, with loggias at each level giving views onto the courtyard and the gardens. The richly carved Renaissance decoration is magnificent and easily the best bit of the interior of the château - worth the visit in itself, though the kitchens are interesting too and the portrait gallery has all the main actors in the pageant of the Loire valley in the 16th century, including Gabrielle d'Estrées (Henri IV's mistress) in her bath.

The monumental staircase is the jewel of the main façade, but when you walk in the park that surrounds the lake on the other three sides of the château, you will understand why Balzac described Azay as a 'facetted diamond set in the Indre'. It is a castle straight out of a fairy tale. The park, which looks more English than French, was set out by the Biencourt family in the 19th century, replacing the Renaissance garden (see Villandry, below) and fields along the bank of the Indre. The first marquis also replaced the mediaeval tower on the angle of the façade, making all the towers identical. The other 19th century change was to make one arm of the river into a proper lake, which added to the romantic appearance.

The château is open: October to March, 10am-12.30pm, 2pm-5.30pm; April to June, September, 9.30am-6pm (closed 1st May); July, August, 9.30-7pm
Entry: 8,50€ (free to members of the E.U. aged under 26). The audio-guide tour lasts up to 1½ hours.
In July, August, nightly at 9.30pm, I recommend the sound and light show lasting 1 hour, called Songes et Lumière *(dreams and light). I have not seen this version, said to be the best in the Loire Valley, but the earlier one I saw only enhanced the romantic and fairy tale atmosphere of this charming château.*

Another thing:
As well as the king and queen's emblems and their initials (F and C – for Claude), you can also see G and P. These refer to Gilles Bertholot and his wife Philippe Lesbahy. It's good to see that their memorial to themselves of the lovely château they built still remains, in spite of their disgrace. The Biencourts also left their mark: the initials B and M are those of Armand de Biencourt and his wife Anne de Montmorency

Where to eat:
I have had a pleasant lunch at *La Salamandre* in the main square.

How to get there:
From Fontevraud, take the D751 outside the village, along the river to Chinon. Outside Chinon, take the bypass, still D751, all the way to Azay.
Journey time: 30 minutes

Villandry:

To put you in the picture:
Jean le Breton, who built this château in the 1530s, was unusual in that he was finance minister to François I, but not disgraced. Unusual too because, in spite of his name, his family originated from Scotland (see Tour 5, Excursion 2 for details of the 'Scottish connection'). Le Breton was also involved in the building of Chambord (Excursion 5). While working on Chambord, le Breton built himself the château de

Villesavin nearby, so that he could more easily be 'on site'. Curiously, Villesavin is a 'look alike' of Villandry, but on a smaller scale.

The château was much altered by its 18th century owners to suit the style of the day, but was restored to its 16th century appearance by Doctor Carvallo, who bought it in 1906. Villandry is still owned and run by his family.

Another thing:
Villandry is built on the site of an earlier fortress, of which le Breton kept only the tower. The fortress, then called château de Colombier, was where Henry II of England, defeated in battle by the unlikely alliance of his son Richard (Lionheart) and King Philippe-Auguste of France in 1189, accepted all their humiliating terms. Henry died three days later at Chinon.

To put you in the picture about Joachim Carvallo:
Born into a modest Spanish family, he studied medicine in Madrid and then in Paris, specialising in physiology. While in Paris he met a beautiful, cultured and rich American student, Ann Coleman, who was also working in the laboratory. They married in 1899 and six years later decided to find a house in the country with enough room to set up their own laboratory and continue their research.

They came across Villandry in a very run down state and about to be converted into a sawmill. The owner could not raise the funds to carry out his project and put it on the market.

The Carvallos bought the place, but, instead of continuing medical research, Joachim immediately set about restoring Villandry, and that became his life's work. To understand this unexpected *volte-face*, it must be said that, since his marriage and doubtless influenced by his wife's cultural leanings, he had developed an interest in art and already had a considerable collection of paintings.

Within a short time he opened up the gallery along the left side of the main courtyard, which had been blocked up in the 18th century to create kitchens, so that it regained its original appearance. The many windows at each level made the château seem like a dismal looking army barracks. Carvallo discovered that every alternate window was false, part of the

18th century modernisation. Within a week he had chipped off the plaster mouldings and whitewashed over the false windows, so that the whole building once again took on its Renaissance character. He then invited members of the Touraine archaeological society to come and see the transformation; they could hardly believe their eyes.

For us now it is difficult to believe that this elegant Renaissance château was so different when Carvallo bought it. *In the shop you may find photos that show it in that state. If not, thumb through the book* Joachim Carvallo et Villandry, Ecrits et Témoignages, *by his grandson Robert Carvallo. It's in French, but the photos show the amazing transformations Carvallo made to the château and its gardens. The picture of Anne Coleman the day before her wedding confirms that she was a good looking lady.*
*Look at this book if you can **before** you go into the gardens.*

Photos in the book show what the gardens were like in 1906 – an English style garden very much in vogue in 19th century France.

The gardens became Carvallo's passion. He had very little to work on if he was to restore them to their 16th century state, only the two retaining walls, the canal and no contemporary plans. So he decided to recreate a Renaissance garden as it might have been.

Two books were his principal source of inspiration: the 16th century *Les plus excellents bastiments de France* by Jacques Androuet du Cerceau and *Monasticon Gallicanum* (see Fontevraud, above). Androuet du Cerceau's book documented not only buildings – he was an architect – but also their gardens, of just the right period for Carvallo's need.

Visit:
Armed with your leaflet giving a plan of the gardens, it's a good idea to look down on the ornamental gardens from the belvedere, so that you can decipher the intricate designs of the low box hedges and colourful plantings. The first ones you see are four squares laid out as symbolic representations of love. The hearts of tender love and the broken hearts of love's passion are easy to pick out. The swords and daggers of tragic

love are more difficult; the *billets doux*, fans (symbolising flirtation) and horns (cuckoldry) stretch the imagination a little. In the next garden the hedges form crosses, of which the central Maltese cross is the easiest to make out. If the symbolism here is not always evident, it is even more obscure in the garden devoted to music. The garden plan tells you, but even then I have difficulty recognising all the symbols. Still, these three gardens are beautifully kept and must be the envy of anyone who has a knot garden.

Just beyond, at the upper level, is the water garden, perhaps more 17th than 16th century, in the style of Le Nôtre and, with its mirror pool, reminiscent of Chantilly (Tour 8, Excursion 5). On the far side is the herb garden, containing more than thirty varieties of aromatic, medicinal and cooking herbs, which were an important feature of the mediaeval garden. Then you come down to the *pièce de résistance* of Villandry, the kitchen garden. Often, the vegetable plot is relegated to the far end of a garden, but here it takes pride of place.

Nine squares, each designed in a different geometric pattern, some featuring crosses, recall the monastic origins of the vegetable garden. Monastic vegetable plots would however be enclosed by herbs; the box hedges, fountains and arbours come from the Italian style adopted in 16th century France. Coincidentally, the builder of Villandry, Jean le Breton, had been ambassador to Italy, where he developed an interest in Italian gardens. The standard roses among the vegetables fit with the French Renaissance idea of an ornamental kitchen garden, combining the monastic and Italian traditions. The roses also, according to tradition, symbolised the monks themselves. I like to imagine the monk tending his plot and enjoying the results of his labour as much as I do.

There are two plantings a year, in spring and in summer, using about forty species. The colours are beautifully coordinated and all the vegetables are consumed.

The whole garden is superb, a unique creation by a man of vision.

Another thing:

For Carvallo, Villandry's gardens were not just a reconstruction; they were an expression of his concept of life:

'there is no greater thing than beauty. Through beauty you improve human beings. You can create union between them'.

The gardens are open daily throughout the year from 9am
Entry: 6€
You can get a combined entry to the gardens and château for 9€, and the audio-guide to both is 3€.
I recommend visiting the garden only, using the explanatory leaflet, because the most interesting things about the château can be seen from outside.
Allow 1½ hours for your visit.

How to get there:
From the opposite end of Azay to the château, take the D39 (direction Langeais, Villandry). Just beyond Vallères turn onto the D7 to Villandry. The château is through the village, on the right, with ample car parking.
Journey time: 15 minutes

Excursion 3: Château de Chenonceau via Château de la Grille

If you fancy a little wine tasting before lunch on your way to your hotel at Chenonceaux, call in at Château de la Grille, just outside Chinon, for something special.

You can see the château from the road and you drive in through the vines. The building goes back to the 15th century, but was much modernised in the 19th. It was bought in 1951 by the Gosset family, who had owned a Champagne House since 1584 (one of the oldest).

Château de la Grille wines are unusual for the Chinon *appellation*, which is usually drunk young. Here they are kept in cask for at least a year, then in bottle for two or three more, so that the youngest wine you can buy is at least three years old. This gives these wines great smoothness and makes them akin to a good Bordeaux.

The present owners, Laurent and Sylvie Gosset, are proud of their tradition and of the fact that their wines are considered 'a reference for good quality Chinon'. Their bottles are unusual, copies of those used in the 18th century by the family Champagne House.

M.Gosset once described his very pleasant *rosé* as 'an amusement', but the reds are seriously good, though not cheap.

How to get there:
From Fontevraud take the D751 to Chinon. Follow the ring road (still D751, direction Azay). At the 2nd roundabout (after 7kms), turn onto the D16 (direction Huismes). Château de la Grille is signposted and is on your right.
Allow 30 minutes for tasting
The cellar is open for tasting: 9am-12 noon, 2-6pm (closed Sunday, Monday and public holidays).
Journey time: 30 minutes.
NB Time your departure from Fontevraud so that you arrive at Chenonceau for lunch. Your total journey time will be no more than 1½ hours.

Chenonceau:

To put you in the picture:
Chenonceau is known as *le château des six femmes*, six women who played a great part in the history of the château, from the Renaissance through to the 19th century.
Before these women came on the scene it had been a modest feudal manor and fortified mill on the site of the circular tower (named *Tour des Marques*, after the original owner) and the main building across the former drawbridge.
The purchase of Chenonceau by the king's chamberlain, Thomas Bohier in 1513 has all the machinations of a Dickensian plot. The Marques family sold off their land, bit by bit, to pay their crippling debts. For twenty years they desperately tried to avoid selling the château itself, but felt the noose gradually tighten round their necks as Bohier bought up each bit of land and clearly had designs on the château. Eventually they gave in to the inevitable. Bohier bought it and immediately demolished everything except the tower.

He had to be away on the king's service, so his wife Katherine Briçonnet, took over. She was the first of the *six femmes*. After her husband's death, she and her son completed the building. She considered it was 'now worthy of receiving the notables of the kingdom', which she enjoyed doing. François I came twice to visit. As he managed to do with Azay, he later confiscated Chenonceau in payment for money he deemed owing to him by the Bohier family.

The young Henri II succeeded François in 1547 and promptly gave Chenonceau (and the crown jewels) to Diane de Poitiers, his long time mistress who was twenty years older than him, but always famed for her beauty. Diane loved Chenonceau and was clever enough to keep the estate in profit. She was the second of the *six femmes* and had the bridge built linking the château to the far bank of the river Cher.

The third was Catherine de Médicis, the neglected wife of Henri II (they were married at fourteen and never got on). When Henri was accidentally killed in a joust by his Scottish captain of the guard in 1559, Catherine got her own back on Diane by making her swap Chenonceau for the less glamorous château de Chaumont a few miles away up the Loire, despite Diane's pleading for forgiveness of her sins and returning the crown jewels.

Catherine made up for lost time, holding lavish *fêtes*, known as *Triomphes de Chenonceau* in her favourite château. France's first fireworks display took place here in 1560 to mark her son François II becoming king. Catherine, ever the astute manipulator, used the *fêtes* to her advantage in an increasingly volatile political climate, through her *escadron volant* (flying squad), a bevy of aristocratic beauties who exercised their charms to winkle out information from the noble guests. She also continued the improvements to the château, notably the construction of the grand gallery on the bridge.

On her death Catherine bequeathed Chenonceau to her daughter-in-law Louise de Lorraine, married to Henri III. When Henri was assassinated, Louise was distraught with grief, a little surprising as her husband had shown more interest in men than in her. She spent the next eleven years, until her death, in mourning (white for royals), her bedroom decorated with funereal trappings. She was number four.

The fifth and sixth women were the wife of Claude Dupin who acquired Chenonceau in 1730 and Mme Pelouze, whose father bought it for her in 1865.

After Louise de Lorraine's death the château remained royal property for the next hundred years, but was not always lived in and rather lost its splendour. Worse, the Duke of Bourbon bought it in 1720 and promptly sold off much of the château's contents before selling it to Claude Dupin.

His wife, Louise, was the grandmother of George Sand (see Tour 5, Excursion 3). Louise started organising grand receptions and inviting leading literary figures to Chenonceau; Voltaire, Montesquieu, Fontenelle, Buffon and Jean-Jacques Rousseau, who was engaged as her son's tutor. In his *Confessions* Rousseau said of his stay in 1747: *'On s'amusa beaucoup dans ce beau lieu; on y faisait très bonne chère; j'y devins gras comme un moine'* (We had a good time in this lovely place; we ate very well; I became as fat as a monk).

Daniel Wilson, a Scot who made his fortune installing gas lighting in Paris, bought Chenonceau for his daughter, Marguerite Pelouze. She went to great pains to restore it to its original 16th century state, following the plans of Androuet du Cerceau (see Excursion 2, Villandry). She also followed in Catherine de Médicis' tradition of holding great parties. Like Mme Dupin, she invited celebrities of the time, including the French President (she was his mistress).

Her extravagancies led to her bankruptcy in 1888. The château was confiscated (how history repeats itself) and an article in the New York Times tells how its rare objects were sold for knock-down prices.

Chenonceau was bought by a Cuban millionaire; he sold it to another member of his family and in 1913 it was bought by the Menier family (Chocolat Menier), who still own it.

Another thing:

If you are wondering about the two different spellings, Chenonceau was for the château and Chenonceaux for the village. Both originally had an *x,* but at the Revolution, Louise Dupin removed it from the spelling of her home so that it

would no longer have *ancien régime* resonances. Her thoughtfulness appeased the republican sensibilities of the villagers, who held her in great affection.
The story is unsubstantiated, but nowadays either spelling is acceptable.
Another reason why the château was spared during the Revolution could have been that it was the only bridge across the Cher for some miles. Dull, but quite likely.
Whichever explanation we prefer, it is certain that Louise Dupin played her part in ensuring Chenonceau's survival at that time. She died there in 1799 and is buried in the grounds.

Where to eat:
From the ticket office you have a good 10 minute walk along the tree lined avenue to the château. On your way, stop for lunch either at the self-service cafeteria or the *Orangerie*. The cafeteria is quite adequate, but as Chenonceau is something special you might like to treat yourselves to something from the *à la carte menu* in the *Orangerie*. A starter and dessert make an excellent light lunch. Both are in pleasant settings.

(Chenonceaux)

Visit:
Although you get the best views of the château by looking at it side on from the far end of the Diane de Poitiers garden, reserve this pleasure for the end of your visit. It will stay in your memory.

Also reserve a visit to the Tour Marques until the end – it is the shop.

Here I shall more-or-less follow the order of rooms taken on the audio-guided tour, but only pointing out some of the features that have particularly struck me (and not mentioning all rooms, the kitchens for example). The audio-guide goes into excellent detail. I recommend it.

On the left and right of the château entrance are the arms of its builders, whose initials, T and K, you will see again on the library ceiling. Over the entrance door is the salamander of François I, with an inscription which translates: 'François by grace of God King of France and Claude Queen of the French'. He was a great self publicist; his emblem is all over the Loire Valley.

The ceiling of the entrance hall is spectacular, with its offset keystones. Like Azay, the straight staircase is one of the earliest in France, though here it is not at the entrance, but further inside the hall.

On the left the Salle des Gardes (guard room) has the motto of Thomas Bohier and Katherine, also seen again in the François I bedroom: *s'il vient à point me souviendra* (if I complete Chenonceau, I shall be remembered). They did, and we certainly do. On the ceiling, you see the intertwined HC, for Henri II and his wife Catherine de Médicis. Look carefully though and this could be HD, for Diane de Poitiers, his mistress. The same motif is found on the fireplace in the Diane de Poitiers bedroom and when you see Diane's and Marie's gardens, there is little doubt as to which is the more attractive. Draw your own conclusions – we shall never be sure what was intended, but for someone who likes the way words may be used, the speculation is amusing.

On the walls of the next door chapel, messages carved into the stone by Mary Queen of Scots' guards in the 1540s bring history alive, as does the thought that the Green Study was the room from which Catherine ran France as regent during the minority of her son Charles IX.

Her superb gallery, scene of great festivities and dalliance by the *escadron volant*, was transformed by Gaston Menier into a hospital in the Great War. In the Second World War it again served the country. The Cher was the boundary between the

Nazi 'occupied zone' and the Vichy so called 'free zone'. A number of *résistants* escaped into the free zone through the door at the far end of the gallery.

Admire the Renaissance fireplace in the Louis XIV living room, with another reminder of François I in the form of the ubiquitous salamander and ermine. (You will certainly see them again at Blois and Chambord)

The most startling room in the whole château is to my mind Louise de Lorraine's bedroom. This has been reconstructed, but the ceiling is original. Note the silver tears, the crowns of thorns and the intertwined HL that contribute to such a devout and mournful atmosphere, the colours in sharp contrast to the white mourning robes she always wore.

Much of the original furniture of the château is of course no longer here, but many elements remain (doors, ceilings, stone and plasterwork). Thanks in particular to Mme Pelouze and the Menier family, the place has been beautifully restored, so that Chenonceau is justly 'the pearl of the Loire Valley'.

Another thing:
On the second floor landing, a 19th century tapestry represents the river Cher with a gondola on it. The party loving Mme Pelouze actually had a gondola, complete with gondolier, brought over from Venice.

The château is open all day, every day of the year. In winter from 9.30am-5pm; from March to October, from 9am-7pm (-8pm in July, August)
Entry: 10€ or 14€ with audio-guide.
Allow 2 hours for your visit, excluding lunch.

How to get there:
From Château de la Grille, get back onto the road to Azay (D751). Continue on this beyond Azay to the junction with the A85. Take this motorway round Tours as far as it goes and join the N143 (direction Cormery, Loches). At Cormery take the D45 (direction Bleré, Amboise). Shortly before Bleré it joins the N76. Follow this across the river (direction Amboise) and then turn onto the D40 (direction Chenonceaux, Montrichard).

After the communes of Vaux and Civray you come to Chenonceaux.
The château is signposted on the right and the car park is after the level crossing.
Journey time: 1 hour

Your hotel, Le Bon Laboureur, is just beyond the turning for the château, on the left.

Excursion 4: Amboise, Le Clos-Lucé and Chaumont Garden Festival

On your way into Amboise, stop for a moment just after you take the turning to the *centre ville* off the D31 (which bypasses the town). In the park on your left you will see the curious **Pagode de Chanteloup**. This 18th century folly is all that remains of the grandiose château of the duc de Choiseul, which was pulled down in the 1820s.

The duke, a minister of Louis XV, was banished from the court, for having schemed against Mme du Barry, the king's mistress. He then retired to his château de Chanteloup, where he held court in great style. He had the pagoda erected in tribute to his many friends who kept faith with him and visited Chanteloup during his exile from court.Drive into Amboise and park along the river bank. It is worth a little stroll to see the château, though not necessarily to go in.

To put you in the picture about the château:

It looks impressive from the river, but most of the buildings inside the walls were demolished in the early 19th century through lack of funds for repairs.

It had been a fortress in the Middle Ages, enlarged by Charles VIII in the 15th century and the scene of notable events in the 16th.

The first three years of the reign of François I saw the height of the town's glory. The king ruled France from the château and held sumptuous *fêtes*. He also brought Leonardo da Vinci to live in Amboise.

But another event plumbed the depths. In 1560, a Protestant force planned to go to Blois, ostensibly to meet the young François II to discuss the freedom to practise their religion, but probably to kidnap him to exert pressure that way. Their plot was discovered and the venue changed to Amboise because it was easier to defend. The plotters were seized as they arrived, and in all over a thousand were massacred: decapitated, drowned or hanged from the castle battlements. Even those who surrendered on the promise that their lives would be spared were executed the next day. It is said that François and his young wife Mary Queen of Scots even interrupted their meal to watch the action.

The court had to leave soon after, because of the smell of the corpses, and the town never really regained royal favour. In the 17th century it was a prison and by Napoleon's time was in poor repair. It was listed as a historic monument in 1840 and considerable restoration was done over subsequent decades, but it was again damaged during the German invasion in 1940.

Another thing:

Charles VIII died in the château in bizarre circumstances in 1498. He and Queen Anne were rushing to watch a game of *jeu de paume* (an early form of tennis), when he banged his head on the lintel of a low doorway. He later developed concussion, was laid on a straw bed in *un lieu malodorant* (an evil smelling place), left there in the general confusion and expired that evening.

Walk up rue Victor Hugo, away from the river and past the great ramp that leads up to the main entrance. Continue up the hill another 500m to the **Manoir du Clos-Lucé**.

To put you in the picture:
The 15th century manor house became royal property when Charles VIII gave it to his wife, Anne de Bretagne in 1490. It remained a 'second home' to the royal family whenever the Court was in residence at Amboise. The future François I, who grew up in Amboise, played war games in the gardens of le Clos-Lucé and his sister, the future Marguerite de Navarre, wrote the first stories of her racy *Heptaméron* here.

François I was a cultured man and a great patron of the arts, especially enamoured of things Italian. He invited architects, artists and men of letters to le Clos-Lucé, including the distinguished poet Clément Marot.

Its most famous guest though was undoubtedly Leonardo da Vinci, brought here by François in 1516 shortly after he had become king. François asked Leonardo to work on a number of projects, giving him a pension of 700 crowns a year *'so that he could bring to fruition everything his genius was capable of producing'*. During the three years Leonardo lived at le Clos-Lucé, until his death in 1519, two of his best known projects were plans to drain the marshy Sologne region (see Tour 5) and to create a new town and château at Romorantin (in the Sologne).

It is said that a secret passage exists between the Château and le Clos-Lucé, by which François would come to visit Leonardo, and two paintings – one by Ingres - show François at the great man's bedside as he lay dying, a testimony to the king's real affection for the man he called *mon père*. His presence on that occasion is not substantiated, so, without calling into question the king's esteem for Leonardo, I think the story was probably part of the 'spin' of François as patron of the arts.

Another thing:
The Romorantin tourist board has a colourful explanation for the name of their town: up to the 16th century Romorantin had been spelt *R*emorantin. François wanted Leonardo to create a

new capital of France that would be worthy of the young, victorious king, a *'new Rome'*. Work started, but Leonardo died, so the nearest the town got was the name: *'Rom(e)orantin'* The plans for the Romorantin château were subsequently used by François at....Chambord.
When Leonardo came to Amboise he brought some paintings with him. One was the *Mona Lisa*, now in the Louvre.

Visit:
When you enter the reception hall, it is easy to imagine Leonardo receiving the great men of his time. In the bed chamber, I don't think the bed is the actual one where he died or where François perched according to the paintings, but the study is interesting for its display of his plans and models (made by IBM). In the chapel you can still see genuine traces of frescoes done either by Leonardo himself or by a pupil.
The garden is where Leonardo's brilliance really comes through. Don't be put off by the slightly 'theme park' feel; as someone who considers himself 'scientifically challenged' I find this an opportunity to marvel at the work of a genius. You are taken on a journey of discovery round the garden, hearing of aspects of Leonardo's creativity at the 'audio-stations' and having the chance to see and 'play with' life size reproductions of his 'fabulous machines', including a tank, machine-gun, paddle boat.
This 'hands-on' park is certainly not just for kids.

Le Clos-Lucé is open daily all year, but it is only worth going when the garden is open too: February to June, September, October, 9am-7pm (6pm>15th November); July, August, 9am-8pm.
Entry, including audio-visual and hands-on displays: 12,50€
Allow ½ hour for the inside and 1 hour for the garden tour

How to get there:
From Chenonceaux, go into Bleré and follow signs for Amboise. Cross the river and continue to Amboise on the D31. NB At the Pagode de Chanteloup take the road into the town centre.
Journey time: 20 minutes

Where to eat:
Drive to Chaumont for lunch in the Garden Festival grounds.

The Chaumont International Garden Festival:
Over the years there have been some 'fabulous machines' at the garden festival too, like the artificial baobab tree and water walls, not to mention various exhibits when the 2002 theme was eroticism in the garden.

The festival has been running since 1992, with the stated intention of appealing to new generations of gardeners, which has brought it a world-wide reputation. It is unsurprising then that some of the display gardens are futuristic, unusual, or downright 'wacky'. It is not like Chelsea, where the displays are designed to be at their peak during the week of the show. Here the twenty five or so gardens are set up in April and have to last until the festival ends in October. This demands a different sort of display, perhaps more akin to our own gardens, which may evolve throughout the season.

As well as all the display gardens, which are created according to a particular year's theme, there are permanent experimental gardens like the *sentier des fers sauvages* (wild iron path – a play on *fleurs sauvages* – wild flowers) and the *vallon des brumes* (valley of mists), which evolve as the years go by. These provide a pleasant stroll round the perimeter of the display gardens, with glimpses of the château in the background.

Walking in the festival gardens, as in any good garden, you come away with ideas. Even 2002, when some of the eroticism was quite explicit, produced good plantings.

The theme for 2010 is 'body and soul', promising relaxing and therapeutic garden spaces.

Where to eat:
The four restaurants or cafés on site will suit all tastes. I like, for a change, the fresh pastas and homemade sauces *à volonté* (as much as you like) at the *Comptoir Méditerranéen*.

The Garden Festival is open in 2010 from 29th April until mid October.
Entry: 9,50€

Allow 2 hours for your visit, excluding lunch.

How to get there:
From Amboise, drive along the river on the D751 to Chaumont. At the château entrance just beyond the château itself (above you on the right), turn into rue du Village Neuf (D114). At the top of the hill follow signs to the car park, opposite the Festival entrance.
Journey time: 15 minutes

Excursion 5: Blois and Chambord

To put you in the picture about the Château de Blois:
To visit Blois (pronounced *Blwah*) is to take a trip through great periods of French history and architecture.
From the 10th to the 13th centuries Blois was the HQ of the powerful counts of Blois-Champagne.
Chroniclers relate that Thibaut I (died 971 and nicknamed *le tricheur* – cheat – by his enemies) had built *une grosse tour* (great keep) at Blois. In the early 13th century another Thibaut built what is now called the Salle des Etats (see below). Then it was the great hall of the castle. Other vestiges of that period are the ramparts and three towers. Two are integrated into later constructions, but the Tour du Foix stands alone. It had an observatory stuck on the top of it by Gaston d'Orléans in the 17th century.
The last count, with no-one to inherit, sold Blois to Louis, Duke of Touraine and brother of Charles VI le fol (the mad). Louis traded Touraine for the county of Orléans because it was richer and thus founded the house of Orléans. From his liaison with his mad brother's wife, Louis fathered several children, perhaps including Joan of Arc (see Tour 8, Excursion 3).
His son Charles didn't distinguish himself at the battle of Agincourt, getting captured and imprisoned for twenty five years in England. On his release he gave up politics and came back to Blois, where he gathered round him a circle of artists and men of letters. He was the patron of the great poet François Villon. Charles d'Orléans was himself one of France's great poets, his graceful musicality and unexpected

imagery inspiring Villon, Marot and much later poets like Verlaine and Apollinaire.

The so called Charles d'Orléans gallery in fact dates from the time of his son, who became Louis XII. However, in keeping with his character, Charles did pull down parts of the old fortress and made the château *plus habitable* (more comfortable).

Louis XII had grown up in the château and when he became king in 1498 after the unfortunate death of his cousin Charles VIII at Amboise (see Excursion 4) he made Blois his royal palace. He started rebuilding at once. Only two years later Blois was described as *tout de neuf et tant somptueux que bien sembloit oeuvre de roi* (all new and so luxurious that it seemed truly deserving of a king).

The château entrance is in the brick and stone Louis XII wing. Its combination of basically Gothic architecture with Renaissance ornament marks a transition period before the Italian influenced Renaissance wing, built by François I only a few years later. In fact this wing looks more like an Italian palazzo from the *outside*, with its numerous loggias and windows, hence its name: la Façade des Loges. On the courtyard façade the innovations are the Italianate ornamentation of the windows and the amazing polygonal external staircase.

The first half of the 16th century saw Blois at its height. Louis' *fêtes* were as *somptueuses* as his building. He cleverly married his cousin's widow, Anne de Bretagne. That way Brittany came under his control though still technically independent. Their daughter Claude was very attached to Blois, which is probably why the first great building project of her husband François I was the new wing there, built between 1515 and 1519. Claude died in 1524 and François had a year's enforced exile in Spain after being captured by Emperor Charles V at the battle of Pavia (Italy) in 1525. When he did return to France he moved his court to the Paris region, transferring the furniture and library from Blois to his palace at Fontainebleau.

Another thing:
Poems of Villon and Verlaine were set to music by the 20th century poet and musician, Georges Brassens. The musicality of Villon's *Ballade des dames du temps jadis* (Ballade of the ladies of bygone times) and Verlaine's *Colombine* comes over beautifully. The opening lines of another Verlaine poem, *Chanson d'Automne* (Autumn Song), were used as a coded message to the French resistance announcing D-Day: *Les sanglots longs/Des violons/De l'automne/Blessent mon coeur/ D'une langueur/ Monotone.*

Even though François I moved out, the parties continued at Blois. At one, the famous poet, Pierre de Ronsard, met Cassandre Salviati, who inspired his sonnet *A Cassandre* and other love poems of his, including: *Mignonne, allons voir si la rose...(*as famous in French as 'To be or not to be...').

Henri II came back to Blois shortly after his coronation. His arrival, accompanied by 'naked women mounted on oxen', did cause something of a stir, even though it was probably meant to be an allusion to the abduction of Europa by Zeus.

Events at Blois later in the century would be rather more political than cultural. The château had its gruesome equivalent to the massacre at Amboise (see Excursion 4).

In 1588 the Wars of Religion were in full swing in France since the St Bartholomew's Day massacre of Protestants in Paris in 1572. The weak Henri III was showing too conciliatory an attitude towards them for the powerful, and Catholic, duke de Guise who was running things in Paris, virtually having forced the king out of the capital. Henri called a meeting of the Etats Généraux (General assembly) at Blois – some say the duke forced him – each having the hidden agenda of getting rid of the other. De Guise at least wanted to overthrow the king by political means, to prevent the succession going to the Protestant Henri de Navarre.

On 23rd December Henri invited the duke to attend an early morning meeting. He arrived, to be told that the king wished to see him in the next room. As he went in he was set upon and stabbed to death by a number of 'the Forty Five', the renowned 'heavies' who guarded the king. The job done, the king apparently came out from behind a curtain and said 'My God! How big he is! He seems even bigger dead than alive'.

Henri III was assassinated in Paris the following year, his wife went into deep mourning (see Excursion 3) and the Protestant Henri IV came to the throne.

Henri IV stayed a couple of times in the 1590s and began his own ambitious building programme with a 200m long gallery in the gardens, but it was never completed and had to be pulled down in 1756. No trace of it remains.

The next two centuries saw Blois host a number of exiles.

First; Marie de Médicis, the queen mother, imprisoned in 1617 by her son Louis XIII because of a disagreement over a court appointment. After two years she escaped and they were reconciled, for a while at least.

The next exile was Louis XIII's brother, Gaston d'Orléans, who was banished from court for conspiring against the king in 1634. He had already been given Blois by the king and so set about putting his mark on it. The next year he commissioned the architect François Mansart to rebuild the château. Work on Mansart's design, the Gaston d'Orléans wing, which faces you as you enter the courtyard, went on for three years, but stopped suddenly in 1638. Gaston was behind in his payments to the builders and they realised that there was no longer a future in the work, as he had just lost his status as next in line for the throne, in favour of the future Louis XIV, born that year.

In a life committed to political intrigue the duke was exiled twice more and died at Blois in 1660.

Another thing:
According to legend, Marie de Médicis escaped by climbing down a rope from a second floor window, quite a difficult feat for a lady of her considerable girth. The reality is more prosaic: she had an accomplice and escaped by crawling along a ditch – still an undignified exit. Her escape inspired a rather fanciful interpretation by Rubens in the cycle of paintings of her life she commissioned from him.

Blois, now crown property again, received the exiled widow of the king of Poland in 1714. She stayed until her death two years later. More Polish exiles, King Stanislas and his family, stayed before moving to Chambord in 1725.

1788 was a crucial year in the history of the château. Louis XVI was strapped for cash and decided to sell off unused royal châteaux, of which Blois was to be one. (Le château de Madrid in Paris was another. It was sold and demolished. One stone capital and three fragments of porcelain from it are now in museums – otherwise, no trace). No buyer was found for Blois, so it was eventually used as an army barracks.

During the Revolution all statues and royal emblems were destroyed, inevitably. While a barracks, the buildings underwent many modifications (Louis XII fireplaces were removed because they stuck out too much for the soldiers' beds to fit in).

Fortunately the 19th century Romantic Movement's love of *vieilles pierres* meant that in 1840 Blois was classified as a historic monument. Restoration went ahead and by 1880 the château was back to something like its 16th century state of decoration.

The Gaston d'Orléans wing was only restored in 1921, but bombing in the Second World War damaged the Louis XII wing and the chapel.

I remember when I first came to Blois as a schoolboy I thought it a very gloomy place. However, the latest round of restoration work, only completed in 2007, has really returned this fascinating château to its former splendour, which is why I have included it in this tour.

Visit:

The façade you see from the forecourt to the château is the wing built by Louis XII. His statue above the entrance is 19th century, replacing the one destroyed in the Revolution. Note the way the horse is lifting both legs on the same side. This is a gait called the 'amble', used in ceremonies and dressage. The first floor windows with balconies were the king's and queen's apartments, from which they could watch the jousting tournaments held in the forecourt. On the far right is the gable end of the 13th century Salle des Etats. Its splendid interior wall decoration – 6,720 *fleurs-de-lys* - was redone in the 19th century and restored again recently.

In the interior courtyard, the first thing you will see is the beautifully proportioned 17th century classical architecture of the Gaston d'Orléans wing that faces you. Your eye will then inevitably be drawn to the magnificent staircase on the Renaissance façade to your right. If you walk to the centre of the courtyard and turn round, you will then be able to enjoy the harmony of the Charles VIII and Louis XII wings, both built in about 1600. Traditional Gothic brick and stone was still in vogue then, but the open arcades at ground level and enclosed above hint at Italian influence.

If you go upstairs to the Fine Arts Museum, you will see the two grand fireplaces (rebuilt in the 19th century – see *'barracks'* above) in the central hall.

The staircase and façade of the François I wing are the architectural features for which Blois is best known. The tall windows and horizontal mouldings make a complex vertical and horizontal pattern that is echoed in the heavy uprights of the staircase contrasted with the lightness of its open loggias. It is no longer central, because of the construction of the later Gaston d'Orléans wing.

This staircase was much more than a means of going up or coming down. The loggias meant that it was *the* place from which the king could see what was going on and also be seen when appropriate.

The rich décor of the inside has of course had to be greatly restored, though the Queen's study still has its original wood panelling. You can witness the sinister murder of the duke de Guise on a silent movie (lasting about 15 minutes) and you can walk up or down the famous staircase, just to be 'seen'.

The main feature of the classical wing begun by Gaston d'Orléans is its grand staircase, which was actually built in 1921, following Mansart's drawings. Had his plans been completed, it would have entailed knocking down the entire Louis XII and François I buildings. What a good job Louis XIV came along when he did…..

Another thing:
The infamous secret poison cabinets of Catherine de Médicis, behind some of the 237 carved panels in her study, are conveniently left open for us. In all probability, however, they

were only used for jewellery or other personal effects. They were a popular design feature in rooms of that period.

The château is open: January to March, November, December, 9am-12.30pm, 1.30-5.30pm; April to June, September, 9am-6.30pm; July, August, 9am-7pm; October, 9am-6pm
Entry: 8€.
Guided tours go every hour if there is enough demand. In English on request.
Combined ticket for the Château and Son et Lumière: 13€.
Shows are at dusk, nightly from April to September (in English on Wednesdays).

How to get there:
From Chenonceaux, take the D176 to Montrichard and then the D764 to Blois. Follow signs to the Château (you will get good views of it) and car parks. The Parking Jean Moulin is the closest. From there, walk up to the château.
Journey time: 30 minutes

Where to eat:
Try *Le Marignan* in place du Château or go on to Chambord and have lunch there (for details see Chambord, where to eat, below)

Château de Chambord:

To put you in the picture:
Chambord is by far the largest château in the Loire valley. Unlike Amboise and Blois, Chambord was never intended as a permanent royal residence, but for short stays, as a hunting lodge. From the 12th century a ford over the river Cosson was guarded by a small fortress, which the counts of Blois subsequently used as a base for hunting.
François I demolished the old fortress and started the construction of a château that would demonstrate to the world the power of the young king who had gloriously won the battle of Marignano.
It also served two of his passions: hunting and architecture. He was aptly called the 'builder king', for, as we have seen, he

had already added a new wing to the château at Blois and had plans drawn up for a royal town at Romorantin in his first three years as king. With the death of Leonardo, Romorantin was abandoned and Chambord begun.

As a keen hunter he knew that the forest here was rich in game and therefore a suitable place for his 'little hunting lodge'. He staked out the boundaries himself, although the 32km wall round the estate was completed by Gaston d'Orléans.

The project was grandiose, even excessive, as early plans included diverting the Loire to flow past the château. This was soon abandoned, but the builders chose instead to ship material in from the nearest point on the Loire, which brought prosperity to the little town of St-Dyé.

In fact water was a problem for the construction of Chambord from the start. No doubt to help solve it, a great lake was planned in front of the château, as is shown in a 1576 drawing by Androuet du Cerceau. That did not materialise and the course of the Cosson made the land in front of the château very marshy, causing subsidence and damage to the structure, so that it eventually needed considerable repair work. This was undertaken in the 1650s by Gaston d'Orléans (see Blois, above) who loved coming to Chambord to hunt during his periods of exile, and his efforts saved the place from ruin. The water problem was finally resolved in the 18th century by the canalisation of the Cosson.

Another thing:
It is said that the site might have been chosen by François so that he could be near his mistress, the countess of Thoury, whose land adjoined Chambord. It is also said that she later had some of François' wall demolished, because it had encroached onto her land. Whether she was still a mistress then I am not sure.

For such a huge and magnificent construction, the château has a rather sorry history.

It was mostly completed in François' lifetime, but was only used infrequently and for short periods. After his captivity in Spain (see Blois, above), François moved his court away from the Loire and governed from Paris. He reigned for thirty two years, but only spent eight weeks at Chambord and, as was custom in those days, when the royal entourage travelled they carried everything with them, furniture and all. The château was therefore empty for most of the first two hundred years of its existence.

The only foreign monarch to be received at Chambord was Emperor Charles V (François' erstwhile captor) in 1539. By then the château must have been very impressive, even if unfinished. The emperor commented that he had seen there 'all that human ingenuity can possibly bring together'.

Louis XIV brought his court to Chambord in 1668. He came nine times in all, for the autumn hunts. While he was in residence the château came alive, with performances of ballets and plays. The playwright Molière and the composer Lulli collaborated on two works, in 1669 and 1670. However Louis' visits only lasted on average three weeks and after 1685 he never came again.

In the next century Chambord became a sort of prestigious royal 'gift'. The exiled King Stanislas of Poland, who was father-in-law to Louis XV, stayed for eight years from 1725. For the first time the château was permanently furnished, with left-overs from Versailles.

Maurice de Saxe was made governor of Chambord as a reward for his victory over the English at Fontenoy in 1745. He came to live in the château in 1748 and installed his regiment too. For the next two years, until his death, it is said that court life was 'brilliant'.

His nephew lived there for the next five years, but after that it lay empty until 1784, when another governor moved in. New apartments were created and more permanent furniture brought in, with a view to receiving a visit from Louis XVI.

That didn't happen, but the Revolution did. Furnishings were sold off, floors taken up to be sold for their value as timber, and over the next few years the château was used to store horse fodder, as a gunpowder factory and prison.

In 1809 Napoleon gave Chambord to field-marshal Berthier, as a reward for his victory at Wagram. The unfortunate field-marshal only lasted two days before expiring. In 1820 his widow was given permission by Louis XVIII to sell the property and it was bought by public subscription for the one

year old duke of Bordeaux, grandson of Charles X, so that it could again be the property of a future king of France.
That didn't happen either and eventually, in 1932, the state took over the château and has been restoring it ever since.

Visit:
From Blois, come along the river and turn off at Montlivault. This way you will have good views of the Loire and see the château full on as you approach.
From a distance its harmonious proportions make it a lovely sight. The nearer you get, the more you appreciate its monumental scale. Essentially the tall roofs and great round towers with their conical tops make it a traditional Gothic castle, while the veritable forest of decorated turrets and chimneys show the Italian influence. It looks like a fortress, but everything is intended as pure decoration. In this respect it is like Azay and Chenonceau.
If the outside of Chambord is spectacular, so is the inside, nothing more so than the double spiral staircase. As at Blois, this is the feature that gives Chambord its renown, only here it is the central point of the main building, the traditional castle keep. The idea of the spiral stairs topped by a lantern has been attributed by some to Leonardo, but his sketch does not make it clear, to me at least, that it is a *double* spiral. The innovation of its construction was that people could go up or down either of the twin staircases and not meet each other. Try it out.
From walking round the huge rooms of the château, the overall impression is that Chambord was not a place to be lived in. The wall hangings and often sparsely furnished rooms seem to re-create perfectly the idea of temporary residence, as was the intention when it was built.
Some things though give it a personality.
The Salamander and initial F that abound on the coffered ceilings leave no doubt as to whose château it was. A more intimate souvenir, of a man perhaps not always as on top of things as his public persona would suggest, is the phrase François etched on a window pane in his bedchamber: *Souvent femme varie, bien fol est qui s'y fie* (women are often fickle, you are foolish to trust them).

The second floor landing with the bust of Molière reminds us that the great man actually performed the rôle of *M. Jourdain* right there, in the first ever performance of *Le Bourgeois Gentilhomme*. On one occasion, when I explained this (with a bit more detail and actions), a member of my group said: 'you really like Molière, that's obvious'. I do, and I'm glad it came across.

In the room dedicated to the count of Chambord is a rather poignant exhibit, a reproduction of his abdication speech. The château had been bought for him as an orphaned baby, the last Bourbon heir to the throne. The Bourbons were banished by Louis Philippe in 1830 and the ten year old duke went into exile, assuming the title of count of Chambord (see Tour 1, Excursion 4 for his connection with Rennes-le-Château). After the fall of Napoleon in 1870, royalists asked the French nation to support the restoration of the monarchy and, as the legitimate pretender, the count was asked to return and reign as Henri V. In 1871 the count paid his first and only visit to Chambord, staying for three days before going on to Paris to become king. Popular support waned and he decided to abdicate. It all hinged on his intransigent refusal to accept the *tricolore* (the republican symbol *par excellence*), insisting instead, as the text of his speech states, on the royal standard of his illustrious ancestor Henri IV. His intended coronation coach is on display in the carriage room of the château.

How different the future of France might have been, if he had not been so stubborn.

Another thing:

Molière's *Le Bourgeois Gentilhomme* (English title: The Prodigious Snob) was produced in a fortnight for the *Divertissement Royal*). It started as a ballet (Louis XIV liked dancing), with music by Lulli. Molière fitted the story round the ballet sequences. This famous knock-about yet witty Comédie-Ballet got a cool reception on the first night because it openly mocked the nobility, but the king found the second performance funny, so his courtiers approved too.

The château is open: January to March, October to December, 9am-5.15pm; April to mid- July, mid-August to September,

9am-6.15pm; mid-July to mid-August, 9am-7.30pm (closed Christmas, New Year and 1st May)
Entry: April to September, 9,50€ (low season 8,50€)
Audio-guide or guided tour, 4€ (1½ hours)
Car park: 2€
Allow 2 hours for your visit

Where to eat:
In the château, the *Hostel du Prince* has a varied light lunch menu, served in period costume (open in July and August, closed on Wednesday)
In the village, near the car park, try *La Crêperie Solognote.*

How to get there:
From Blois follow the D951 along the river to Montlivault. Turn onto the D84, then D112A to Chambord. Follow signs for car parking.
Journey time: 30 minutes

Return to Chenonceaux by the D112 (direction Bracieux). At Bracieux, take the D102 to Cour-Cheverny, then the D52 to Sambin. Join the D764 (direction Pontlevoy, Montrichard). At Montrichard take the D176 to Chenonceaux.
Journey time: 1 hour

7 The Magic of Brittany

Words like 'magic' and 'charm' readily come to mind when describing Brittany. This tour takes you to places that fit that description, whether figuratively or in the actual sense of the words: the château at Fougères, whose 13th century lords claimed to be descendants of the fairy Mélusine, and the Côte d'Emeraude (Emerald Coast) seen from Fort La Latte or St-Malo.

Dinan and Dol-de-Bretagne both have the charm of their 'vieilles pierres' as well as connections with English history, while the writer Gustave Flaubert likened St-Malo to 'a crown of stones set on the sea'.

Brittany is a land of myths and legends, nowhere more so than in the forest of Brocéliande, home to King Arthur and where Merlin worked his magic.

Finally, the Mont-St-Michel, top tourist spot in France: it is simply a wonder, which is also the name given to part of the abbey buildings themselves.

Where to stay:
The *Château de Bonaban*, near St-Malo, is conveniently positioned for your visits and, appropriately for this tour, looks as though it comes straight out of a fairy tale. There has been a fortress here since the 4th century AD, although the present

building is 18th century. The period interior décor is sumptuous and the cuisine excellent. For particularly good value in this luxury hotel, try their half board offer.

How to get there:
Leave the N176 at the exit for St-Malo (D137). After 2kms, at Châteauneuf, take the D76 (direction Cancale) for 4kms and, as you approach La Gouesnière, pick up the signs for the Château.

Excursions: 1 St-Malo
                     2 Fougères and Dol-de-Bretagne
                     3 The forest of Brocéliande
                     4 Dinan, Cap Fréhel and Fort La Latte
                     5 Mont-St-Michel

Excursion 1: St-Malo

To put you in the picture about St-Malo:
The part of St-Malo you want to see is the old fortified town called Intra-Muros (within the walls). The rather uninspiring agglomeration you have to drive through to get there has grown up since the 18th century and the unsightly commercial and industrial port area has only developed since the 1970s.

St Malo - Intra Muros

However, you will forget all that as soon as you see this powerfully impressive citadelle. The grey granite of the ramparts and tall merchants' houses with their grey slate roofs give it a sombre, even forbidding appearance on a dull day, but if the sun is shining the colours become mellow and welcoming

As you would imagine, St-Malo owes its name to a saint. A Celtic monk called Malou or Maclou brought Christianity to the area in the 6th century, becoming bishop of the Gallo-Roman city of Aleth, which was on the site of what is now St-Servan, the headland just to the south of St-Malo Intra-Muros. By the 12th century the population had grown and spread northward to the next headland (in those days an island), so the bishopric was transferred there and given the name St-Malo. They found a local saint for Aleth, which became St-Servan.

The inhabitants, *les Malouins,* have always been fiercely independent, as their unofficial motto implies: *'Ni Francais ni Breton: Malouin suis.'* (I am neither French nor Breton: I am from St-Malo). The mediaeval bishops of St-Malo were also its rulers and vigorously defended their privileges as such, which inevitably brought them into conflict with the dukes of Brittany (not officially part of France until 1532). In 1394 relations were so bad that, to oppose the duke, St-Malo declared itself a French enclave and remained an open port for the next twenty years. In the way politics works, the French king did then hand the city back to the duke in return for his support against the English.

Two centuries later they threw out their governor for supporting the Protestant Henri IV, proclaiming the city an independent republic, which it remained for four years.

The 15th and 16th centuries were times of great prosperity for St-Malo. Always seafarers, the *Malouins* became international traders and speculators.

In 1534 François I sent Jacques Cartier, a native of St-Malo, to find a northern route to China or, failing that, 'to discover certain islands and lands where it is said there is a large amount of gold and other riches to be found'. On his 1534 voyage, Cartier reached Newfoundland, explored the coast of Labrador and sailed up the St Lawrence, claiming the land in the name of the French king. He called it Canada, apparently hearing that word used by the natives he encountered. It means 'village' in the Huron-Iroquois language.

He made two further voyages to Canada. On the last one he advised the king's representative, sent to colonise the country, not to stay there because of the terrible winter climate.

The rich maritime trade became threatened towards the end of the 17th century during wars with England. St-Malo was attacked by the English in 1693 and 1695, resulting in defensive reinforcements to the city in the form of the series of forts you see off the coast.

These wars also saw more and more *corsaires* (privateers). This legalised piracy – *corsaire* derives from the *lettres de course* they received from the king, allowing them to attack enemy shipping without being considered as common or garden pirates – went on alongside normal trading, certainly from François I's time. Two of the most famous *corsaires* from St-Malo were René Duguay-Trouin (1673-1736) and Robert Surcouf (1773-1827).

The former was the son of a rich ship owner, who, after the privateering years of his youth, rose to become lieutenant-general of the navy. He was ennobled by the king for his distinguished services (he had captured over 300 merchantmen and 20 warships, bringing a lot of money to the royal coffers). Surcouf's was a different story: he ran away to sea at 13, became a slave trader and then, during the Napoleonic wars, a *corsaire,* retiring aged 36 a very rich man. He became a ship owner and went on making a fortune. Both men, along with Jacques Cartier, have their statues on the ramparts of the old town, as distinguished sons of St-Malo.

The Peace of Utrecht in 1713 had brought to an end the war of the Spanish Succession and the great era of privateering. From then on the town's prosperity gradually waned despite 19th century industrial advances.

The next notable date for St-Malo was 1944. Intra-Muros was a German stronghold, part of the Atlantic wall. After the D-Day landings, the Americans broke through at nearby Avranches and between 6th and 14th August fire-bombed the old town to dislodge the German garrison there. 80% of St-Malo Intra-Muros was in ruins.

After the war the mayor, Guy La Chambre, managed to persuade the government to restore Intra-Muros to its 18th century grandeur. Such was his influence that the plans were drawn up in three months and the whole project, started in 1948, was completed by 1953. Fortunately the ramparts had not been significantly damaged, but only 33 houses could be repaired. The imposing walled city you see today is almost entirely 'new-build', with prefabricated concrete lintels and cornices to save time and money, but carefully following the 18th century ground plan and building style.

Anyone looking at photos of the 1944 destruction and seeing Intra-Muros now, for all the world a town built on the prosperity of its 17th and 18th century merchants, should feel nothing but admiration for this *pastiche normalisateur*, as it was called, and for the determination of M La Chambre.

Another thing:
Las Malvinas, the Spanish name for the Falklands, derives from the French *les Malouins*, the sailors from St-Malo who first colonised the islands.

Visit: St-Malo Intra-Muros
It is not so much the individual buildings but the city as a whole that is the interest of a visit, strolling through its streets (there is relatively little traffic) or taking in the stunning views when you walk round the ramparts.

A good place to start is the Porte St-Vincent on the corner of the quay St-Vincent alongside the Bassin Vauban (the yacht basin on the east side of the city).

Here you will find the Tourist Office, where it will be useful to pick up a plan of Intra-Muros – it is not always easy to know exactly where you are in the narrow streets.

Also enquire here about low tide, which is when you can walk out to the Grand Bé, and plan your day accordingly (see opening times etc below).

The Porte St-Vincent was built in 1708 to give additional access to the city. Until then the main entry was by the smaller Porte St-Thomas on the other side of the château. In the pedestrian entrance of the gate, is the cell where they locked up those who missed the 10pm curfew, announced by the ringing of the bell called the *'Noguette'*, mounted above the Grande Porte.

Immediately to your right is the château fronted by twin towers. The right hand one (when you are facing the château) houses the museum of the history of St-Malo, with exhibits from the great days of sea trading and piracy to reminders of the Nazi occupation. The other has the curious name Quic-en-Groigne. This refers to the famous reply of Anne de Bretagne to the *Malouins'* objections to the construction in 1500 of three watchtowers facing in towards the city rather than out to sea: *'Qui qu'en grogne, ainsi sera, car tel est mon bon plaisir'* (Whosoever complains, it shall be so, for thus is my pleasure), and the name stuck.

Place Chateaubriand, in front of the château, is the heart of St-Malo, a place to meet or linger over a drink in one of the cafés. No2 is where the writer Chateaubriand grew up. This building and the others in and around the square are typical of the grand, but rather severe style of the 18th century shipping merchants' residences. There were sometimes two levels of cellars below ground; at street level the arcaded fronts housed shops, workshops, or were rented out as living accommodation; the next two floors were the owner's living accommodation and above that, more storage room – precious in a town where ground space was at a premium.

Another thing:
It was a good idea to be inside the city by the 10pm curfew as they then let loose 24 bulldogs outside the walls. This had gone on since the Middle Ages, but was stopped in 1770 when a sailor returning late after visiting his girl friend in St-Servan was mauled to death by the dogs. The bell was recast in the 1980s and is one of the cathedral bells. It still rings nightly, but the city gates remain open and there are no dogs.

The ramparts:
To get the best perspective of the citadelle, continue on past the Tour Quic-en-Groigne and after place Vauban, make your way up onto the ramparts. As you walk round, whichever way you look, you have breathtaking views of the coastline and the Rance estuary across to Dinard, and of the citadelle itself. The cathedral spire dominates an already impressive skyline of tall slate roofs and was of course a vital landmark for sailors.

The series of islands you see from the ramparts as you go round are the fortifications designed by Vauban, Louis XIV's top military architect, to protect the port against the English. The first one, facing you is the Fort National. It was called Fort Royal when it was built in 1689, but, unsurprisingly, come the Revolution its name was changed. You can reach it, but only at low tide. During the visit you will be shown where Robert Surcouf fought a duel against 12 adversaries. He killed 11, but spared the 12th so that he could tell the tale.

The Tour Bidouane, a little further on, at the north east corner of the ramparts, is the best place to see all the island defences. There is a statue of Surcouf on the esplanade in front of the bastion.

Le Grand Bé and Le Petit Bé, just beyond it, are two more island forts of the Vauban era, although Le Grand Bé is better known now for being the burial place of Chateaubriand. Again, you can walk to this island at low tide. The famous writer's tomb is just an unmarked stone with a granite cross above it. In a day of wonderful views, those from the high point of le Grand Bé are the best.

Further out, the guns of the fort of la Conchée and the island of Cézembre were to stop enemy ships getting into the Rance estuary beyond range of the inner island and coastal batteries. There are remains of chapels on Cézembre, home to Franciscan monks up to 1693, when military needs became more pressing.

Continuing on round the ramparts to the Bastion de la Hollande you have fine views over the Rance estuary to Dinard and the Côte d'Emeraude as far as Fort La Latte and Cap Fréhel (Excursion 4).

Keep on the ramparts as far as the Bastion St-Philippe on the south west corner. Before making your way down to street level, look along the next section of rampart towards the Bastion St-Louis on the south east corner. Here you see probably the best set of 18th century houses with their tall roofs and monumental chimneys, belonging to the rich *malouin* shipping merchants. Only two were not destroyed in 1944 (near the Bastion St-Louis). The others have been restored to their former glory, stone by stone.

Now walk through the side streets towards the cathedral. They tend to be less crowded than the main thoroughfares in high season. On your way through the city look out for some quaint street names like rue du Chat-qui-Danse (dancing cat), rue du Gras-Mollet (fat calf – as in leg, not cow), rue du Pie-qui-Boit (drinking magpie). These tend to be the names of former inns or taverns that gave their name to the road. There are also a number of picturesque shop signs that are a feature of St-Malo. They were designed by Dan Lailler, founder of the Cape Horn museum in St-Servan.

To put you in the picture about Chateaubriand:
Viscount François-René de Chateaubriand, 1768-1848, was *the* man of letters in early 19th century France. His 'imaginative melancholy' made him a forerunner of Romanticism, the great literary movement of the first half of the century. He is best known for his autobiography *Mémoires d'outre-tombe* (Memoirs from beyond the grave), deliberately not published until a year after his death. Probably the most evocative parts of it are those recounting childhood times spent in the gloomy family château at Combourg.
Less well known is his military and political career. He fought in the royalist army (Brittany was always strongly royalist) during the Revolution, but had to escape to England. He returned to France in 1800 and was appointed by Napoleon to the Embassy in Rome, but became increasingly critical of him. After the fall of Napoleon he became a minister of Louis XVIII and then French Ambassador in London. The king said the anti-Napoleon invective in a political pamphlet written by Chateaubriand in 1814 was worth an army to him in propaganda value.

The cathedral:
When you reach the cathedral square, place Jean-de-Chatillon, go into the cathedral by the west door **and stop.** Your eye will be drawn to the chancel, which is lit by astonishing stained glass windows. Blues, reds, oranges, yellows shoot up like flames into the rose window and gradually the colours turn to more muted tones in the side panels. The whole effect is stunning and moving. Jean le Moal's design is a powerful

reminder of those days of destruction in August 1944. If I were to come to see only one thing in St-Malo it would be this stained glass.

As you move down into the church you notice the transition from the Romanesque nave to the Gothic chancel, marked by the unusual modern altar, with the man, lion, bull and eagle, symbols of the four Evangelists. The design is elegant and it works.

In the central aisle of the nave is a mosaic plaque marking the spot where Jacques Cartier received blessing from the bishop for his epic voyage to Canada. In chapels on the north side are the tombs of Jacques Cartier (his head only) and Duguay-Trouin, whose remains were brought back from Paris in 1973.

Leave the city by the Grande-Porte, a splendid piece of early 15th century military architecture which was then St-Malo's main entry point. Above the doorway, the statue of Notre-Dame-de-Bon-Secours (Our Lady of Perpetual Succour), now a replica, is credited with halting the great fire of 1661 which destroyed nearly 300 timber framed houses, whose cellars were full of barrels of pitch and grease. Thereafter, stone became the obligatory material for houses along the front – thatch had already been replaced by slate after an earlier fire – resulting in the style of building we see now.

Where to eat:
Bistrots, brasseries and restaurants abound in St-Malo to suit most tastes and pockets. If this is your first day of the tour why not try a traditional Breton *galette* (savoury pancake) and/or *crêpe*(sweet pancake).
Le Petit Crêpier, rue Ste-Barbe, *Le Brigantine, Le Gallo,* both rue de Dinan, *Crêperie Ti Nevez,* rue Broussais, *Bergamotte,* place J-de-Chatillon are all recommended. Most close on Tuesday and Wednesday, *Le Gallo* on Monday. All are open every day in July and August.

How to get there:
From the hotel take the D4 (direction St-Malo) and then the D137. Once in St-Malo pick up signs for Intra-Muros. Signposting is not always clear, but when you do get there park in the first available place along the city walls. In high

season parking is at a premium. Walk to the Porte St-Vincent to begin your tour.
Journey time: 20minutes.
Allow 1 hour for your walk along the ramparts, ½ hour for walking through town to the cathedral, ½ hour to visit the cathedral, ¾ hour for the museum of St-Malo in the château, 2¼ hours to visit Le Grand Bé (it takes 45 minutes each way on foot).
The château museum is open: 10am-12.30pm, 2-6pm April-September. The rest of the year it is closed on Mondays and public holidays.
Entry: 5€

Excursion 2: Fougères and Dol-de-Bretagne

To put you in the picture about Fougères:
The story of the town in mediaeval times is the story of the castle, built, along with Dol and Vitré, to defend the border between Brittany and France. Nothing remains of the original castle, but over a period of 500 years it was built and rebuilt as a state of the art fortress, extending its walls all round the upper town. As you approach Fougères today you can see that it must have been an impressive fortified town. It has even been called the Carcassonne (see Tour 1) of the west of France. However, the original town that grew up in the early 11th century next to the castle always remained outside the fortifications. Centred on the Eglise St Sulpice, the church just by the castle, this part of Le Bourg-Vieil (old town) still has an old feel about it, with some attractive half-timbered houses in the place du Marchix (market square).

Despite repeated military modernisation this seemingly impregnable fortress has the sorry record of being captured half a dozen times in 300 years. It fell to Henry Plantagenêt, who razed it to the ground in 1166, but it was rebuilt by its stubborn lord. He recognised the strategic importance of its position and hugely increased its size and strength, making it the corner stone of Brittany's border defences.

The problem was that, while the dukes of Brittany were technically vassals of the king of France, occasions arose when their own ambitions put them at odds with their sovereign. However, successive lords of Fougères remained loyal to the French King. This led in 1231 to one rebellious duke of Brittany capturing the castle in a surprise attack. The royal army retrieved the situation and the duke obviously redeemed himself with the king and subsequently went on crusade with him.

During the Hundred Years' War, the kings of France tended to be 'absentee landlords', having pressing concerns elsewhere. Supported by the English, another duke of Brittany took over the castle, which had to be recaptured in 1373 for Charles V by his *Connétable* (army commander), Bertrand du Guesclin (see Excursion 4). In 1428 the lord of Fougères sold it to the duke of Brittany to pay his ransom, having been captured by the English in Normandy. Twenty years later, shortly before the end of the Hundred Years' War, the castle was captured yet again, this time by a mercenary in the pay of the English, François de Surienne. After a two months' siege the duke of Brittany retook it and strengthened the defences against ever improving artillery.

However, Brittany and France were soon at odds again and in 1488 Louis de Trémoille, head of the royal army, captured Fougères. The king established a garrison there and Fougères effectively became 'French' some years before the official annexation of Brittany under François I.

Another thing:

Some of the towers that make up this imposing yet surprisingly fragile fortress have picturesque names. One in particular, the Tour Mélusine refers to the Lusignan family from the Poitiers region, lords of Fougères in the 13th century. The family claimed to be descended from the fairy Mélusine, a water-sprite of Celtic folklore. This surprising lineage could have come about through linguistic change: *Mélusine* became *mère Lusigne* (mother Lusigne), which in due course became *Lusignan.* Odd things do happen with language (see Tour 5, La Chapelle d'Angillon). Of course, you also have to believe in fairies.

The Tour Mélusine was the finest of the castle's defences, but the fairy story is a sad one. She met and agreed to marry

Raimond of Poitou on condition that he would never see her when she took her bath, because that was when she took on her mermaid form again. You can guess that Raimond could not resist the temptation and ... Mélusine disappeared for ever.

The town only came to prominence again when it became the scene of bloody encounters between royalists and republicans in the royalist insurrection in Brittany during the Revolution. The insurrection was known as the *chouannerie,* from the hooting call sign of the rebel *Chouans* (a Breton word for owl). This uprising, which went on sporadically until 1800, was the inspiration for novels by Honoré de Balzac (*Les Chouans*) and Victor Hugo *(Quatre-vingt-treize).*

Balzac used Fougères as the setting for his 1829 novel, staying there to gather material, and even had the idea of becoming *député* (MP) for the town.

Victor Hugo was inspired for his novel of 1874 by his visit to Fougères nearly 40 years earlier with his mistress Juliette Drouet, who was born there, daughter of a *Chouan.* In his story Hugo gives one of the characters Juliette's maiden name, Gauvain (which is also the French name for that Round Table hero, Gawain).

In the 19th century, Fougères was very much a working class town and from the 1850s was home to a thriving shoemaking industry, which employed most of the town's inhabitants up to WW1. In the 1920s there were around 100 factories, but most had closed by the '60s.

Fougères also boasts the last remaining glassworks in Brittany. A statue in place Riboisière pays tribute to l'Abbé Bridel who in 1921 was the inspiration behind a glass-workers' Catholic cooperative, set up when the very authoritarian owner of the existing glass works refused to accept the Christian trade union formed by the priest. The workers' cooperative has had to become a Limited Company, but still exists. The private factory shut down in 1934. There must be a moral in that.

The inscription on the statue reads: 'To the memory of Abbé Bridel. The grateful working class'.

Visit: The Castle:

It is unusual to find a castle at the foot of a hill, but here the site was used to full advantage. The course of the river Nançon round a rocky spur provided both a moat and the foundations for the walls of the fortress. The exterior walls, with their 13 towers (13th, 14th and 15th centuries) are still intact and as you walk round the outside you can see just what a formidable obstacle the castle must have been to potential attackers. *Walk anti clockwise, starting from the car park below the north west corner of the castle and follow rue Bouteiller.* The Tour Mélusine is the right hand one of the two round towers on this corner. The nearby Eglise St-Sulpice was founded in the 11th century, but was rebuilt in the 15th, as you can see from its flamboyant Gothc-style nave. The chancel took a further two hundred years to complete. My favourite bits are the two rather rare 15th century granite reredos in the chapels.

Go through the Porte Notre-Dame, which is the only remaining mediaeval town gate, and on to the castle entrance to your left.

The inside has suffered more from damage and destruction over the centuries than the outside. Nonetheless you can still get an idea of how the defences were organised. These consisted of three successive enclosures: *l'avancée* (the outer courtyard) allowing crossfire from defenders on all four walls and with a second moat, the *enceinte principale* (main enclosure) with its four towers, finally the *réduit* (redoubt) – the highest part of the castle, with the main keep, until that was pulled down by Henry Plantagenêt and never rebuilt.

These defences are a good example of the mediaeval strategy of progressive withdrawal, even though they were not enough to prevent the castle being captured so many times.

How to get there:

Take the D4 to Dol-de-Bretagne. Briefly join the N176 and then turn onto the D155 to Fougères. When you reach Fougères follow signs to the town centre and then the castle. Follow the boulevard de Rennes to the car park at the foot of the castle.

Journey time: 45 minutes.

The castle is open: July, August, 10am-7pm daily; May, June, September, 10am-1pm, 2pm-7pm, closed on Monday; October-April, 10am-12.30pm, 2-5.30pm, closed on Monday.
Entry: 7,50€. This includes an audio-guide or a guided visit (45minutes). They have lots of visual effects and make the most of the connection with Mélusine.
Allow 1 ¼ hours for the visit to the castle, inside and out.

Another thing:
Rue de la Pinterie, which starts by the castle, used to be the only link between the lower and upper parts of town. It got its name from the 15th century workshop there that made pewter measures for liquids. The road used to be lined with half-timbered houses with open arcades (round here called *porches)* at street level. This covered area and the rest of the ground floor was the workplace. Living accommodation was above. The last of these traditional artisan dwellings were destroyed by allied bombing in 1944.

Visit: La Ville Haute (upper town)
This part of Fougères, originally known as Bourg-Neuf (new town), took over from the Marchix area in the 14th century as the town's commercial hub. Within its fortifications, some of which you can of course still see, the town prospered, through the cloth trade. The castle was in the hands of its 'absentee landlords', so the townspeople got used to running the town themselves. An early sign of their control of the town's affairs was the construction of the belfry (between rue du Beffroi and rue Nationale) in 1397. This elegant granite tower was funded by the wealthy Fougères merchants and had the symbolic importance of allowing ordinary people to know the time, hitherto a privilege of the nobles and clergy.
Rue Nationale was the main street of the Bourg-Neuf and has fine examples of 18th century architecture. Two fires in the first half of that century destroyed nearly all the old timber framed houses with porches. Timber was therefore banned in favour of stone. The style of the new houses was very plain, the only decoration being the wrought iron balconies or carved doors. The horseshoe shaped stairway at No 14 is an exception, while No 51 is the only house that survived the

fires, to remind us of how different the street must have looked previously.

No 51 now houses the Emmanuel de la Villéon museum. This post-impressionist painter (1858-1944) has been described as the aristocrat of the movement (*de* in one's name is an indication of nobility), but is nowadays practically unknown.

His family means allowed him to devote his life to painting. He exhibited every year at the main Paris Salons, receiving favourable comments, including being likened to Corot. He was innovative and an admirer of Cézanne, but his work was not always understood. Praise was often tempered with reservations.

In 1976 his three daughters donated to the town of Fougères the hundred or more of his paintings and drawings that are exhibited here.

Most are landscapes, where he manages to bathe his colours in vibrant light and his scenes have a quality of serenity and harmony. In contrast, his pictures of Breton peasants reflect their stoic acceptance of the hardships of their existence. His *Les fileuses* (women spinning) and *Les mendiantes* (beggar women) are striking in this respect.

All in all, the works on display are an eye opener: Emmanuel de la Villéon is an artist who deserves to be more widely known.

How to get there:
From the castle it is a 10 minute walk up rue de la Pinterie to the Ville Haute. You can drive up, but there is no convenient car park for rue Nationale, which is where you are going, and the ornamental bollards make on-street parking difficult.

The top of rue de la Pinterie comes out into place du Théâtre, which leads into rue Nationale. The Emmanuel de la Villéon museum is on the left side (the only timbered house with a porch).

The museum is open Wednesday–Sunday, 10am-12noon, 2-5pm
Entry free.

Another thing:
The theatre, built in an Italian style in 1886, was considered perfect for 'a working class town'.

Where to eat:
There are several places in rue Nationale, where you can pause for refreshment before or after visiting the museum. Try *Le Buffet* at No 53 bis (closed on Sunday), *Le Saint-Léonard* at No 20 (closed Saturday lunchtime and Wednesday), or *La Galette du Beffroi* at No 41.

Visit: Dol-de-Bretagne:
Victor Hugo said of Dol: 'it is not a town, it is a street'. I would add that it is also a cathedral and that both are worth discovering.

To put you in the picture about Dol:
The cathedral is named after the 6th century Celtic saint, Samson, who founded a monastery here. After he died Dol became an important place of pilgrimage. In the 9th century the Breton king Nominoé wanted to make Dol an independent archbishopric. The Pope refused, but the dispute rumbled on for another 250 years, when the Pope prevailed.

Because of its religious importance, Dol was besieged by William the Conqueror in 1064, a scene shown on the Bayeux tapestry, and the Romanesque cathedral was burnt down by the English king John Lackland in 1203.

The cathedral was rebuilt in Gothic style, but as you can see was never completed. Nonetheless Dol prospered until it was stripped of its bishop by the Revolution. The fierce battle there in 1793 in the *chouannerie* uprising is graphically described in Victor Hugo's novel *Quatre-vingt-treize*. It cost over 15,000 lives.

The industrial 19th century passed it by and the sleepy little town now relies a lot on the tourists who come to discover its illustrious past.

Visit:
If the cathedral looks rather fortress-like from the outside, the elegant and airy interior is a real contrast. The stained glass window in the chancel is a gem. The glass is 13th century,

inevitably with some later restorations, though it is difficult to tell which. Look also at the carved armrests of the 14th century choir stalls and the unusual 1980 altar sculpted in wood and terra cotta.

Outside, the towers at the west end were part of the town's defences. The 15th century north tower was never finished, as they ran out of money, but the south tower was rebuilt on its 12th century base after John Lackland's ravages and rose gradually over the next two centuries. Perhaps the builders got their own back on the king: a grimacing figure set into the angle of the south tower buttress at the second level is said to be John.

On the south side, the smaller of the two porches was the entrance used by the bishop. Continue along rue Ceinte (enclosed road), so named because it had gates at each end which were shut at night. The houses in this street were originally lived in by church officials. No 16, the Manoir du Grand Chantre, was the residence of the Presentor. After the Revolution rue Ceinte became the preserve of the better off. As it nears the main street, notice two 15th century shops with their granite counters. I love the idea of the seat carved out of granite - for the shopkeeper to rest between customers or to make sure they didn't steal anything on display?

You come out into Victor Hugo's 'street': the Grande-Rue-des-Stuarts to your right, rue Lejamtel to your left. Some of the lovely old houses date as far back as the 12th century (No 17, les Petits Palets, one of the oldest in Brittany). Inside No 18, another 12th century vaulted room is part of a former Templar inn, now unfortunately a *crêperie*. A stroll up and down the street reveals a host of charming *vieilles pierres* that reflect the town's former grandeur. Look out for the floral motifs on the pillar of No 32 and the two carved gloves and birds on the lintel of the door of No 33. I haven't been able to find an explanation for these.

Another thing:
Why Grande-Rue-des-Stuarts? According to the commemorative plaque next to the Mairie (town hall) the Royal House of Stuart, kings of Scotland and England, descended from a count of Dol, whose son went to England

with the Conqueror. His grandson, Walter was appointed 1st Steward of Scotland by the Scottish king and the appointment was subsequently made hereditary. For Steward read Stuart and there you have it.

On the same wall is a plaque which I find poignant, commemorating the liberation of Dol by General Patton on the 4th August 1944.

How to get there:
From Fougères, return towards Dol by the D155. Do not take the road right into the town centre as this will spoil the pleasure of discovering the main street. Rather, get onto the N176 and come off at the next junction and follow signs to the cathedral. Park in the cathedral square.
Journey time: 30 minutes. Allow 1 hour to visit the cathedral and see the town.

On your way back to La Gouesnière by the D4 you will see a rocky outcrop rising out of the plain between Dol and the sea. This is Mont Dol and of course, being so near the Mont-St-Michel, it has its own legend about the saint and his combat with Satan: *St Michel made a hole in the Mont Dol and flung his foe into it. Satan somehow escaped and reappeared on the Mont-St-Michel. The saint leapt after him, taking off with such force that you can still see the footprint he left in the rock....*

Excursion 3: The forest of Brocéliande

This excursion takes you to the land of Merlin and the Knights of the Round Table, to a place that doesn't exist on the Michelin map; such is the magic of Brittany.
It is a day of gentle walks in the enchanted forest, a visit to a church with surprising Arthurian connections and also to a site of industrial archaeology.
In fact, the forest is really called the forest of Paimpont. Its 7000 hectares (17000acres) are all that is left of the vast forest that once covered inland Brittany (l'Argoat). From the early Middle Ages the forest has gradually been eroded for settlement, agriculture and more recently industry.

Until the Revolution it was called *Brécilien,* but in the Arthurian legends was known as *Brocéliande,* the softer sounding *Brocéliande* no doubt more suited to romantic tales of chivalry. Paimpont only grew up in the 19th century through its nearby industry and gave its name to the forest. Now, through the popularity of tourism based on the legends of the forest, the name *forêt de Paimpont* is beginning to be dropped in favour of *Brocéliande.*

To put you in the picture about Brocéliande and the Arthurian legends:
To the British mind, Arthur is associated with places like Tintagel, his supposed birthplace, or Cadbury castle in Somerset, the legendary Camelot. Excalibur is set in stone outside the castle in Taunton and the Round Table is in Winchester. How then does Brittany fit in?
Arthur is supposedly based on a 6th century Romano-British warrior who fought and defeated the Saxons. The many Celts who fled from the Saxons to Brittany at that time (eg St Malou and St Samson) would have taken with them stories of his heroic deeds.
He first appears in literature in Geoffrey of Monmouth's 12th century *History of the Kings of Britain*. No one knows for certain, but it is likely that Geoffrey's sources included tales current on both sides of the Channel.
The French poet Chrétien de Troyes, writing in the late 12th century, brought new elements, Lancelot, Perceval and the Holy Grail into the stories. He set some of the action in Brocéliande, starting a real tradition in the forest. It was Chrétien de Troyes whose poems popularised the legends, which were adapted into other languages, particularly German. Thomas Malory's popular *Le Morte Darthur* 1485 reinterpreted some of the French and English tales, but the big revival of interest came with Tennyson's *Idylls of the King* in the 19th century. The 1863 illustrations by Gustave Dore look just like Brocéliande.

Visit:
Start your tour of this 'enchanted' forest at **Tréhorenteuc.** This village has now become a colourful, even gaudy centre for the

Brocéliande tourist. This is all down to l'Abbé Gillard, who transformed his church and brought life to the village, once described as the 'chamber pot of the Department', in his time as village priest from 1942 to 1962.

When he came, l'Abbé Gillard was struck by the spirituality of Brocéliande and over the years did much research on the relationship between the legends and Christianity. The result is the strange fusion of the two in the decoration of the inside of the church. The white stag in the mosaic at the west end of the nave symbolises Christ, while in Arthurian mythology the hunt for the white stag confronts the Knights with their destiny. Paintings in the chancel too depict this fusion: the Holy Grail appearing to the Knights of the Round Table, and the one representing the four elements, where the fairy Viviane imprisons Merlin in magic rings of air. These two paintings were done by Karl Rezabeck, one of two German prisoners of war recruited by l'Abbé Gillard to decorate his church. The other, Peter Wisdorf, was a carpenter.

Between 1945 and 1947 they worked with the priest to create the unusual Stations of the Cross. The paintings use local scenes as background, rather than the Holy Land, and there are other interesting details. In the second Station, it is Wisdorf the carpenter who offers Christ the cross he has made himself. In the fourth, the Roman soldier between Christ and Mary is Rezabeck and he has signed the eleventh with his name preceded by 'PG' (*prisonnier de guerre*). He has also included his prisoner's water bottle with the cross of Lorraine on it. The ninth Station caused a furore. Here, standing in front of the fallen Christ is the very sensual sorceress Morgane le Fay. Again a fusion of Christianity and legend, but which provoked an outraged newspaper comment: *'a pin up in the Stations of the Cross'*. It is said that the image was inspired by the local schoolteacher, but history does not relate what she thought about it.

The tourist office opposite the church has guide sheets you can borrow for your visit to the church. They give details of all Gillard's symbolism and his books are on sale too. *From here, pick up a plan of the area for your walk. They speak English and will give helpful directions.*

A gentle walk in the **Val sans Retour** (Valley of no Return) will give you time for reflection about what you have just seen and to enjoy the scenery of this 'enchanted' valley, the realm of Morgane le Fay, half-sister of Arthur. Ditched by her lover for another woman, she took umbrage and imprisoned him in this valley within her magic rings of air. She was so vengeful that she took captive all errant knights who came her way. They lived there, captives of her charms, oblivious of time. Only Lancelot, because of his devotion (albeit illicit) to Guinevere, was able to overcome Morgane's magic powers and released all the unfaithful knights. The legend does not say if they were actually grateful for their release.

On this 3.5km circuit you pass the still lake called Miroir aux Fées (fairy mirror) and near it the Arbre d'Or. This 'tree', made from the burnt remains of a chestnut tree and covered in gold leaf, was created in 1991 and symbolises the forest reborn among the charred remains of the previous year's fires.

The valley used to be called Vallée du Rauco from the stream that ran through it, but since the rekindling of interest in the legends of Brocéliande in the 19th century, this was designated the site of Morgane's spiteful magic, so even the map now uses its romantic name. It is probably the most visited of Broceliande's sites, and maybe the most magic – even compasses play tricks on the hiker, but the prosaic explanation for this is the amount of mineral deposits found here.

Where to eat:
Paimpont is a pleasant village, with lakeside gardens and an impressive looking abbey, especially when seen from across the lake. The abbey, parts of which date from the 13th century, is on the site of a much earlier priory. The attractive archway at the start of the main shopping street was the old entrance to the abbey.

Opposite, try the *Relais de Brocéliande*, an old staging inn, with décor befitting its name.

Otherwise, follow signs for the Syndicat d'Initiative (tourist office), just by the abbey. There are a couple of places nearby where you can have a reasonable snack sitting in a pleasant little garden.

How to get there:
From your hotel, get on the N176 (direction Dinan). 4kms beyond Dinan, take the D766 (direction St-Méen-le-Grand, Mauron, Ploermel). After the Mauron bypass turn left onto the D307 to La Sauldraie and join the D141 to Tréhorenteuc. Park near the church, or in the car park on the edge of the village on the D141 (direction Ploermel. Everything is in walking distance.
For Paimpont, take the D141 to Touche-Robert, then the D134 to Campénéac and at the other end of the village (direction Plélan) take the D312>D40 to Paimpont.
Journey time: to Tréhorenteuc, 1hour. From Tréhorenteuc to Paimpont, 15 minutes.

4kms down the road you come to **les Forges de Paimpont,** a reminder of another, but far from magic forest activity. This is the site, still being restored, of the centre of the important iron industry that made *les fers de Paimpont* (Paimpont iron) known throughout Brittany and beyond. In the 15th and 16th centuries they made crossbow arrows, pikes and halberds. Later it was armaments for the arsenals at Rennes, Lorient, Brest and Nantes and there were even orders for the American War of Independence. In the 19th century railway track was produced, but they could not compete with output from Britain and eventually closed down in 1884.

The rich iron deposits in the area, proximity of water and vast quantities of wood from the forest had made this enterprise possible. It employed some 400 workers at its peak.

It is not Ironbridge, but a remarkable example of industrial archaeology in a lovely rural setting nonetheless.

The château de Comper has been the Arthurian Centre in Brocéliande for over twenty years. It has had a turbulent history, being sacked by Bertrand du Guesclin, again by Henri IV in the Wars of Religion and partly burnt down in the Revolution. All that is as nothing compared to its role in the Arthurian legend, for in its lake is the underwater palace built by Merlin for his lover, the fairy Viviane. You can only see the lake by paying to go into the château grounds, but even then Merlin's palace is only visible to believers.

The Centre holds exhibitions and other activities every year, but find out from the Tréhorenteuc or Paimpont tourist office exactly what's on, to make sure the subject appeals, before you decide to go in.

However, a gentle walk to two nearby sites will round off this day in Brocéliande.

Le Tombeau de Merlin was first given its name by M. Poignand in 1820. This august judge from Montfort claimed that this was the burial place of Merlin, a 5th century archdruid, but he did not specify the exact location. This was wise in the light of what happened later. In 1889 a certain Félix Bellamy discovered its exact location and that it appeared to be a Neolithic covered row. Soon after, the landowner totally vandalised it in his search for supposed hidden treasure. All that remains now are a couple of stones from the Neolithic monument with an old holly tree growing out of them. Disappointing to look at, but don't be surprised to see garlands of flowers, messages, or offerings to Merlin. This says something about the spirituality of Brocéliande, a spirituality that l'Abbé Gillard certainly found too.

A little further on is the **Fontaine de Jouvence** (fountain of youth). As one guide puts it: 'just a hole with water in it'. Nonetheless its history makes the visit worthwhile and it is a pleasant stroll.

It is thought to be an ancient Celtic baptismal site. Traditionally, children born during the year were brought to a fountain like this at the summer solstice to be washed and 'registered' as newborn by the druid. Children born later were not registered until the following year, hence appearing 'officially' a year younger. Subsequently it gained the reputation of being able to restore their youth to those who drank its water.

Before you get too excited, to achieve the desired effect you had to drink the magic water on seven successive days between the moon setting and the sun rising, having made your journey there barefoot.

How to get there:
For les Forges de Paimpont: just by where you came into Paimpont, Les Forges is signposted. At les Forges parking is near the entrance.

The museum is open: 14th July-31st August, 2.30-6.30pm, daily. Otherwise, only on Sunday, from Easter to 1st November.
Entry: 5,50€
For the château de Comper: return to Paimpont and continue on the D773 (direction St-Méen). After 5kms, turn right onto the D141. The château is 1km down the road.
Journey time from Les Forges: 15minutes.
The château is open: April, May, June, September, October, 10am-5.30pm, closed Tuesday and Wednesday. In July, August it stays open till 7pm, but is closed on Wednesday.
Entry: 5,50€
For the **Tombeau de Merlin***: past Comper, turn right onto the D31. After 4kms, turn right onto the little road to La Ville-Moisan. The Tombeau de Merlin is signposted. NB When you get there, the track you want is off the road* **opposite** *the car park, a 400m walk. The* **Fontaine de Jouvence** *is a little further on. There is a 4km circuit if you prefer. This is marked on the information panel at the car park.*
Journey time from Comper: 5minutes

Another thing:
Le Pont du Secret (bridge of the secret) has possibly the most romantic associations of any place in Brocéliande. This is where Lancelot and Guinevere first avowed their love for each other. The place is on the map, south of Paimpont near Les Forges, but don't bother going there, as there is nothing to see. The remains of the fateful bridge are inaccessible to any but the determined hiker.

To return home: the easiest way is to go back to Comper, turn right onto the D773 and at Gael rejoin the D166> D766 to

Dinan and then the N176, turning onto the D137 (St- Malo) and the D74 to La Guesnière.

Excursion 4: Dinan, Cap Fréhel and Fort La Latte

To put you in the picture about Dinan:
In a sense Dinan is actually two towns: the port on the bank of the Rance with its associated activities, and the upper walled town.
The first pictorial reference to Dinan is in the *Tapisserie de la reine Mathilde*, better known as the Bayeux Tapestry. Here William's troops are seen attacking a castle on a hilltop in 1065. This no doubt resulted in a strengthening of the defences, for a 12th century Arab geographer writes of Dinan as 'a town enclosed by stone walls'.
By the 1300s the town was doing well through trade with England and Flanders. However, The English repeatedly attacked the town during the early part of the Hundred Years War, but Dinan was saved from capture in the 1357 siege by the victory in single combat by Bertrand du Guesclin (pronounced *Geklan*) over Thomas of Canterbury (NB not St Thomas).
From then on Dinan underwent the ups and downs of France's and the region's life. Access to the upper town was made easier in the 19th century by the construction of the viaduct. This was a period that also saw Dinan and nearby Dinard colonised by the English, in holiday mode this time.
Now tourism seems to be the major industry, the annual *Fête des Remparts* (Festival of the Ramparts) in July making the most of the town's mediaeval setting and history.

Visit:
Your first view of Dinan's ramparts, lovely as they are, as you cross the viaduct over the Rance doesn't transport you back to the Middle Ages as much as Carcassonne (Tour1), but once you have parked, crossed place du Guesclin and found yourself in rue de l'Horloge you can easily feel that you have stepped back in time.

Now, the problem may be parking. Normally, you can park without difficulty in place du Guesclin (On your right after the château), but on Thursday this is where the market is held and the town is buzzing. Just park where you can, even on pavements if you see others have already done so. However, once you have overcome the parking problem, market day is the time to be in Dinan.
It is also an idea to pick up a town plan from the Tourist Office next to the château.

To put you in the picture about Bertrand du Guesclin (c1320-1380):

The equestrian statue of the man who rose to be Constable of France stands in the square named after him. He is in fact facing the other part of the square, place du Champ Clos, where his single combat took place. The siege of Dinan was going badly, so du Guesclin asked for a forty day truce, after which the town would surrender unless help arrived. His younger brother Olivier ventured unarmed outside the walls and, in contravention of the truce, was taken prisoner by the English knight Thomas of Canterbury, who then demanded a ransom of 1000 florins. This unsporting act provoked du Guesclin to challenge Canterbury to a formal combat. Du Guesclin won, Canterbury had to pay him the money and was thrown out of the army in disgrace and Dinan never fell into the hands of the English, who obviously wanted to restore their reputation for what the French call *le fair play*. Even better, a pretty Dinan girl called Typhaine had vowed to marry du Guesclin if he won and apparently they lived happily….

Du Guesclin was considered such a valuable military asset to Charles V that the French king twice ransomed him after he had been captured. The king was obviously right as du Guesclin, by the time he died, had regained most of French territory occupied by the English.

Leave **Place du Champ Clos** by the Passage de la Tour de l'Horloge (half way along the top side of the square). From here you get a good view of the 15th century clock tower and from the top of the tower (variously 158 or 160 steps) a wonderful view over Dinan, the river and surrounding countryside. *(Open: May-September, 10am-6.30pm. Entry: 2,75€)*

You come out into **rue de l'Horloge**, which has some lovely old houses that have been beautifully restored. Turn right to see two of my favourites. On your left, on the corner by the former Couvent des Jacobins (Dominican monastery), you see the three granite pillars of the Hotel Kératry. This charming little 16th century house looks as though it has been here ever since that time. In fact it came from the village of Lanvollon where it was nearly in ruins. It was bought by the municipality and erected here in 1938. On your right is the house known as the Maison du Gisant (recumbent statue). The 14th century statue under the portico was discovered during restoration work on the house. If you look closely, you see that these funerary statues were prefabricated, the personalised head and coat of arms being produced for the appropriate death. The notion of mass production maybe sheds new light on the so called 'dark ages'.

Go back towards the clock tower and down an alley on your right. This leads to place St-Sauveur. The church clearly shows the different periods of its construction. Above and to the left of the Romanesque porch the façade is Gothic. Inside, the contrast between the Romanesque on the right and the Gothic, on the left and in the chancel and transept, is quite striking. In the north (left) arm of the transept is a tomb containing the heart of the saviour of Dinan, du Guesclin.

Another thing:
In the Middle Ages, the kings of France traditionally had three tombs containing their heart, body and entrails respectively. Du Guesclin has four.
He had died on campaign in the Auvergne, but had wished to be buried in Dinan. His body was embalmed and the entrails buried at Le Puy. Unfortunately the embalming wasn't very efficient, so at Clermont-Ferrand his flesh was boiled to detach it from his skeleton and buried there. The cortège continued towards Dinan, but the order came from the king that the body was to be buried at St-Denis in Paris, burial place of royalty.

The skeleton was handed over and only the heart reached Dinan.
A gruesome tale, but it makes du Guesclin unique.

Just to the right of the church a timbered house with its portico is the birthplace of Auguste Pavie (1847-1925). His is a remarkable story. Son of a cabinet maker, but looking for adventure, he joined the army at seventeen and was posted to the Far East. Back in France for service in the Franco-Prussian War (1870) he rose to Sergeant-Major and afterwards went back to the Far East, where he ran a telegraph office in a remote part of Cambodia for ten years. He 'went native', learning the language and charting the region. His knowledge and talent were recognised and so he was taken on in the Diplomatic Service and eventually became the French consul in Laos and subsequently plenipotentiary minister when Laos became part of French Indochina. In 1904 he returned to France to write his multi-volume memoirs
People still come to see the home of this 'local boy who made good'.
The **Jardin Anglais** behind the church used to be a cemetery. From the far side you get splendid views over the river Rance and the port.
A café in the square is the place for a timely pause for refreshment before turning right into rue de la Larderie and then left to get back to the corner of rue de l'Horloge. Go straight across and you come to the most atmospheric part of the old town. **Rue de l'Apport, place des Merciers** and **place des Cordeliers** together make up the finest set of mediaeval buildings in Dinan. With their wooden pillared arcades, timbered and corbelled façades they are all great to look at and it's worth a glimpse at the 15th century interior of *Chez la Mère Pourcel*, even if you are not eating there.
At the end of place des Cordeliers turn right down rue de la Lainerie and on down rue du Jerzual. Everywhere you go in Dinan there are good buildings. I have picked out the best, but others have explanatory plaques that are interesting to read. *En passant*, 6 rue de la Poissonnerie is one of the oldest, dated 1494.

Until the viaduct was built, **rue du Jerzual** was the main link between the town and the port, a perpetual bustle with loaded carts struggling up and down its steep gradient. The grand houses show that it was a favoured residential area, while the counters of the old *échoppes* (shops) reflect its commercial activity. Then this was the workplace of the tanners, so the road was perhaps not as picturesque as it is now (they took the skins down to wash them in the river). Half way down you go through the Porte du Jerzual. Corot painted it in 1860 'in the rain and with his feet in the mud' according to a friend. The road now becomes rue du Petit-Fort, still with some impressive old houses. Notice the openwork loft for drying skins at Nos49/51.

At the bottom the road opens onto the port area, still in keeping with the atmosphere of the past, even though it is now just an attractive, sunlit mooring for yachts and pleasure boats. The tall former warehouses tell you that it once was a busy working port.

Another thing:
Some of the street names in the old town indicate the activity that used to go on there: Merciers (haberdashers), Cordeliers (Franciscan friars), Poissonnerie (fishmonger's), Ferronnerie (ironmonger's), Lainerie (wool). Jerzual is less clear. It probably comes from a Celtic word 'Jaruhel' meaning 'high road'.

Where to eat:
The restaurants along the quayside have reasonably priced menus and terraces that overlook the river. Try *Le Myrian* (closed Wednesday out of season) or *Café-Terrasses*.
After lunch it has been known for the driver to be despatched to bring the car down to the port. If so, then drive back up the hill and follow signs for Lamballe and St-Brieuc for the afternoon excursion.

How to get there:
The most direct way into Dinan is across the viaduct. From your hotel get onto the D137 at Châteauneuf and just after the junction with the N176 take the exit for Miniac-Morvan.

Follow this slip road for 2kms and then join the D795 to Dinan.
Journey time: 20minutes.

Cap Fréhel and Fort La Latte:
Cap Fréhel is arguably the most impressive stretch of the whole of Brittany's beautiful coastline. Its 200ft high cliffs fall vertically into the sea, calm on a fine summer day, but whipped into fury at other times by the full force of the Channel winds. Its colours are particularly striking. The shades of grey, black and red of the rock seem to change with the light.

There is of course a legend, miraculous rather than magic, about the red. An Irish saint, either Hérel or Venon, both 5th century evangelists who founded the communities of Pléherel and Plévenon, was preaching on the cliff top facing the little St Michel's island (west of Pléherel) and was asked by an as yet unconverted local: *'St Michel was sent by God. When he stepped onto that island, the rock turned red. If you are sent by God, can you do the same here?'* The saint scratched his hand on the rock and the blood that fell on it turned the whole cliff red. Everyone was of course immediately converted by the miracle.

The 400hectares (nearly 1000acres) of moorland are a reserve for plants and birds. From spring onwards the colours of the heathers, sea pinks and gorse can be spectacular. At the tip of the headland the lighthouse is the third to be erected there. The first, the 17th century Tour Vauban was lit by coal, then by fish oil. Its replacement was destroyed by the Germans in WW2 and the present one dates from 1950. Drive to the lighthouse and enjoy the views.

Another thing:
Plé, Plo, Plou are variants of the old Breton word for parish, going back to the Christianisation of the country in the 5th and 6th centuries. As in *Pléherel* and *Plévenon*, they were usually followed by the saint's name.

Fort La Latte:
To put you in the picture:
Etienne III Goyon, a Breton noble built the fort in the early 14th century on the site of an earlier wooden keep, whose purpose was to watch out for and repel invaders from Normandy. In the 14th century the purpose of the imposing stone fortress with its impregnable keep and two drawbridges was still to repel attacks on Breton independence, whether the enemy was English or French, depending on the political situation of the time. Du Guesclin laid siege to the fort and eventually took it in the name of the king of France in 1379, but it withstood an attack from the sea by the English in 1490. However, during the Wars of Religion, it was attacked and partly burnt down by Catholic forces hostile to the Protestant Henri IV.

A century later, when Louis XIV was strengthening defences in St-Malo and along the coast, his military architect Vauban noted the wretched state of the fort: *'The commandant has not been paid for three years and has had a broken leg for eighteen months. His chief gunnery officer has only one arm, so that between them they have only half the number of working limbs they should have'*. The fort was rebuilt with the emphasis now on coastal defence. It was never captured from the sea, but one boat did manage to get past its guns. During a storm in 1815 the boat carrying James Stuart, the Old Pretender was washed up on the shore. He was forced to take refuge in the fort until the storm abated, but he didn't enjoy his stay. He called it *'the bleakest place where man ever lived, without wood to prepare food, nor any object of necessity'*.

During the Revolution a number of *Chouans* were imprisoned there, the garrison amusing themselves by lining them up before a firing squad and then firing blanks.

In 1815 during the 'Hundred Days' the fort was captured briefly by a group of royalists from St-Malo, but that was its last military involvement. By 1886 it was manned by only one guard and a few years later, like the St-Malo forts, was decommissioned and sold.

The 20th century saw its classification as a Historic Monument, much restoration and use as a film set for, notably, *The Vikings* in 1957 with Tony Curtis and Kirk Douglas. This magnificent location has been used for a number of other films since then, but don't bother watching Philippe de Broca's *Chouans* in spite of its apparent local historical interest – as a film *Mary Poppins* is more realistic.

Visit:

The wonderful location of the fort and the remains of its fortifications are really more impressive than its history. The double drawbridges must have been a formidable obstacle, but the keep is the most imposing of the buildings and you can see why it was never captured. The round construction and splayed base made it more resistant to attack and allowed stones thrown down through the machicolations to bounce, causing havoc among the attackers - real 14th century state of the art. Notice the four carvings of the Evangelists set into the stonework, marking the points of the compass. Inside, the upper room, which was the living area, has a fine vaulted ceiling, while the views from the *chemin de ronde* above are wonderful, as you would imagine.
The strange little building below the keep is a kiln, installed in 1794. This was one of a series built along the coast to heat cannon balls which would set fire to enemy (English) ships. The cannon balls were inserted at the top end and came out into a channel at the bottom when heated. Unfortunately it took 2 ½ hours to get them to the right temperature, by which time the enemy would doubtless have noticed the smoke and sailed out of range. The project was soon abandoned.

The 15th century Governor's residence and the 18th century chapel were restored in the 1930s - photos on display show the terrible state they were in before.

Another thing:
The fort was originally known as La Roche Goyon, from the name of its lords. They married into the Matignon family, who in turn married into the Grimaldi family of Monaco in 1715. So the locals say that the princes of Monaco are really Bretons.
In written documents the name seems to have changed to La Latte (the nearby village) in the 1500s, which is when the Goyon line died out.

How to get there:
Your route out of Dinan will bring you to the N176 junction with the D734. Take the D734 (direction Plancoet). At Corseul this becomes the D794. Follow this to Matignon. There join the D786 (direction Erquy). At Fréhel turn right onto the D34 to Pléherel and Cap Fréhel.
From Cap Fréhel take the D16 to Fort La Latte.
Journey times: Dinan to Cap Fréhel, 40 minutes. Cap Fréhel to Fort La Latte, 5minutes.
Fort La Latte is open: July, August, 10am-7pm; April-June, September, 10am-12.30pm, 2-6pm; October-March, weekend only, 2-6pm.
Entry: 4,50€

Return by the same route. The colours of Cap Fréhel are at their best in the late afternoon.

Excursion 5: Le Mont-St-Michel

To put you in the picture:
Way back in the 6th century there were already two shrines on this offshore rock, one dedicated to St Etienne (Stephen), the other to St Symphorien. The rock was known as Mont Tombe and it was not until two centuries later that an oratory to the Archangel Michael was built below the summit of the rock. It

soon became such a popular place of pilgrimage that the name changed to Mont-St-Michel.

A 10th century manuscript recounts the origin of the oratory: in 708AD the saint appeared in a dream to Aubert, bishop of Avranches, asking him to erect a church in his honour on the Mont Tombe. It needed the saint to appear three times for the bishop to be convinced, but finally he was, and the rest, as they say, is history.

Pilgrims flocked to the site to pray to the saint who overcame the Devil, though crossing the sand spit to the island church could be dangerous. The mount was surrounded by water at high tide and some pilgrims were sucked under or drowned by the tides which, in the words of Victor Hugo, could rise or fall *à la vitesse d'un cheval au galop* (as swiftly as a galloping horse). This accounts for the nickname it had, St-Michel-au-Péril-de-la-Mer (St Michael in peril of the sea).

As the mount became one of the great centres of pilgrimage, so the buildings had to be extended to house the community of monks and offer hospitality to the pilgrims. Between 1017 and 1144 a Romanesque church was built on the pointed summit of the rock, using the earlier church as the crypt (now Notre-Dame-sous-Terre: Our Lady below ground), to support part of the new nave. The abbey buildings went up on the south side, around the original church. The latter part of the 12th century, under the rule of the abbot Robert de Thorigny, was the golden age of the abbey. The community of sixty monks was never matched again and its library was so rich in manuscripts that the monastery was known as the 'city of books'.

In 1204 part of the abbey burnt down in a fire. This was the work of Breton forces in support of King Philippe Auguste who was in the process of reconquering Normandy from John Lackland (king of England and duke of Normandy). The Bretons massacred the inhabitants of the village and torched it. They failed to capture the abbey itself, but unfortunately the fire reached it. Now, burning such a centre of pilgrimage was not a popular move so the king deemed it politic to make amends for this misguided 'support' by giving the abbey a large donation. The sum was enough to erect buildings so magnificent that they became known as the Merveille (the Wonder).

The fortifications protecting the abbey and the village below were strengthened during the Hundred Years' War, successfully thwarting the English, who occupied the neighbouring island of Tombelaine and laid siege to the mount.

During that period the Romanesque chancel collapsed, but once peace was restored it was rebuilt in Flamboyant Gothic style with money from pilgrims grateful to St Michel, whom they called *'protecteur de la France'*. It took seventy five years to build and was finished in 1521.

The abbey's fortunes began to decline in the 16th century, once abbots were appointed by the king rather than elected by the monks as was the Benedictine rule. Funds were not spent on the upkeep of the abbey and with often an 'absentee' abbot the rule became lax. The Wars of Religion at the end of the century did not help, as the number of pilgrims seriously decreased with the Protestant Reformation.

In 1780 the Romanesque façade and part of the nave were pulled down after fire damage, and the anti-clerical Revolution expelled the remaining ten monks and turned the abbey into a prison. In the 19th century Victor Hugo and other literary figures petitioned against this sacrilegious use of the abbey, but it was not until 1863 that Napoleon III closed the prison down.

It became a listed building soon afterwards and restoration began, the present spire being added in 1897.

Although the Mont-St-Michel is France's number one tourist attraction, it still has a small religious community and there is a sung mass every day except Monday.

Another thing:
It has been hotly disputed for centuries whether this great monument is in Brittany or Normandy. Traditionally the river Couesnon marks the boundary between the two regions, but its course often changed after high tides silted up its estuary. In 1863 it was canalised, permanently fixing the boundary. Unfortunately for the Bretons, the Mont is officially in Normandy, though guide books to both regions include it as theirs.

Visit: the village
Ever since the abbey became a place of pilgrimage, there has been a secular community on the mount, providing 'support services' or just as likely finding ways of relieving the visitors of as much of their money as possible. So if you deplore the rampant commercialisation cheek by jowl with a great religious building, it was always so. Only the crowds of pilgrims from France and beyond have been replaced by crowds of tourists. Look, listen to the different languages, and let your mind imagine….

The three successive fortified gates show how well protected the village was and the two *'michelettes'*, cannons captured from the English in 1434, are a reminder of the failure of their siege.

The village really consists of one road, the narrow Grande Rue, which curves up towards the abbey, with narrower alleys leading off it on either side. The buildings were then as now mainly shops. They mostly date back to the 15th and 16th centuries, but many have suffered early 20th century restoration. On your way up, look out for the old stonework of the communal bakehouse, the Hôtellerie de la Lycorne (unicorn), the Maison de la Truie-qui-file (spinning sow). The timber of the Maison de l'Arcade, the Logis St-Pierre and the Auberge de la Sirène is genuine. Others look good, like the Mouton Blanc, but the timber has come from other buildings.

Visit: the abbey
As you glimpse the mount from the N176, it appears mystical, almost floating on the blue-grey of the sea and sand. As you approach it along the causeway it is so impressive, the more so when you think that the actual apex of the rock is the *base* of the transept of the abbey church. The top of the spire doubles the height of the natural rock. A truly amazing piece of mediaeval

engineering, the blocks of granite being shipped in from the mainland or the Chausey islands up the coast.

The entrance to the abbey is via the steps of Le Grand Degré at the top of the Grande Rue. This entrance was also protected, first by a gate and at the top by the twin towers and machicolations of the *châtelet* (fortified entrance). Here the use of alternate pink and grey granite gives it some elegance as well as strength. These defences were good enough to stop the Bretons in 1204.

There is so much to see and wonder at in the abbey that I strongly recommend going round using the audio-guide, or joining a guided tour in English if it is at a convenient time.

Your tour takes you through a seeming maze of passages and stairs, so that there is no particular sequence of building or architecture. It is important to remember that this is not traditional abbey construction, where the various buildings extend outwards from the church, *on the same level*. Here they are built above each other, on three levels, round the church, which perches on the very summit of the hill. The chapels and rooms on the lower levels of the abbey support the church and cloister above.

When I go round I constantly marvel at the construction. However, in a building that is altogether amazing, for me there are still some highlights.

You enter the church by the south door and are immediately struck by the sombre Romanesque nave contrasting with the lightness and elegance of the Gothic chancel and apse. Only the central part of the transept and the first three bays of the nave are built directly on 'terra firma'. On the terrace at the west end you can see the extent of the nave before 1780. Notice the markings on the flagstones. These are the masons' marks, by which they were identified so they could be paid. Little details like that give this huge structure a human dimension.

The Crypte des Gros Piliers is aptly named. Its massive pillars (5m in circumference) support the whole of the chancel and apse above.

You suddenly come upon the Grande Roue (treadmill), a somewhat grim reminder of the seventy years or so when the abbey was a prison. Five or six prisoners would work the wheel to haul supplies up from the ramparts on a sled, which you can see by looking out.

The Eglise Notre-Dame-sous-Terre is all that remains of the original pre-Romanesque church of the 10th century. The roughly finished blocks and narrow bricks show that its construction was still in the Roman style. Traces of painting have been found, so that its original appearance would have been less sombre. 20th century excavations behind the altar revealed what are thought to be remains of Aubert's oratory. In a way the whole history of the abbey is encapsulated in this small church. *(NB You can only visit it with a guided tour).*

Finally the Merveille (the Wonder), the result of Philippe Auguste's conscience money. It was constructed on the north side of the church and looks like a fortress, giving no indication of what the interior is like.

The lowest of its three levels of rooms consists of the austere halls of the chaplaincy and cellar.

On the next level the enormous Salle des Chevaliers was the scriptorium, whose two fireplaces allowed the monks a modicum of warmth in winter for the delicate work of copying and illuminating manuscripts. Its columns are still quite sturdy looking, but with decorated capitals. Next to it, the even larger Salle des Hôtes was the reception room for distinguished guests. Here the columns are finer and the vault higher, giving the hall its elegance. The kitchen end, with its two huge fireplaces, could be separated from the dining end by a great curtain, whose position you can still see.

The real 'wonder' comes at the third level. The refectory is amazing. You can hardly understand how the room can be so well lit just by the two windows you can see at the far end. As you go in you realise that the light comes from tall narrow windows set deep into the bays of what is apparently a solid wall along the length of the room. This was a triumph of design: achieving such light, while not weakening walls which had to support considerable pressure from the roof. The acoustic too is excellent, as it needed to be for the monk reading from the Scriptures during the meal.

The cloister is the jewel among jewels in this wonderful building. It has been described as being suspended between sea and sky. Solid walls on the outside; inside, the double row of slim offset columns gives an impression of incredible lightness and the richly decorated vaulting above completes the beauty of it all. Words cannot do it justice: it just has to be seen.

The abbey is open daily: May to August, 9am-7pm; September to April, 9.30am-6pm.
Entry: 8,50€, members of the E.U. aged under 26 free. Audio-guides: 4,50€, for 2 sets of headphones linked to the same tape: 6€.
The guided tour lasts 1¼ hours, as does the audio-guide.
Allow 2 hours to visit the village, including a walk round the ramparts and abbey gardens, which give you views of the far side of the abbey.
In July and August there is also an evening Son et Lumière *show. This is open from 7.30pm, with the last entry at 10.30pm. This involves walking in your own time round various parts of the abbey, including some rooms not normally open, where special lighting and sound effects have been installed.*
If you are as bowled over by the Mont-St-Michel as I am, the Son et Lumière *is well worth a visit too. I would come back after your evening meal at the hotel, or on another day, but **after** you have toured the abbey in daylight.*

Another thing:
Since 1877 the mount has been joined to the mainland by a causeway and during the first half of the 20th century even a little steam train took visitors along it. Creating the causeway, redirecting the river Couesnon and later building a dam across it, have brought about the gradual silting up of the sea between the mount and the shore.

After many years' discussion, plans are now going ahead to rectify this by siting the car park on the mainland, making part of the causeway into a bridge and using an environmentally friendly shuttle service to take people to the mount.

All this is due to be in place by 2012 and is designed to give the Mont-St-Michel back its island atmosphere. Here's hoping...

Where to eat:
Choose from any number of *crêperies* and restaurants in the Grande Rue. The *crêpereie La Sirène* is atmospheric and genuinely old, though not the cheapest. There is also *La Mère Poulard*, famous for its omelettes. It's big business now and overpriced.

At some stage on your holiday you should sample the regional speciality, pré salé *lamb. The lambs are reared on the salt marshes of the Mont-St-Michel bay, which gives them their flavour.*

How to get there:
From your hotel, cut across to Dol on the D4, join the N176 (direction Avranches). At Pontorson follow signs to Mont-St-Michel (D976)
Journey time: 25 minutes
To return: At Pontorson take the D797 (direction Cancale) and then the D155 at Le Vivier-sur-Mer. Then, at La Coudre turn back onto the D76 to La Guiesnière. This country route gives you good views over the bay.
Journey time: 35 minutes

8 Houses, Gardens and Artists

This tour takes you from the Normandy coast near Dieppe to Chantilly, north of Paris. In the Dieppe region you visit two wonderful places: the gardens of Le Vasterival, created by the princess Greta Sturdza, and le Bois des Moutiers, home of the Mallet family, (pronounced as in 'ballet') designed for Guillaume Mallet by Sir Edwin Lutyens, with help from Gertrude Jekyll for the garden.

The impressionist artist Claude Monet used the garden of his home at Giverny near Rouen as inspiration for some of his most famous paintings. A detour to Rouen itself offers a visit to the magnificent cathedral, also the subject of a series of Monet's paintings. In Rouen it is worth looking too at the memorials to Joan of Arc in the Place du Marché (Market Square), traditionally her place of execution.

The small town of Auvers-sur-Oise is a shrine to the artist Vincent van Gogh, who died there in 1892, while the Château de Chantilly houses the finest individual art collection in France. The formal gardens at Chantilly were considered by their designer André Le Nôtre to be his best and of course it is the home of Chantilly cream.

Where to stay:
Because of the distance between the start and finish of this tour it is more convenient to use two hotels.

For your two days in the Dieppe region, stay at the *Domaine de Joinville* which is 30 kms up the coast from Dieppe, at Eu (pronounced *eugh*, as if you are tasting something unpleasant). Rooms are in the various buildings of this former royal hunting lodge, now one of the 'Symboles de France' hotels.

From here it is a 35 minute drive to Le Vasterival and Le Bois des Moutiers, which are situated within 2 kms of each other.

For your visits to Auvers-sur-Oise and Chantilly, the *Château de Chaumontel,* also a former hunting lodge, is only 10kms from Chantilly. This independent hotel (which the owners call a 'château that takes in guests') is an ideal base for visiting Chantilly and Auvers-sur-Oise.

Both hotels are set in extensive gardens and provide an excellent cuisine.

How to get there:
For the Domaine de Joinville: go through the centre of Eu and take the route du Tréport. The hotel is on the edge of the Forêt d'Eu on the route du Tréport. For the Château de Chaumontel: see directions for Excursion 3.

Another thing:
TV or radio reporters always enjoy the chance in an election to mention the mayor of Eu (le maire d'Eu). In French this has the same sound as a vulgar term of abuse.

Excursions: 1 Le Vasterival and Jehan Ango's manor
             2 Le Bois des Moutiers and Varengeville church
             3 Rouen and Giverny
             4 Auvers-sur-Oise
             5 Chantilly

You can follow the excursions in the order I have given, or in reverse order. Either way, the day you spend in Rouen and Giverny is en route to your second hotel.

You stay two nights in your first hotel and three nights in the second.

NB. *When planning your tour please note that in Auvers (Excursion 4) the House of Van Gogh is only open Wednesday to Sunday and Daubigny's studio is open Thursday to Sunday.*

Excursion 1: Le Vasterival and the Manoir d'Ango.
*The visit to Le Vasterival can only be made by appointment (see details below), so organise your visit to Le Bois des Moutiers for the **other** day of your two day stay in the area. This way you can appreciate both places fully.*
This guide assumes you will visit Le Vasterival in the morning, have a leisurely lunch and go to the manor in the afternoon, but of course the order can be reversed according to the time of your tour of Le Vasterival.

To put you in the picture about Le Vasterival:
Princess Greta Sturdza is a Norwegian by birth who married into the Roumanian aristocracy. When she and her husband acquired this property in 1957 it was an overgrown and in places marshy wilderness, so much so that they thought the whole garden was more or less flat. Only when they started clearing around the house did they discover that it was part of a valley sloping down towards the sea. From the outset she intended creating a beautiful garden with all year round interest. What you see now is the result of her labours over the past 50 years and certainly lives up to her original aim. More land has recently been acquired and the Princess, with Sybil Clamagerant, her assistant for many years, is still creating new areas of planting. In her nineties now, she still rides round her 9 hectare (22 acre) domain every week on her lawnmower. She is well known in the gardening world and is a vice-president of the Royal Horticultural Society. As the title of her book states, Le Vasterival is a *'Jardin d'une passion'* (the recent English version rather more prosaically calls it 'the four season garden'). Anyone who has a garden, large or small, cannot fail to take away ideas and be inspired by LeVasterival.

Another thing:
The Princess, standing on a rock, warns you by way of greeting not to tread on the borders and jabs her long handled fork into the ground. Her meaning is clear.

On one tour of the garden a visitor was heard to say 'there's not a weed to be seen and the plants come to attention as she goes past'. She is truly a 'formidable lady' who has a passion for her garden.

Visit:
You can only visit Le Vasterival by appointment, either by writing well in advance to Princesse Sturdza, Le Vasterival, 76119 Sainte Marguerite-sur-Mer, or by phone: 0033 235851205 from England /0235851205 from France. English is no problem.
You will be part of a group going round (minimum 15 in summer, 10 in winter) and the princess enjoys giving her tour commentary in English. The tour lasts 1½ – 2 hours. The cost is 24€.

How to get there:
From the Domaine de Joinville, get onto the D925 to Dieppe. On the outskirts of Dieppe follow signs to the town centre (centre ville), Pourville and Varengeville. This takes you on a picturesque coast road (D75) to Varengeville (8kms to the west of Dieppe). If you prefer to avoid Dieppe town centre, take the ring road (D925) signposted Hautot-sur-mer, Veules-les-Roses. 5kms west of Dieppe turn right to Hautot and Varengeville (D55). Continue through Varengeville to the turning on your right signposted Phare d'Ailly (lighthouse). About 400m down the road take the Allée Albert Roussel, a narrow road on the right through woodland. After some 200m turn right into the drive to Le Vasterival. It is not signposted.

Where to eat:
There is a pleasant woodland picnic area, with tables, further down the road towards the Phare d'Ailly. If you prefer something more formal, the *Hôtel de la Terrasse* has a varied lunch menu and a great setting overlooking the sea.
For this hotel, go back towards Varengeville. After 1km take a sharp turn left and follow this road down to the end. The hotel is well signposted from the main road through Varengeville.

Visit: Le Manoir d'Ango:
You may well be surprised at the generally run down air of this 16th century summer palace, but there is enough for you to imagine its former grandeur.

After the death of its original owner in 1551 it was sold, had a number of owners and the parts of the building now missing were probably demolished in the Revolution. Unfortunately no pre-Revolution plans or pictures of it have been found, the earliest prints being from the 19th century when it became a farm. It was however classified as a historic monument in 1862 by Prosper Mérimée (writer and government inspector of monuments). Some restoration has been done over the years and continues with the present owner, but he has a daunting task.

Its Italian Renaissance architecture may seem out of context in Normandy, but the Italian influence was strong when this manor house was built, in the reign of François I (1515-1547).

When you go into the vast courtyard around which the *manoir* is built, you will immediately be struck by the huge dovecote in the middle. Its Bysantine style roof and ornate geometric brick and stone work make it an extraordinary sight. To possess a dovecote was a class privilege, so this one, with its capacity to house 3200 pigeons, gives an idea of the importance of Jehan Ango.

Look too at the Italian style loggia and the medallions on the south wall that include Ango, his wife and the king and queen of France. On the west wall you can see the sculpted salamander, emblem of François I. On the outside of the east gateway (there was once a gatehouse matching the one by which you came in) is a corner stone sculpted in the form of a seal, which may be a reference to Ango's seafaring.

To put you in the picture about Jehan Ango:
Jehan (modern French: Jean) Ango was born in 1480, the only son of a rich ship owner who settled in Dieppe, one of France's most important ports. Whether he actually sailed to Africa and India himself is a matter of dispute, but he did take over his father's business and made himself immensely rich through the spice trade. He was made viscount of Dieppe in

1521 and was a great local benefactor, in particular helping to found the first French school of cartography in Dieppe.

Ango also became a successful privateer (a sort of pirate with the king's authority), ensuring a French presence at sea, which the king could not afford himself, at a time when maritime commerce was dominated by Spain and Portugal. A notable incident showing Ango's power occurred in 1530 when one of his ships was captured by the Portuguese and the crew massacred. Incensed by this Ango sent a punitive expedition, blockading the mouth of the Tagus and capturing Portuguese ships. The king of Portugal thought France had declared war and sent emissaries to François I, who told them to deal directly with Ango. They were lavishly received by Ango, who in turn received considerable financial reparation from the king of Portugal.

In 1534 he invited François I to stay with him at his recently built *manoir* at Varengeville. The king obviously appreciated Ango's hospitality, promoting him to captain (governor) of Dieppe. This may not have been just an act of generosity. Ango pledged himself to the service of his king who, ten years later, got him to spend a large part of his fortune equipping ships for what turned out to be an abortive campaign against Henry VIII.

Another thing:
On a subsequent visit to the *manoir* in 1544 François I described it as 'the finest house in Normandy'. Mind you, this was just at the time the king needed Ango's money.

How to get there:
Go through Varengeville towards Dieppe on the D75. The Manoir d'Ango is signposted on your right. Turn right and, after about 400m, park in the avenue leading to the Manoir. The Manoir d'Ango is open daily from May to September and at weekends all year, 10am-12.30pm and 2-6pm. Entry 5€
Allow about ¾ hour for the visit.

Excursion 2: Le Bois des Moutiers and Varengeville church

To put you in the picture about le Bois des Moutiers:
Guillaume Mallet was a member of a family of bankers, forced to flee from France during the Franco-Prussian war of 1870. They found refuge at Shanklin on the Isle of Wight. The young Guillaume fell in love with the English countryside and over the years the idea grew that he would create an English style garden in France. Shortly after his marriage to the daughter of another well-to-do family, the couple were on holiday with her sister in Dieppe. Guillaume came across a house, and more importantly its 12 hectare (30 acre) estate overlooking the sea, that would fit the bill: le Bois des Moutiers.

Through family contacts Guillaume Mallet commissioned the young up and coming English architect, Edwin Lutyens, to redesign the existing Normandy country house, which he did, completing it in 1898.

In his design of the house Lutyens was inspired by the Arts and Crafts movement and the ideas of William Morris, its founder. Le Bois des Moutiers has similarities with Lutyens' English houses: the huge chimneys, the many windows with small panes that give it a mediaeval appearance. He loved spatial surprises: here the front door cannot be seen from the path leading to it, but is hidden at the top of stairs at right angles to the path.

Visit:
Inside, the imposing main staircase is full of light and there are associations everywhere with the Arts and Crafts movement. A Burne-Jones tapestry copied from cloth from William Morris' studio hangs in the stairwell. The solid oak linen-fold

doors are beautifully crafted and the Robert Anning Bell painted plaster reliefs on the walls outside the bedrooms are charming, giving each room its own identity. The blue-green mosaic and rope hand rail on the back stairs remind you that this property leads down to the sea, although you may think Lutyens has taken his quirky design too far and that you are walking down steps into a swimming pool.

Outside, a series of garden 'rooms' with walls and yew hedges are linked by a path through arches and a pergola designed by Lutyens to harmonise with the house. For these intimate, formal gardens, conceived as extensions of the house, Lutyens called on Gertrude Jekyll, the garden designer, with whom he had already worked. She never came to le Bois des Moutiers, but sent Lutyens her planting schemes. You can see one of her letters among memorabilia in the music room (the main reception room of the house) and in more than one garden 'room' there is a genuine Lutyens garden seat, the sort you find imitated in English garden shops, but they are not *quite* like sitting on the real thing.

The formal gardens round the house lead into the park, with a half moon stone and brick seat designed by Lutyens on the right of the entrance. Now you walk gently down a valley towards the sea through a succession of informal garden areas, each with its own theme, designed and planted by Guillaume Mallet over a period of forty years. They are all good to look at, but No 17, Ariane's Path, is the *pièce de résistance*, especially when the rhododendrons are out in May and early June. Further down the valley you get a view through the trees to Varengeville church.

Another thing:
Guillaume Mallet commissioned Lutyens to design two more houses in Varengeville (only one was built) and one in the south of France near Mougins. He also got Lutyens the commission for the British Pavilion at the 1900 Paris Universal Exhibition.

How to get there:
From Varengeville centre take the road (D57) that leads to the church. Le Bois des Moutiers is signposted from the village

centre. There is an official free car park on the left opposite the house.

The house and gardens are open daily from 15th March to 15th November, 10am-12noon and 2-6pm.

You should book the guided tour of the house (1 hour) when you arrive. Allow 1½ hours for a walk round the gardens at your leisure. The guide to the house, usually a member of the family, will have many interesting snippets of information for you – in English - while the plan of the gardens has details of the plants you will see. You can organise your tour of the different parts of the gardens according to the time of your tour. The combined ticket costs €25.

Where to eat:
Light lunches and snacks are available at le Bois des Moutiers itself, which gives you the most flexibility.

Visit: The church of St Valéry, Varengeville
St Valéry, who converted the population at the end of the 6th century, is known as 'the apostle of the cliffs', so it is perhaps not surprising to find this church perched on the cliff top some distance from the main part of the village. Legend has it that the villagers were obstinately opposed to its site and eventually started building their oratory in the centre of the village. St Valéry, equally obstinate, is said to have moved all the stones by night to *his* preferred site. Thanks are surely due to the saint for siting his church in such a spectacular position, although being so close to the cliff edge it is always in danger from erosion by the sea. The cliff is receding on average by one to two metres a year.

The present church was built in the 12th century, with a second nave added on the south side in the 16th. It has a number of unexpected features. One of these is the lovely, vivid blue stained glass window by Georges Braque depicting the *Tree of Jesse* behind the altar of the chapel in the south nave. In summer the sun rises through this window, but unfortunately we can only imagine what must be a stunning effect as the church does not open until 9am. Braque also designed the tabernacle on the altar itself. Unusually in this scene of the last supper, Jesus is sitting at the end of the table.

The window behind the altar in the chancel of the north nave was designed in 1961 by Raoul Ubac, a Belgian born surrealist artist and photographer who worked with René Magritte as well as with Braque. Four more in the north wall are Ubac designs, inaugurated in 1992. However, the Braque window is the one that really stands out.

Look at the pillars between the naves, which replaced the wall when the south nave was added. Two of these have rather strange carvings. One is decorated with ropes and scallop shells, which you might well expect in a seafaring community. The other has some really strange carvings: the Inca sun, mermaids, a head with three faces, a sailor being sick. These carvings are thought to refer to the voyages to the Americas, India and Africa of the 16th century shipping magnate Jehan Ango who probably paid for the enlargement of the church.

Outside, you will easily find the tomb of Georges Braque and his wife Marcelle: the headstone has a mosaic of a Braque trademark bird. Nearer the churchyard gate is the tomb of the rather less well known Jacques-Antoine Danois. This native of Varengeville fought in and survived all Napoleon's campaigns, was made a Knight of the Legion of Honour, then came back to live in Varengeville where he worked as a tax collector. The inscription says, 'As a soldier he was brave, at home (and) in his public duties he was a good and upright man'. His tomb is maintained at public expense and it makes a greater impression on me than the more famous one.

Another thing:
Monet was inspired to paint several views of the church, from the sea and across the fields from the direction of le Bois des Moutiers.

To put you in the picture about Georges Braque (1882-1963) and Varengeville:
After staying a few weeks in 1928 at the home in Varengeville of his friend the American architect Paul Nelson, Braque was so taken with the region, which he had already got to know when growing up in Le Havre, that he decided to have his own house built here. It was designed by Nelson in a rustic Norman style and completed in 1931. From then until his death Braque would come every year to his home in Varengeville for the whole summer and autumn, spending the rest of his time in Paris. Braque had given up landscape painting for many years, but returned to it when he came to Varengeville. He found great inspiration in the changeable light and the soft luminous quality given by the chalk cliffs. He said he felt a deep affinity with the village.

A poem *Varengeville,* published with reproductions of Braque's paintings, was written by Jacques Prévert in 1968 to express his admiration for Braque's late Varengeville works. Prevert's words echo the simple but powerful subjects of these paintings, which Braque insisted were not minor works in spite of their small format.

This extract refers to *La charrue* (the plough):

Sombres nuages salés	Dark salt clouds
Grèves ensoleillées	Sunlit shores
Squelette de charrue	The skeletal plough
épave de la terre	an earthly wreck
et carcasses de barques	carcasses of boats
décombres de la mer	debris of the sea.

Braque wrote of this picture: 'The idle plough rusts and loses its usual meaning'.

Prévert's poem, with the reproductions, can be found in the *Pléiade* collection.

Another thing:
This region, the Côte d'Albâtre (Alabaster Coast) gets its name from the constantly eroding chalk cliffs which give the water below a milky look, like alabaster.

How to get there:
From the crossroads in the centre of the village take the D27 which leads to the sea. It is signposted to Le Bois des Moutiers and the church (église). Follow the road as far as it will go (about 1km) and park opposite the church.
The church is open all day. Entry is free. Allow 45 minutes for your visit.

Excursion 3: Rouen and Giverny

This excursion visits Rouen before Giverny on the assumption that you have been staying at Eu. If you are coming from the Château de Chaumontel, your first call will be Giverny.

To put you in the picture about Rouen:
Rouen is probably best known for the trial and burning of Joan of Arc. Perhaps after that, it is known to art lovers, for the series of paintings by Claude Monet of its cathedral. There is of course more to Rouen, which was in the Middle Ages France's second city and for centuries a major port, although some fifty miles from the estuary of its river, the Seine. For three hundred years until the 19th century Rouen porcelain with its traditional embroidery motif in blue monochrome was a thriving industry. It was the birthplace of two great French writers, the 17th century playwright Pierre Corneille and the 19th century novelist Gustave Flaubert, as well as the romantic painter Théodore Géricault.
For this whistle-stop visit we shall concentrate on Joan of Arc, the cathedral and another Rouen landmark, le Gros-Horloge.

Visit: Place du Vieux Marché and the Church of St Joan of Arc
Leaving your car in the underground car park in the place du Vieux Marché (Old Market Square) conveniently brings you out to where tradition has it that Joan of Arc was burnt at the stake. The place is marked by the tall cross erected in 1979 as the national monument to the patron saint of France. Only a few yards away is the church of St Joan of Arc, also consecrated in 1979, built partly on the site of the old church

of St Sauveur which was demolished during the Revolution. You will either love or hate the very French juxtaposition of this uncompromisingly modern church and the covered market that adjoins it, with buildings round the square that have been restored to retain a mediaeval appearance. Certainly, architectural harmony is achieved with the pointed slate roofs of the market halls rising up towards the high vault of the church like the crests of waves. Appropriately so, as Rouen has seafaring connections and a church nave gets its name from the Latin word for ship.

Nor can you remain indifferent to the architecture of the interior of the church. The soaring vault of the roof and the stained glass windows all along one side give an impression of intense light. Initially you may not realise that the stained glass is not as modern as the rest of the building. It is in fact 16th century and from a nearby church that was destroyed by bombing in 1944, coincidentally on 30th May, the same day that Joan was burnt in 1431. Again a juxtaposition of old and modern, but in both cases I think it works and the effect of the stained glass lit up at night is stunning.

Another thing:
There is a theory, which I find quite convincing, that Joan of Arc was not burnt at the stake. There are contemporary references to *la pucelle* (the maid) appearing some years later, for example in Orleans which had been liberated by her. However there is no mention of her in the Rouen city accounts for wood used and the executioner's wages for burning five witches between 1430 and 1432, which seems surprising. One chronicler even states: *'En la ville de Rouen en Normandie elle fut echaufée et arse en un feu, ce veut-on dire, mais depuis fut prouvé le contraire'* (In the town of Rouen in Normandy she was heated and burnt in a fire, or so they say, but this has since been disproved). I like the distinction between heating and burning.

To find out more about this theory read *Jehanne d'Arc n'a pas été brûlée* by Gérard Pesme or *Le double secret de Jeanne la Pucelle* by Etienne Weill-Raynal. (Both in French).

Visit: Le Gros-Horloge

From the church, walk past or through the covered market and take the pedestrianised rue du Gros-Horloge. This busy street with its chic shops is the main thoroughfare of the old part of town. It links the Place du Vieux Marché with the Place de la Cathédrale. As you walk along it, notice the timbered houses that still seem to retain their ancient charm, from the first storey up at any rate.

The most imposing edifice is undoubtedly the elegant Renaissance tower that straddles the roadway. This was built in 1529 to house the public clock, le Gros-Horloge, that gives the street its name. The magnificently decorated clock faces on both sides of the tower have only an hour hand. Just below is an opening portraying the divinities that represent the days of the week. The daily change at midday always attracts onlookers.

The original clock mechanism is still housed in the adjacent, and rather more austere, earlier belfry. This also houses two 13th century bells: one used to summon the population in the 1382 *révolte de la Harelle* – a popular uprising against harsh taxes, harshly put down by the king; the other, called la Cache Ribaud (hide bawdy fellow), still rings a symbolic curfew at 9pm every day.

On the underside of the arch of the Gros-Horloge the sculpture of the Good Shepherd with his flock probably also symbolises the important wool industry of the time.

You can go up the belfry of the Gros-Horloge and get an impressive view of the spires and towers of Rouen. Open from Easter to 1st October except on Tuesdays and some bank holidays.

Another thing:
In a French dictionary you will find that *une horloge* (clock) is feminine. However, *Le Bon Usage* (the 'bible' of French grammar) quotes *le Gros Horloge de Rouen* as a regional exception.

To put you in the picture about Monet and Rouen cathedral:
Continue along the street, cross rue la Champmesle and rue des Carmes and you are in the cathedral square. From February to April 1892 Monet rented a second floor room facing the cathedral, above a shop near the present tourist office. In February and March the following year he rented a similar room close by, at 81 rue Grand-Pont. From these rooms he painted over thirty views of the cathedral façade. Most of them are signed and dated 1894 because he finished them later in his studio at Giverny. His aim was not in a sense to paint the building but to capture the different light effects, so that in some of the paintings you can barely pick out the details of the building: light was all. The series has been described as the 'climax of impressionism'.

Visit: Rouen cathedral
If Monet has been the focus of attention on the exterior of the cathedral, we shall focus on Gustave Flaubert for the interior, but without the haste with which Léon dispenses with the guided tour in Flaubert's novel *Mme Bovary*. When he met Emma in the cathedral he definitely had other intentions.
A window in the north ambulatory has the unusual distinction of being the subject of a story by Flaubert, *La Légende de Saint Julien l'Hospitalier*, which ends: '*Et voila l'histoire de saint Julien l'Hospitalier, telle à peu pres qu'on la trouve, sur un vitrail d'église, dans mon pays*'. *(And there you have the story of Saint Julian the Hospitaller, more or less as you see it on a stained glass window in the region I come from).*
Flaubert's tale is so much more psychologically complex than the stained glass version that he would not allow any detailed illustration of the window to be printed with his story. He explained to his publisher: '*By comparing the visual image*

with the text, the reader would say...how did he get this from that?'

For all that, there is a helpful notice explaining the story told in the 13th century stained glass. If you are wondering why the bottom row depicts fishmongers, they donated the window.

On your way through the cathedral give yourself enough time to take in the imposing architecture of the nave and especially the chancel of what is considered a Gothic masterpiece. Also worth noticing *en passant* are the very early Renaissance tomb of the cardinals of Amboise, archbishops of Rouen in the 16th century (north ambulatory), and the library staircase (north transept). The lower flight is late Gothic, the upper is 18th century. Both are elegant.

Another thing:
If this visit has given you the appetite to read, or re-read, Flaubert's *Madame Bovary* or *Trois Contes* (Three Tales), of which *La Légende de Saint Julien* is one, they are available in Penguin.

The Chabrol film *Madame Bovary* (English subtitles) is a faithful adaptation of the novel, with Isabelle Huppert as the ill-fated romantic Emma.

The streets around the cathedral are the setting for Flaubert's famous and beautifully understated seduction scene where Léon and Emma rush out of the cathedral, jump into a cab and drive round and round for hours with the curtains tightly drawn.

How to get there:
From Eu take the D1015 to the junction at Blangy-sur-Bresle (20kms) with the A28 motorway to Rouen. This takes you into the heart of Rouen (72kms). Go through the tunnel, follow signs to the town centre and pick up the signs for the Jeanne d'Arc car park in the place du Vieux Marché. As you approach the town centre you will see the spires of the cathedral and other churches, which will give you the general direction.

Journey time: 1¼ hours. Aim to arrive by 10.30am, which will allow about 2 hours for a leisurely visit before lunch.

Where to eat:
My favourite is *Chez Paul* on the south side of the cathedral square, but there are several other café/bistrots along there serving light lunches. It is very pleasant to sit outside if the weather is good.

Visit: Giverny, Le Clos Normand

To put you in the picture:
Ernest Hoschedé, a businessman and friend of Monet, went bankrupt and fled to Belgium in 1877, abandoning his wife Alice. The next year she came with her children to live with the Monets in the latest of their rented houses, at Vétheuil. Camille Monet gave birth to a second son, but died from tuberculosis in 1879, leaving Monet two young children to bring up. Alice moved in as a companion to Monet to bring up his children with her own family of six, settling in Poissy, a place Monet grew to dislike. When the lease was about to expire in 1883, Monet scoured the Vexin region in search of somewhere better to live. From the local train between Vernon and Gasny he discovered Giverny. They moved, first to an inn, then to a rented house that he had seen from the railway that ran past the bottom of its garden. This was Le Clos Normand. He was in such financial difficulties at the time that it was only the support of the art dealer Paul Durand-Ruel that saw the large Monet-Hoschedé ménage through.

Monet became more successful, partly thanks to the exhibition in America in 1887 arranged by Durand-Ruel. In 1890 he bought Le Clos Normand and redesigned the garden.

He also bought a plot of land on the other side of the railway track at the end of the garden. Eventually, five years later and after many difficulties with local authorities about diverting a stream, he created there the famous lily pond and wisteria covered Japanese bridge.

Le Clos Normand was thereafter the centre of Monet's life as a painter and gardener. However, just as Monet's life was to have its ups and downs, so did the house and garden after his death in 1926.

Monet married Alice in 1892 after her husband died, and his 1900 exhibition of water lily paintings brought him fame in

England and America as well as France. Alice, though, died in 1911 and his son Jean in 1914. Both deaths shattered Monet, while the war and the cataracts he began to suffer from depressed him even more. His friend Georges Clémenceau (twice prime minister of France) had to encourage him to persist with his project for the *Grandes Décorations des Nymphéas* (water lilies) which Monet was prepared to abandon in moments of depression. Fortunately Clémenceau prevailed and persuaded Monet to donate the series of paintings to the state in 1922. (They are in the Orangerie museum in Paris).

After the artist's death, his second son Michel inherited the property. He had not been on good terms with his father, and now only came occasionally to Giverny, but his sister-in-law Blanche (Alice Hoschedé's daughter who had married Jean Monet and to whom his father had been devoted) looked after the house and garden until she died after the Second World War.

After that the garden gradually fell into neglect and Michel sold most of the paintings. When he died in 1966 and left the estate to the Académie des Beaux-Arts (like the Royal Academy), everything was in a sorry state. The leaky roof was repaired, but there were not enough funds to heat the house and so furniture deteriorated, floors and ceiling beams rotted, a staircase fell down. The remaining paintings were moved to the musée Marmottan in Paris (now the official Monet museum), but the Japanese engravings were badly mildewed and their frames worm eaten.

It took more than ten years to restore the house, its contents and the garden to the way it was when Monet lived there. This was made possible by the devoted work of the Curator of Giverny and his team, not to mention funding and donations from French authorities and from America and Japan in particular. That is why you will see notices in the garden referring to Japanese and American societies. The American ambassador to France gave the money for the tunnel that now connects the two parts of the property separated by the old railway, now a road with rather more traffic. You should not be surprised therefore – nor upset - at the number of Japanese and American visitors. You are never alone in Monet's garden.

Visit: The House
As you walk through the house it is hard to imagine the dilapidation I have described above, especially as the furniture, fittings and pictures are the restored originals, except in Monet's first studio where his paintings are all reproductions. If the restoration work perhaps makes the house, especially the kitchen and dining room, look like a museum, that is because it is one. It gives us a picture of a comfortable middle-class country home in the late 19th century as well as that of one famous man.

The most striking thing about the decoration of the house is the profusion of Japanese engravings. Apart from these, there are two fine pieces of furniture upstairs in Monet's bedroom: a chest of drawers and an 18th century writing desk. This bedroom also has a good view over the garden that Monet designed and painted many times. If you look down with half closed eyes at the flower borders stretching away from the house, you get an impression of the way Monet painted flowers, in drifts of colour rather than in detail.

To put you in the picture about the Japanese engravings:
The Universal Exhibitions in London in 1862 and Paris in 1878 had introduced Japanese art to the western world and further exhibitions in Paris were great attractions. Other artists too were bowled over by this style of art, so different from the conventions of western painting. Camille Pissarro wrote: *'moi, Monet et Rodin en sommes enthousiasmés' (me, Monet and Rodin are very keen on them).* Van Gogh too had a collection. Monet picked up his first engravings on his visit to Holland in 1871, seeing them by chance in an Amsterdam shop where he was interested in buying a piece of Delft porcelain. The shopkeeper threw them in for the price of the Delft piece. Monet ended up with a collection of over 200, now hung in the rooms of the house as far as possible in the way he had displayed them.

For Monet the interest of the engravings was less the subject than the composition of the picture, from which he took inspiration (oblique lines balanced by verticals, the main subject often pushed to one side) and the way they captured changing light according to the weather (this comes out strongly in his 'series' paintings).

Another thing:
As you come down the stairs into Monet's studio, you may recognise a view of the cliffs you have seen at Pourville on the coast road between Dieppe and Varengeville.

Visit: the garden
The rectangular borders intersected by straight paths are in the formal French style of garden, yet the overwhelming impression is of informality, created by the profusion of colours that change with the seasons and soften the straight edges. In May the mauves, blues and whites of the irises – Monet's favourite flower – and, later in the summer, the nasturtiums that trail across the central path below the rose covered arches are the sights that stand out in my memory. Much research has gone into recreating as closely as possible Monet's own planting schemes.

Through the tunnel is a different sight altogether. Mature weeping willows trail their branches in the water of the pond, which is more the size of a lake. The beds along its curving edges are filled with trees and plants that give it the look of a water garden in a woodland setting. At each end of the pond is a Japanese style bridge. As you can see from his paintings, the famous one did not originally have the metal arcading to support the wisteria. In the pond itself there is every known variety of water lily, the subject of so many of Monet's later canvasses. Inspired by the play of light on the lily covered water rather than the representation of the actual scene, these works have been hailed as the forerunners of abstract art.

Another thing:
As everywhere, you have to leave via the shop. At le Clos Normand this is housed in a rather ugly metal framed shed. This is the studio Monet had built in 1916 so he could paint his large format canvasses in comfort. A particularity of the impressionists was to *'peindre sur le motif'* (paint the scene on the spot). Monet did this but worked on his paintings afterwards in his studio. However, most of his large water lily canvasses were not done outside, but in this studio. The paintings on the walls are reproductions, but the easels were Monet's.

How to get there:
From the place du Vieux Marché follow signs out of Rouen for the motorway A13 towards Paris. At junction 16 take the D181 to Vernon. Drive through the town, cross the river Seine following signs for Giverny (D5). Once you are there the car park will be signposted, off the Chemin du Roy, where the little railway ran from which Monet first saw le Clos Normand.
Journey time 40 minutes.
Le Clos Normand is open from 1st April to 1st November, daily, 9.30am-6pm.
Entry: 6€

For your hotel at Chaumontel near Chantilly:
After your visit leave Giverny by the D5 towards Gasny. Bypass the village on the D5, leading onto the picturesque D128 and D37 to Bray-et-Lu, where you take the D86 to Magny. Take the N14 to Pontoise. At Pontoise this briefly becomes the A15. At Junction 7 take the N184, direction Méry-s-Oise and l'Isle-Adam.
After 11kms take the D104 (the Paris outer ring road called La Francilienne) and after 17kms at Mareil-en-France turn onto the N16, direction Luzarches and Chantilly.
At the roundabout on the way past Luzarches take the exit to Chaumontel. After a few hundred metres, drive through the entrance to the Château de Chaumontel in front of you.
Journey time 1hour (75kms, mostly on dual carriageway)

Excursion 4: Auvers-sur-Oise

In the morning I suggest you visit the Maison de Van Gogh (pronounced Gog in French), the church and the cemetery where the artist is buried. After lunch, a walk round the village takes you to 'motifs' of paintings by Van Gogh, Cézanne and Corot. Finally look round Charles-François Daubigny's unusual studio.

This village, squeezed between the bank of the River Oise and the steep slope up to the Vexin plateau, still retains the rural atmosphere it must have had when Vincent Van Gogh lived here and yet it is only thirty kilometres from Paris.

Before the opening in 1990 of the Maison de Van Gogh (House of Van Gogh), popularly known as the Ravoux Inn, the village was a shrine to the Dutch painter, even though he only spent three months here.

However, it had artistic connections before his arrival, although the claim of its tourist office to be 'the cradle of impressionism' may be exaggerated. Certainly Charles-François Daubigny (1817-1878) lived in Auvers. He was a precursor of the impressionist movement in that he painted his subjects directly outdoors, and even had a boat made into a studio so that he could paint river scenes, as Monet was to do a decade later. Daubigny's style was criticised by the writer Théophile Gautier: *'It is a real pity...he contents himself with an impression and neglects the details'*. He was a friend of contemporary artists and supporter of that new generation of painters, the impressionists.

Cézanne too lived in Auvers from 1872-1874, developing here a more impressionist style and lighter palette. He received support from another inhabitant, Doctor Gachet, who was also a painter and one of the impressionist circle at that time. Gachet's name is probably best known because Van Gogh came to Auvers expressly to be under his medical care after leaving the asylum at St Rémy.

To put you in the picture about Van Gogh at Auvers:
He arrived by train on 20th May 1890 and took a small room in the attic of the inn opposite the Town Hall run by the Ravoux family. He immediately found subjects to paint in and around the village and every day would set out early with his painting gear strapped to his back.

All went well for a while: encouraged by Dr Gachet, 'Monsieur Vincent' painted daily and seemed to find a peace of mind that is reflected in his work. After a while, though, he began to quarrel with Dr Gachet and his total financial dependence on his brother Theo weighed on his mind. On 7th July he returned particularly tired and tense after a day in Paris with his brother. No one knows exactly what was wrong, but Vincent's paintings now reflected his troubled state of mind.

On 27th July he shot himself while out in the fields. This suicide attempt, like so much else in his life, failed. He managed to drag himself back to the inn and up to his room without anyone noticing. Hours later the innkeeper heard his moans, found him critically wounded lying on his bed and called Dr Gachet. He and another local doctor could not operate on him there and the bumpy ride to hospital in Pontoise would have killed him. His brother was alerted and arrived the next afternoon. The two brothers then spent the rest of the day talking together in Vincent's room until he died in the early hours, aged thirty seven. Two days later he was buried in Auvers cemetery.

During his two months in Auvers he painted seventy canvasses and his career as a painter had lasted only ten years.

Another thing:
In his lifetime he only sold one painting. He painted Ravoux's thirteen year old daughter Adeline and gave it to her father. In 1905 it was sold for 40fr. In 1988 a Van Gogh portrait sold for $13,750,000. As a girl, Adeline did not like her portrait much.

Visit: La Maison de Van Gogh, the Church, Van Gogh's grave.
As you approach the village from across the river, you get a good view of the church made famous by Van Gogh's painting (in the musée d'Orsay). After the bridge turn left along rue du

Général de Gaulle and park at the Mairie (Town Hall) opposite the Ravoux Inn.

Before starting your tour of the village, go to the tourist office which is signposted up rue de la Sansonne, just beyond the Ravoux Inn. Here you can pick up a plan of the village which marks all the places associated with Van Gogh and other artists, essential for your visit. They also run a short and beautifully made film about Van Gogh's stay in Auvers. Now go to the House of Van Gogh, whose entrance is on the opposite side of the same road. On your way notice the two panels on the roadside, one where he set up his easel to paint *l'Escalier d'Auvers* (the Auvers steps). Although there is much more greenery now, you can still make out his *motif* (subject). The other, at the entrance to the House of Van Gogh, is of Adeline Ravoux.

Once inside, it is worth reading the comprehensive biography of Van Gogh on the wall panels before you go into the building itself. The ground floor is still a restaurant. The guided tour begins upstairs, with a visit to the painter's garret, listed as a historical monument. The visit ends with a well crafted audiovisual show using as commentary extracts of the many letters Vincent wrote during his stay.

The walk along rue du Général de Gaulle and up to the church is gentle. Notice on the way the panel of Vincent's depiction of the Town Hall on Bastille Day (14th July). The complete absence of festivity surely indicates his state of mind at that stage. In the park on your left the 1961 statue by the Russian sculptor Zadkine captures the tortured figure of Van Gogh setting out to paint. A little further on is the panel of *le Jardin de Daubigny* (Daubigny's garden). An unfinished letter to Theo was found in his pocket after his death with a comment that could well refer to this painting: '*…you have played your part in the production of some of the canvasses which retain a sense of tranquillity, even in the midst of disaster*'.

When you see the church and the panel of Van Gogh's painting of it you may wonder at his use of colour. In a letter to his sister in June 1890 he compared it to paintings he had done in Holland five years earlier: '*Only now the colour is probably more expressive*'. This close up of the church is thought to be one of the greatest works of his Auvers period.

You now have a steep climb up to the cemetery. Half way up on the right, the panel of *La Pluie* (Rain, now in Cardiff museum) shows remarkable technique in painting rain. In the cemetery, along the wall facing you as you look to your left, are the simple graves, side by side, of Vincent and Theo. Theo died only six months after his brother and was buried in Holland. His widow brought his body to be reburied in Auvers in 1914. The ivy that runs over both graves was grown from a cutting from Dr Gachet's garden and is seen as symbolic of the closeness of the two brothers. In the summer you will often see stalks of wheat strewn on Vincent's grave, a reference to his paintings of the nearby fields.

Across from the cemetery there is a panel in the middle of the field depicting one of Van Gogh's last paintings, *Champ de blé aux corbeaux* (Field of wheat with crows). The view has not changed, but the threatening sky and birds of ill omen in this painting seem to reflect his tortured soul and maybe intimate his suicide.

Where to eat:
At the House of Van Gogh the *guingette* (19th century café-bar with dancing) in the back courtyard does light lunches, but you should book at the start of your visit. I prefer the brasserie *Au Verre Placide* opposite the station. You can make a reservation on your way up to the church and cemetery.
The House of Van Gogh is open from March to 1st November, Wednesday-Sunday,
10am -6pm
Entry: 5€. The rest is free.
Allow 45 minutes at the House of Van Gogh and 1¼ hours for your walk.

Visit: the village and Daubigny's studio

After lunch, armed with your plan of Auvers, set off for a gentle stroll through the village to look at the *motifs* painted by Van Gogh, Cézanne and Corot, and reproduced on panels, as you will have seen from your morning's walk. It is interesting to see how little some of these views have changed since they were painted over a hundred years ago. There doesn't seem to be anything special about what these artists chose to paint, so I am always full of admiration for the way great painters manage to turn what appears very ordinary subject matter into a work of art.

From the Ravoux Inn, go along rue du Général de Gaulle in the opposite direction to this morning's walk. Carry straight on up rue Zundert and turn left into rue Victor-Hugo which in turn leads into rue du Dr-Gachet. Near the far end of this road on the right, is a panel of Van Gogh's portrait of the doctor. This is where Dr Gachet lived, at No 78. Van Gogh wrote to his sister: *'I would like to do portraits which would seem like apparitions to people in a hundred years' time. I am not aiming for a photographic likeness, but I explore the possibilities of expressing the passions.'* His portraits of Adeline, himself and the melancholy Dr Gachet seem to be alive over a hundred years on, just as he intended.

At the crossroads are panels of two paintings: *Rue de village à Auvers* by Corot and Cézanne's *Carrefour* (crossroads) *de la rue Rémy*. Along rue François-Coppée another Cézanne, *Route de village à Auvers* and Van Gogh's *Maisons à Auvers*.

From the junction of rue François-Coppée and rue de Four the panel shows one of my favourite Cézanne canvasses, *La Maison du Pendu* (The House of the Hanged Man).

A little further on, turn down rue de Gré. A track on the right shows two more Van Gogh *motifs* of village houses: another *Maisons à Auvers* and *Les chaumes* (thatch roofs) *du Gré*.

Having seen the spots where these world-famous artists actually stood to paint what are in some cases masterpieces gives the onlooker an added sense of involvement with their work. No more is this true than in the village roads of Auvers.

Make your way back to the junction of rue Victor-Hugo and rue Zundert, then take rue de Léry. Turn left at the far end into rue Daubigny and you come to the Maison-atelier de Daubigny (Daubigny's studio).

Daubigny bought this plot in 1860 and had a studio built 'with a few rooms round it'. It was the family home, but Daubigny was always ready to welcome fellow artists, which accounts for the unusual décor in the various rooms. Members of Daubigny's own family contributed to this, but look especially at the murals in the studio, which cover 100m2 and were a collective effort by Daubigny and his artist friends, including Corot.

Another thing:
La Maison du Pendu was one of three canvasses exhibited by Cézanne at the first Impressionist exhibition in 1874. Cézanne did not give the painting this title, nor is there any record of a man being hanged there. It would seem that a Breton with black hair lived there and in Breton 'black head' is 'pen du'.

Allow 1½ hours for your stroll through the village and 45 minutes for Daubigny's studio and garden.
The studio is open from Easter to 1st November, Thursday – Sunday, 2-6pm.
Entry: 5€

How to get there:
From Chaumontel take the N16 to Mareil-en-France, then the D104 (direction Pontoise). After 17 kms turn off at the exit for Méry-sur-Oise. Go through the village and over the river (D928) to Auvers-sur-Oise.
Journey time: 30 minutes.

Excursion 5: Château de Chantilly

To put you in the picture:
From the Middle Ages there has been a castle on this small triangular island in the marshy land of the Nonette valley. Its story really begins, though, when the future Constable of France, Anne de Montmorency had the old mediaeval fortress renovated in about 1530 in the new Renaissance style. In 1560 he added another building, the Petit Château, on the small island next to the main château (the Grand Château), joined to it by a two level bridge and a drawbridge. The

exterior of the Petit Château has remained much the same as when it was built, but the Grand Château has undergone a number of changes over the centuries.

Le Grand Condé (the Great Condé), Prince Henri II de Bourbon and one of Louis XIV's greatest generals, inherited Chantilly. He hosted the king and his court there in 1671. This lavish gesture not only showed up the inconveniences of the old building, but also, according to Mme de Sévigné, caused Condé's *maître d'hôtel*, François Vatel, to commit suicide because he was afraid the fish would not arrive from Boulogne in time to be served to the king.

The principal architect to Louis XIV, Jules Hardouin-Mansart, rebuilt the Grand Château, but when he died in 1708, the work was still not completed. Even when it was finished, the accommodation was not enough for the princes de Condé, so in the mid 1700s the Italian style Château d'Enghien (pronounced *ongyan*) was built on the opposite side of the main drive.

The then prince de Condé fled the Revolution, his property was taken over by the revolutionary council in 1792, the furniture sold and Chantilly became a prison.

Things were to get worse before they got better in the somewhat turbulent history of this serene looking château. It was sold to an estate agent, who tore down the Grand Château and sold off the stones. After the Napoleonic wars the last prince de Condé had his property returned to him. It was in a terrible state, but he started restoration work, notably filling in the moat between the two islands. Having no surviving son, he left all his personal fortune to his great nephew, Henri d'Orléans, duc d'Aumale, who was the fifth son of King Louis-Philippe. Aumale was already a distinguished soldier and now found himself a very rich man.

He moved into the Petit Château in 1845, but once again the history of Chantilly took a down turn: the revolution of 1848 forced him into exile – to England. Chantilly was confiscated and was subsequently owned by Coutts bank.

Aumale was not able to return for some twenty years. When he did, he set about reconstructing the Grand Château to house the collections he had built up during his exile in Twickenham. He bequeathed Chantilly to the *Institut de France* (The governing body of the French Academies) on the condition that the collections, the finest privately owned ones in France, should be open to the public just as he had displayed them, and never loaned out. The collections were first shown to the public in 1898, a year after Aumale's death.

Another thing:
In the middle Ages the Constable of France was the commander in chief of the king's army. The position was abolished by Cardinal Richelieu in 1627.
In the 16th century Anne was a man's name as well.

Visit: the Château and the collections
The Condé museum is so called because, when Aumale went into exile, he was able to take with him archives, precious books and manuscripts that had belonged to the Condé family. These formed a basis for the collection and the duke's passion grew not only for precious books but also for paintings and drawings. His wife wrote in 1854: *'we are busy creating a gallery of beautiful paintings'*. This finally included nearly a thousand paintings and two thousand drawings of the Italian, Flemish, French, Dutch, German and English schools from the 15th to the 19th century.
As you walk through the gallery there are superb pieces of art at every step. Everyone will have their favourites but there are some that I go back to every time: in the Galerie de Peintures, *Gabrielle d'Estrées au bain* (she was a mistress of Henri IV) and Poussin's *Massacre of the Innocents*, a painting designed to be viewed from below to gain the best effect; in the first rotunda, the *Madonna of Lorette* was discovered in 1979 to be an original Raphael, not a copy, while Chapu's *Joan of Arc* seems to show that she understood the enormity of her task; in the Salon d'Orléans, the porcelain, made at Chantilly in the 18th century at the instigation of the prince de Bourbon-Condé in the Japanese style and using only five colours; in the Salle Caroline the tiny Watteau paintings of the *Serenader* and the *Worried Lover* have a lightness with an undertone of melancholy, picked up by some of my favourite Verlaine poems, *Fêtes Galantes*, inspired by Watteau's paintings; the Cabinet de Clouet has rare portraits of French royals.

Not to be missed is the Santuario, which houses the gems of the collection: the *Virgin of the House of Orleans* and the *Three Graces*, both by Raphael, a panel from a wedding chest by Filippino Lippi and forty miniatures by Jean Fouquet taken from a Book of Hours.

Another highlight of the collection, in the entrance to the museum, is the most famous of all Books of Hours, the early 15th century *Très Riches Heures du duc de Berry*. The delicate illuminations with their rich colours and naturalistic style draw a picture of the rigours and pleasures of contemporary rural life, even if what you see is only a facsimile. The real one has only been put on public display twice in the last fifty years. I saw it and am pleased to have done so, even though I have to admit that I couldn't really tell the difference, such is the quality of the reproduction.

The visit to the Grands Appartements (Grand Apartments), by guided tour only, takes you into the Petit Château. Anne de Montmorency's building survived the ravages of the Revolution, although the interior décor has changed several times. The guide will point out a host of wonderful pieces of furniture and art, but I could linger in two places particularly: the Grande Singerie is an example of the fashion which developed in the first half of the 18th century for porcelain figures and decorative panelling with often amusing scenes of monkeys (*singes,* pronounced *sanj*) 'aping' human activities. The room is not only beautifully decorated in this style but also contains several lovely chairs from Marie-Antoinette's dressing room at Versailles; the other place to linger is the Galerie des Actions de Monsieur le Prince. This gallery is devoted to paintings, commissioned by the Grand Condé to commemorate his lifetime's military achievements. Among the portrayals of a military career of which he was obviously proud, a view of 17th century Paris makes an interesting comparison with the city today.

To put you in the picture about the gardens:
These gardens are nothing like any of the others on this tour. From the top of the steps (Le Grand Degré) you look down on a fine example of a 17th century French formal garden, whose essence is geometric design. The Grand Condé commissioned

the landscape architect André Le Nôtre, who started work on the Chantilly gardens in 1663. The project took twenty years. Of course Le Nôtre was designing other gardens too throughout this period and is almost certainly best known for his gardens at Versailles.

If you are at all disappointed by the 'minimalist' look of the lawns and pathways stretching out in front of you, you have to imagine that these were gardens designed for 'occasions' where water had an important role to play. The river Nonette was diverted to feed the new Grand Canal, natural springs found under the gardens supplied the hydraulic system for the waterfalls and fountains, all of which required complex engineering. It also needed a perfectly coordinated operating system and considerable maintenance to make sure that the spectacular effects 'surprised, entertained and astonished' Condé's guests.

For two hundred years the *fêtes* that took place at Chantilly were the *raison d'être* of the gardens. The entertainment put on for Louis XIV would certainly have been at the top end of the scale, with open air banquets, fireworks, theatricals, water extravaganzas.

An anonymous visitor wrote in 1790: *'Nature and the arts seem to have come together to create the beauty of Chantilly. There are few sites in France that succeed in bringing together so many magnificent and decorative objects. The splendour and wealth of the buildings, the variety and beauty of the gardens, the abundance and clarity of the pools……the contrast between the monumental and rural sites, daily attract all kinds of curious visitors from all countries….' (Préface à la promenade ou Itinéraires des jardins de Chantilly).* This description of the brilliance of Chantilly contrasts sharply with the ravages inflicted by the Revolution less than two years later.

Visit: the gardens
Walk down the Grand Degré and from the far side of the Bassin de la Gerbe (the central round pond) look back towards the steps. The symmetry and especially the mirror effect created by the water were deliberately contrived features of the Le Nôtre design.

The tree shaded Allées des Philosophes on each side of the formal garden are so named in honour of the visits to Chantilly of the great and good of the 17th century French literary scene: La Fontaine, la Bruyère, Bossuet, Mme de Sévigné, Mme de Lafayette, who strolled there, no doubt exchanging literary ideas, or in the case of Mme de Sévigné, Court tittle-tattle. Molière's controversial play Tartuffe was performed at Chantilly, which is no doubt why his is one of the statues in the formal garden.

Other areas of the gardens have changed considerably from the Grand Condé's time. The Parc de la Caboutière opposite the château was landscaped in the early 18th century and in the 19th the Jardin Anglais (an English style garden) was created in parkland to the left of the formal garden.

To see something more unusual, follow the signs to the *hameau* (hamlet) set in woodland, framed by streams and carefully landscaped to appear totally natural. It was built in 1774, predating the more famous one at Versailles, but serving the same purpose. In the years before the Revolution, under the influence of the ideas of Jean-Jacques Rousseau about nature, it was the vogue for the aristocracy to 'get away from it all' and enjoy the simple life in miniature villages – provided they retained their creature comforts of course. Here, in this charming woodland setting the houses look modest, but they had a proper kitchen, dining room and billiard room…. The *fêtes* of those days always included a meal at the *hameau*.

Another thing:
The film *Vatel,* (in English with Gérard Depardieu) is not particularly good, except for its pretty accurate portrayal of the lavish *fête* organised at Chantilly for the three day visit of Louis XIV, which gives an idea of everything involved in putting on one of these events.

Where to eat:
I like the delicious light lunches, with of course the chance to sample strawberries or raspberries with genuine Chantilly cream, served at the mill in the *hameau*.

The Château is open daily except Tuesday: between April and October, 10am-6pm (the gardens stay open until 8pm); November to March, 10.30am-5pm. Entry 11€
The visit offers some flexibility: I like to start by going round the musée Condé. While you are going round, the time of the next guided tour of the Grands Apartements will be announced (tours last 30 minutes). After your tour you can resume your visit to the Condé collection (allow a good hour for the musée Condé) or go round the gardens and come back to the musée Condé later (you can come and go as many times as you like).
From the formal garden it takes 10 minutes to reach the Hameau, where it is a good idea to book in for lunch as soon as you arrive.

Another thing:
Chantilly is a horse racing centre and this activity accounts for a good 10% of employment in the *département*. The first official race meeting took place in 1834 and they became great social events. By the early 1900s the two annual meetings at Chantilly were so popular that the railway company would lay on a number of extra trains that has never been equalled, not even for soccer or rugby matches at the Stade de France.
As you near the château you pass the racecourse. You might be forgiven for thinking that the magnificent Italian style building on the far side was the château itself. It is in fact the stables, built for the prince de Condé between 1719 and 1735 and described as one of the masterpieces of 18th century architecture.
Chantilly château and stables were a location for the Bond film *A view to a kill*.

How to get there:
From Chaumontel take the N16 to Chantilly. Go under the railway bridge and turn right at the next roundabout onto route de l'Aigle. This takes you through the forest with the race course on your left. At the third junction (Carrefour des Lions) turn left. At the next roundabout you will see the entrance to the château. Turn right into the car park under the trees. Journey time: 20 minutes.

I should like to thank all those who have helped me with this project. Special thanks to Gavin Thomas for his valuable advice at an early stage.

I am indebted to many sources of information, written and oral, in the making of this guide. Any errors of interpretation are my own.